"IN THE BEGINNING GOD CREATED THE HEAVEN AND THE EARTH . . ."

From the moment one begins reading this unsurpassed retelling of the Old Testament, one is transported back into the world of the Bible . . . back to the Garden of Eden . . . to the tragedy of Cain and Abel . . . to the doomed cities of Sodom and Gomorrah . . . to Abraham and Isaac . . . to Joseph in Egypt . . . to Moses leading his people across the desert . . . to Ruth amid the alien corn . . . to David and Goliath . . . to the evil Jezebel . . . to the wisdom and folly of Solomon . . . to the exile in Babylon and the homecoming of the Jews . . .

Here are enthralling stories that have become a fundamental part of our religious and literary heritage—retold in a manner that brings them to vivid, unforgettable life.

"The Bible, in both Old and New Testaments, may be read in many ways. For some it constitutes divine teaching. For others it is the purest literature we have in the English language. For still others, it is a compendium of information on suffering, struggling, rejoicing human nature."

—PEARL S. BUCK

The Story Bible

Volume I   The Old Testament

by Pearl S. Buck

A SIGNET BOOK from
NEW AMERICAN LIBRARY
TIMES MIRROR

Library of Congress Catalog Card Number: 71-141871

Produced by Lyle Kenyon Engel
Editors:
Valerie Moolman
Marla Ray
George Engel

SIGNET TRADEMARK REG. U.S. PAT. OFF. AND FOREIGN COUNTRIES
REGISTERED TRADEMARK—MARCA REGISTRADA
HECHO EN CHICAGO, U.S.A.

SIGNET, SIGNET CLASSICS, MENTOR, PLUME, MERIDIAN AND NAL
BOOKS *are published by The New American Library, Inc.,*
1633 Broadway, New York, New York 10019

FIRST PRINTING, JULY, 1972

8   9   10   11   12   13   14   15   16

PRINTED IN THE UNITED STATES OF AMERICA

Contents

Foreword   vii
The Creation of the World   13
The Garden of Eden   16
Cain and Abel: The First Murder   21
Noah and the Flood   24
The Tower of Babel   31
The Journey of Abram and Lot   34
The Capture of Lot   39
God's Promise to Abram   42
The Visit of the Strangers   46
The Fate of Sodom   51
The Sons of Abraham
   (The Story of Hagar and Ishmael)   57
The Sacrifice of Isaac   61
Rebekah at the Well   65
Esau Loses His Birthright   73
Jacob Tricks His Father   77
Jacob's Ladder   83
Rachel and Leah   86
Jacob and Laban   91
The Meeting of Jacob and Esau   100
The Coat of Many Colors   107
Joseph a Captive in Egypt   113
Joseph's Brothers Bow   118
Joseph's Family in Egypt   127
Moses in the Bulrushes   135
The Burning Bush   142

"Let My People Go"   150
The Night of Passover   156
Into the Wilderness   163
The Ten Commandments   170
The Cloud Moves on from Sinai   178
Land of Milk and Honey   185
Joshua Fights the Battle of Jericho   194
Gideon's Three Hundred   202
Samson and Delilah   211
The Story of Ruth   220
Samuel the Kingmaker   229
David the Shepherd Boy   238
David and Goliath   246
The Enmity of Saul   252
The Triumph and Tragedy of David   262
The Wisdom of Solomon   272
The Division of the Kingdom   281
Elijah and the Prophets of Baal   291
Elijah and Elisha   301
The Story of Jonah   310
By the Rivers of Babylon   318
Daniel   329
The Homecoming of the Jews   338
God's Promise to Israel   349

Foreword

When I was a child growing up in China in the household of my American parents, I was not encouraged to read the Bible. My father, scholar in Hebrew and Greek, considered the translation of the Old and New Testaments inadequate renderings of the ancient texts and, irritated by what he considered downright mistakes in the use of words, he ignored the English version and read the Scriptures in the original languages. Since he did not teach me either Hebrew or Greek, I was reduced to English, but without encouragement I did not read the Bible. True, I heard it read for brief periods, night and morning, when my father summoned the household to family prayers. In the morning he read in English a few verses chosen by him for the benefit of his American family and in the evening he read another few verses in Chinese for the benefit of our Chinese servants. Beyond this my knowledge of the Bible was limited to the memorizing of the Beatitudes and Psalms and parts of the old prophets as Sunday occupation and to the reading—with much pleasure, I might say—of a very fat volume in a brown cloth cover entitled *Stories of the Bible* in worn gilt letters. My mother, who delighted in the English language, required me to memorize those parts of the Bible which she considered most beautiful and poetic, and to assuage my undying thirst for stories she found the fat volume for me.

Now as everyone knows who has read the Bible, there is not a better source for story than this vast collection of verse and prose, song and lamentation, love and death, sin and punishment. The scriptures of any religion are a fascinating and profound revelation of the struggle of the souls of men and women to find the source of their being and the cause of life and death. In recent years, for example, the sacred books of the Sikh religion in India have been beautifully translated into English and to my joy copies of these two volumes were presented to me on a recent trip to India. Reading them, I discover the same spiritual urgency that inspired my own youthful soul when I began to read the Bible for myself. Thus it is with other scriptures, wherever they are found. The books of Buddhism, the richly colored tales of Hinduism, the pantheons of Greece and Rome share with the Hebrew and Greek Testaments the stories of man's yearning to penetrate the Beyond. All have certain stories in common. The virgin birth is not unique to Christianity and it loses nothing of its importance thereby. The story of the great flood and Noah's ark is to be found in more than one literature. Reared as I have been in Asia, I find one religion enhances and deepens another by correlation and corroboration.

It is not as religion, however, that the stories contained in this volume are presented. I remember simply that I derived great pleasure and profit from reading that earlier volume of *Stories of the Bible,* and since I do not see its duplicate, it may be that this collection will take its place for today's readers.

The Bible, in both Old and New Testaments, may be read in many ways. For some it constitutes divine teaching, and it does contain this element. For others it is the purest literature we have in the English language. For still others it is a compendium of information on suffering, struggling, rejoicing human nature. For children, it is a story book. May they read it as I read it long ago in a Chinese house on a Chinese hillside!

Yet stay—as I write it occurs to me that the Bible has another meaning. It is an Asian book, for Christianity came out of the East. It seems a contradiction that today the West, facing conflict with the East, should nevertheless find its own source of spiritual life in a volume of Asia, centering about the Jews, who, though they have wandered far, nevertheless remain in many ways true to their ancient history which is Asian. It may be that in this very fact we shall find the means of a common understanding, a basic agreement on the constitution for a peaceful world.

The Story Bible

The Creation of the World

✠✠✠✠✠✠✠✠✠✠✠✠✠✠✠✠✠✠✠✠✠✠✠✠

In the beginning God created the heaven and the earth.

At first there was nothing: neither earth nor sky, nor light, nor sound, nor any living thing. All was darkness and silence.

And then the Spirit of God came into the emptiness to give it form and bring it life.

God said: "Let there be light," and the first dawn of time brought light into the world. God looked upon his work and found it good, and divided the light from the darkness. "Let the light be called Day," he said, "and the darkness be called Night." So ended the first of all the days of the earth.

On the second day, God said: "Let there be a sky as a roof over the world, and let it be called Heaven." And it was so. God made the sky and the rainclouds and placed them high above the waters of the deep.

On the third day God said: "Let the waters under the heaven be gathered together into one place, and let the dry land appear." And it was so. Mountains and plains and valleys rose out of the waters, so that now there were great stretches of dry land divided by vast expanses of deep water. God called the land Earth, and the waters he called Seas. Then God said: "Let the earth bring forth herbs and grass, and flowers and trees, each yielding seed of its own kind so that the earth will never cease to yield." And it was so. Soft grass carpeted the land. Plants sprang up and bore flowers and seeds. Trees grew and yielded fruit, each according to its own kind; and the seeds of the new growth spread across the earth.

On the fourth day God said: "Let there be lights in the heavens to mark the seasons and the days and the years, and to give light upon the earth." And it was so. God made the sun and the moon and the stars, and they shone down upon the earth. Of the two greatest lights, he made the sun to rule over the day and the moon to rule the night.

On the fifth day God said: "Let the waters bring forth living creatures and may birds fly above the earth in the heavens." And it was so. God created great whales and tiny fishes and all the living things of the sea, and great hawks and tiny sparrows and all the birds of the air. Now there was life in the waters and the heavens, and the silence was gone from the world. By the end of the fifth day there was birdsong in the land.

On the sixth day God said: "Let the earth bring forth living creatures, cattle and creeping things, and beasts that walk on legs." And it was so. God made the cattle and the creeping things and all the beasts that live on the land. But as yet there was no being in the likeness of God.

And God said: "Let us make man in our image, after our likeness, and let him have dominion over the fish of the sea, and over the fowl of the air, and over the cattle and beasts, and over every creeping thing, and over all the earth."

And so it was that God created man in his own image. From the dust of the earth he shaped man's form, and into man's nostrils he breathed the breath of life; and man became a living soul. God called him Adam, and gave to him every herb and fruit that was upon the earth, every lovely flower and shady tree, every bird in the air, and everything that walked and crept upon the land.

Now it was for Adam to enjoy the fruits of the earth and rule over all its creatures. He looked upon all the birds and beasts and gave names to all of them; but among them there was not another like himself to be his true companion.

And then God said: "It is not good that the man should be alone. I will make a helpmeet for him." God caused Adam to fall into a deep sleep. While the man slept, God took a rib from Adam's body and closed up the flesh in its place. And from Adam's rib the Lord God made a woman.

Now the first man had a wife.

Adam named her Eve and loved her deeply. They began their life together in a garden paradise the Lord had planted for them in the loveliest part of the newborn world. It was a land of rivers and precious stones, of flowering trees and abundant fruit; and its name was Eden.

God saw everything that he had made, and it was good. The heavens and the earth were finished, and living creatures in his likeness walked upon the earth according to his plan.

So ended the sixth day.

On the seventh day God rested from his work.

The Garden of Eden

✥✥✥✥✥✥✥✥✥✥✥✥✥✥✥✥✥✥✥✥✥✥

Adam and Eve were content in their garden home. The Lord had given them everything they could want for their food and pleasure. Brightly colored birds flitted from flower to flower and from branch to branch, singing sweet songs that rose high into the heavens. The river splashed and whispered through the land, watering the earth so that all plants but weeds and thistles grew easily in the fertile soil. It was the lightest of labors for Adam to look after the garden, for the Lord had not meant him to spend his days in toil.

There were trees of every kind, beautiful in all seasons but especially lovely when their leaves were a young green and blossoms brightened the boughs; and there was fruit to eat in plenty. In the midst of the garden stood the Tree of Life, and also the Tree of Knowledge of Good and Evil. But Adam and Eve knew nothing of evil. Their world was all good, and in

16

it they were as free and unafraid as the birds of the air and the animals that roamed the woods and fields. God himself would walk on earth and talk to them in the cool of early evening, and then their happiness was complete.

The Lord asked only one thing of them, and that was to obey. "Of every tree in the garden," he told Adam, "you may eat freely, except of the Tree of Knowledge of Good and Evil. The day that you eat of that tree, you will surely die."

Adam gave his promise readily. There was no need to eat of that tree; there were many others. And even though he did not know what it meant to die, he knew that he must obey and love the Lord who had created him.

Even for the woman it should not have been hard to avoid picking from that one tree and eating its fruit. But the serpent was the most cunning of any of the beasts of the field, as well as one of the most beautiful. He knew that he could make the fruit of that tree seem desirable above all others simply because it was forbidden, especially if he approached the woman in his most persuasive manner. So he appeared before Eve, tall and handsome in his multicolored coat.

"God has told you that you shall not eat of every tree in the garden, is that not so?" he began slyly.

"We may eat the fruit of every tree but one," Eve answered. "Of the tree in the middle of the garden, God has said that we should neither eat of it nor touch it, or we will surely die."

"You will *not* surely die," the serpent said. "God has told you that you will die so that you will be afraid to eat of the fruit, for he knows that if you do your eyes will be opened, and you will be as wise as the gods, knowing good from evil."

Eve took another look at the tree. It was pleasant to the eye, and the fruit looked good. If it was true that eating of it would make her wise, it was indeed a desirable tree. She did not realize how subtly she was being tempted by the wily beast. Her hand reached out and her fingers plucked the fruit. She tasted it; she began to eat. The serpent left her to her meal.

She shared the whole world with her husband, so now she shared the new thing she had discovered. The fruit was pleasant to the taste, and Adam must have some of it, too. Eve gave some to her husband; and Adam also ate of the forbidden fruit.

It was true that they did not die at once, but by their disobedience they had denied themselves eternal life. It was true, too, that their eyes were opened, and now they were aware of things they had never known before. For the first time they realized that they were naked, and for the first time they felt shame. They knew they had done wrong. They sewed fig leaves together into clothes to cover their nakedness; and when that was not enough to shield them from their shame and fear they hid themselves among the leafy trees.

Then they heard the voice of the Lord as he walked in the garden in the cool of the day, and they went deeper into the woods to hide from him.

"Adam! Where are you?" the Lord God called.

"I am here, Lord," Adam answered. "I heard your voice in the garden, and I was afraid because I was naked, so I hid myself."

"How do you know you are naked?" asked the Lord. "Have you eaten the fruit of the forbidden tree, that you should have such knowledge?"

"It was the woman," Adam said. "She gave me some of the fruit, and I did eat."

The Lord God turned to Eve. "What is this that you have done?" he asked her sorrowfully.

"It was the serpent," said the woman. "The serpent tempted me, and so I ate."

Adam and Eve had been wrong to disobey. The Lord had asked only for obedience, and they had failed him. Yet the serpent had also done wrong in tricking Eve, and God's first words of punishment were for the beautiful beast.

"Because you have done this," the Lord God said to him, "you are cursed above all cattle and above every beast of the field. Upon your belly you will crawl, and dust you will eat all the days of your life. You and the woman, and your children and her children, shall be enemies forever."

The serpent no longer stood upright and proud but lay upon the ground lower than any other beast on earth. And it crawled away with its belly in the dust.

"For you," the Lord God said to Eve, "there will be pain and suffering, and in sorrow will you bring forth children. No longer are you equal to the man, for he shall rule over you."

And to Adam he said: "Because you listened to your wife and ate the fruit you were commanded not to eat, the ground will no longer bring forth only good things but also thorns and thistles. You will eat of the herb of the field, but food shall not be yours only for the taking. From now on you will work and earn your bread by the sweat of your brow, and this you will do until you return to the earth from which you were made."

Here, then, was the promised death. But it was not to come for many years, and during those years Adam and Eve would have children and Eve would be the mother of the world.

Then the Lord God made coats of skin for Adam and his wife, and clothed them with his goodness. And he said to himself, "It is enough that the man knows good and evil. Now, unless they leave this place, he may put out his hand and eat also of the Tree of Life, and live forever. And that he shall not do."

Therefore the Lord God sent Adam and Eve away from the garden and out into the world to make a new life for themselves. At the east of Eden he placed angels to watch over the garden, one of them with a flaming sword which turned in all directions to guard the pathway to the Tree of Life. It was the end of perfection in the world, for Adam and Eve had disobeyed. No longer would they know a paradise on earth. But they left Eden with God's promise that some day a Savior would appear among their children's children to wash all sins away.

Cain and Abel:

The First Murder

✠✠✠✠✠✠✠✠✠✠✠✠✠✠✠✠✠✠✠✠✠✠✠

Life was very different now for Adam and Eve. Instead of tending a fertile garden and picking fruit when they were hungry, they had to work hard to wrest a living from the soil. Instead of feeling safe and free from fear, they had to find shelter against the wild animals that had once been their companions. The ease and beauty of their former life were gone forever. As God had warned them, they knew both suffering and sorrow; and God himself no longer walked upon the earth to talk to them.

Yet there was still goodness in the world. God loved Adam and Eve, and they loved him in return. Adam learned how to till the soil so that the crops would grow and there was food to eat; and Eve learned how to make a home for her husband and herself. Even though they could no longer talk directly to their Lord, they could still keep close to him by offering him their gifts of love. Upon the rough stone altars that Adam built they would place the fruits of their harvest and the lambs of their flock as tokens of their faith. Because their love was great, so were their gifts. It was to show that they were willing to offer everything they had that they brought not only the food they grew from the soil but also creatures of flesh and blood to the altar of their Lord.

As time went by Eve gave birth to the first baby in the world, a sturdy little boy whom she and Adam named Cain. Before long a second baby came, and they called him Abel.

As the boys grew up they began to help their father on the land. Cain, like his father, preferred to work in the fields, tilling the soil and looking after the crops. Abel liked to tend the flocks, so he became a shepherd.

In time it came to pass that the two young men built altars of their own to bring gifts to the Lord. Cain brought the fruits of the field for his offering, and Abel brought the young lambs of his flock. God was pleased with Abel and his offering, because the younger brother was giving him creatures who lived and breathed even as Abel did. It was almost as if he were giving himself to God. But God was not pleased with Cain. The older brother was not giving freely of himself, and so was not offering all that God desired of him.

Cain felt God's displeasure, and he became angry because it seemed to him that he had done his best. After all, he had brought the fruits and grains he had grown with his own hands. Surely no more could be expected of him! His face fell, and he raged inside himself. God saw his sullen look and the anger burning in him.

"Why are you angry?" said the Lord to Cain. "And why is there a frown upon your face? If you do well, you will be accepted. And if you do not, you must know that you are in the wrong. It is for you to master sin, not to give in to it."

But Cain would not try to please the Lord. Instead, he let his anger grow until it took command of him.

Why should Abel be more favored than he, and why should not the Lord place an equal value on his offering?

The two brothers went together into the fields and talked. Cain's rage was growing, and the talk grew into a quarrel that became so fierce that Cain's anger overflowed. He sprang at Abel and attacked him bitterly, and when the sudden assault was over Abel lay dead in their father's fields. Cain left him lying there.

The Lord spoke to him again. "Where is your brother Abel?"

"I don't know," Cain lied. "How should I? Am I my brother's keeper?"

God knew that Cain was lying. "What have you done?" he said. "The blood of your brother cries out to me from the ground. Because of that, the earth that drinks the blood shed by your hand shall forever curse you. When you till the soil it will not yield its crops for you; from this day on you will be a wanderer and a fugitive throughout the land."

At last Cain was afraid.

"My punishment is more than I can bear!" he cried. "You have driven me away from yourself and from the company of men, and nowhere on the face of the earth will I find a home. Where shall I go? I shall be a homeless vagabond, and every man's hand will be against me as I wander. Any man who finds me will surely try to kill me."

Then the Lord said to him: "Whoever kills Cain will be punished seven times over. I will put a mark upon you so that you will be known wherever you go as a man to whom no harm shall come. You will not be killed by anyone who finds you."

So Cain left the land of his parents and wandered into a far country called Nod. He no longer spoke to God, yet God did not forsake him. Although Cain had killed his brother, God let him live to build a city and find himself a wife; and in time Cain's family became great in numbers and rich in worldly goods. But they did not worship God.

Noah and the Flood

✢✢✢✢✢✢✢✢✢✢✢✢✢✢✢✢✢✢✢✢✢✢

Adam and Eve went on living for a long time after losing their first two children, for people lived many hundreds of years when the world was new. Their hearts were sad because their sons had left them in such a tragic way, but they did not give in to sorrow. In time they had many more children, the first of whom was a boy very much like Abel. They called him Seth. When Seth grew to manhood he himself married, and established a branch of the family that went down through the centuries to produce a man who was to save the world from the judgment of the Lord.

When at last Adam and Eve died, eight hundred years after the birth of Seth, their family had grown into a vast tribe of people. The earth on which they had lived and toiled was no longer a lonely wilderness but a productive land teeming with their children, their chil-

dren's children, and great-great-great-grand children
who themselves were grown and had children of their
own. It should have been a good and wonderful world.

But it seemed that the more people there were the
more wickedness there was upon the earth. Among
them all there were only a few who found favor in the
eyes of the Lord because of their love for what was
good and right. These few were descended from Seth.
One of them was Enoch, who walked and talked with
God as Adam had done in the days of Eden. Another
was Enoch's son Methuselah, a man who lived longer
than any other man in the world, and who produced a
great many sons and daughters in the course of his nine
hundred and sixty-nine years on earth. Among his
several sons was Lamech, who had a son of his own
who proved to be among the most outstanding of the
descendants of Seth. That son's name was Noah.

Men multiplied on the face of the earth, working and
playing and having families, and forgetting all about
their Lord. God looked down and saw a few men like
Noah working hard in their fields and dealing honestly
with their fellow men; and he saw many men, such as
the descendants of Cain, becoming wealthy in their
cities and worshiping the things that they had made
with their own hands. Scarcely any man or woman
gave thought to the Lord who had created them. People seemed to have forgotten how to be good to one
another, much less love their Lord. They had become
so thoughtless that they no longer knew what was
right; nor did they seem to care.

Something had to be done. The Lord gave warning:
"My spirit shall not strive forever with the people of the
earth. The days of man shall be no more than a hundred and twenty years if his wickedness does not
pass."

But it was as if they did not hear him. The people
did not heed the warning of the Lord. Instead of
changing for the better they became even worse. And
God saw that the world was full of evil and wrongdo-
ing. Not only were man's deeds wicked, but his

thoughts were evil and there was evil in his heart continually.

The Lord was grieved at what he saw, and he regretted that he had ever placed man upon the earth. In sorrow, he said: "I will destroy man, whom I have created, from the face of the earth; not only man, but all the beasts and creeping things, and the fowls of the air; for I repent that I have made them."

But even in those bad days there was one man who found grace in the eyes of the Lord, and that was Noah. Like his great-grandfather Enoch and his first ancestor Adam, Noah was a just man who walked and talked with God. In the midst of all the world's wickedness he alone was truly righteous, and he alone tried to keep his family in the ways of God. He had three sons, Shem, Ham, and Japheth, and there was good in them as well.

God spoke to Noah. "The time has come to make an end of all this violence and evil," he said. "I will destroy all living things, and the whole earth with them. But you, Noah, must build an ark of gopher wood. You will make rooms in it, and line it with pitch inside and out so that no water can enter in. The ark shall have three levels: a lower, a second, and a third; and it shall be forty-five feet high. The length of it should be four hundred and fifty feet, and it must be seventy-five feet wide."

Noah listened with growing wonder as God spoke to him. He had never built a boat, for he lived far from the coast and had never needed one. Certainly, he had never imagined building a boat of such great size. But God was telling him how it should be done. It was to be very strongly built with a sturdy wooden frame and a sound, stout roof to keep the water off the decks, and there would also be a window and a single wide door set into the side. When it was finished it would look like a great houseboat. But what was it for?

The answer was soon coming. "There will be a flood of waters upon the earth," said the Lord, "and everything under heaven shall die. But to you, Noah, I

make a promise. When you have finished building you
will go into the ark, you and your wife and your
three sons and their families, for I have seen that you
are a righteous man and I will save you. And of every
living creature, excepting only man, you shall bring two
of every sort into the ark to keep them alive with you.
Each pair shall be male and female. Of every fowl of
the air and every beast that is greatly needed by man,
such as sheep and cattle, you shall take in sevens of
pairs, so that all such shall be reborn upon the earth in
good quantities when the flood has passed away. And
you shall gather every kind of food and place it on
board for yourselves and all the animals and birds and
creeping things that will be with you in the ark."

It was a strange thing for Noah to have to do, but he
did as he was commanded because he believed in God.
It was a long task to build the ark, to round up all the
animals, to gather and store the food, and it was made
no easier by his mocking neighbors. He warned them of
the oncoming flood, and begged them to repent and
save themselves; but they laughed at him and his enormous boat so far from the sea and would not believe
that they were in any danger from the Lord. They
could not believe, because they did not believe in
God. And they could not imagine a flood so bad that
it would destroy everything they had, including their
own lives. Therefore they kept on laughing and they
kept on with their evil ways.

But Noah went on building, while his sons collected
animals and food.

The time came when God told him he should load
the ship. "In seven days," said the Lord, "I will cause
it to start raining upon the earth. And it will rain for
forty days and forty nights. Take the beasts, two by
two, into the ark, and your family also. Whatever living thing is not upon the ark will be washed from the
face of the earth."

Noah went into the ark with his sons and his wife
and the wives of his sons. Two of every bird and beast
and every creeping thing, the male and female, fol-

lowed the human family into the ark. Then Noah
closed the door and waited.

He did not have long to wait. It came to pass after
seven days from God's final warning that the waters of
the flood were upon the earth. It was in the six hundredth year of Noah's life, on the seventeenth day of
the second month, that the fountains of the great deep
were broken up and the windows of heaven were
opened.

Water poured down from the sky. People ran from
the drowning lands into their homes to keep dry, and
when that did not help them they climbed the hills and
mountains to escape. There was no escape. The rivers
swelled and rose until they broke their banks and
washed across the lands. Great pools of water joined
together into even greater pools, and the water level
slowly rose. The ark rose steadily with the rising waters, and the rain lashed down upon its pitch-lined
roof. Inside, the good man Noah and his family were
safe and dry, and with them were the many pairs
of animals of every kind. They alone floated above
the flood, and although they were cut off completely
from the land, they had with them enough food to
last for many months if that were needed.

For forty days and forty nights, it rained.

Outside the ark, small streams grew into rushing
rivers, the rivers into walls of water that turned the land
into a vast lake dotted with small islands which had
once been high land. Rain water joined with sea to
wash away the coastline and the valleys, and the hills
shrank down beneath the growing seas. Higher and
higher rose the waters, until all the high hills under the
whole heaven and even the tall mountains were covered. There was no longer anywhere to run for safety.
Every man and all the cattle, all the birds of the air and
every creeping thing, all were washed away by the
flood, until there was nothing left in the world but a
great sheet of water and one wooden boat bobbing on
the face of the deep.

And then the rain stopped. At the end of forty days

and nights God remembered Noah and every living thing that was with him in the ark. And God made a wind to pass over the earth so that the waters were quieted. He stopped the fountains of the deep and closed the windows of heaven, and he held the rain back from the sky. The great sea over the land began subsiding gradually. For six months and more the ark went on floating on the silent sea, the only life in all the world. Slowly, day after day for a hundred and fifty days, the waters drained away. On the seventeenth day of the seventh month after the rain the ark came to rest upon the mountain of Ararat in Mesopotamia. And on the first day of the tenth month, the tops of distant mountains could be seen from the ark.

At the end of forty days of receding waters Noah sent out a raven from the window of the ark and watched it fly back and forth across the lonely sky. It was the only living thing outside the ark; and though it scouted for dry land, it found none. Noah also sent a dove, knowing that the dove would light on land if any land there was. But the dove came back, and Noah reached out his hand and took her into the ark. Seven days later he sent the dove out once again. This time she came back to him in the evening with a fresh young olive leaf in her mouth. Now Noah knew that the waters had drained away from the earth enough to permit life on the land, and that, somewhere, living trees had raised their heads above the immense lake. He waited yet another seven days, and then sent the dove out once again. She did not return at all.

And so it was that, on the first day of the first month of Noah's six hundredth and first year of life, the waters were dried up from the earth. Noah removed the covering of the ark and looked out upon a strange yet promising world. He was no longer in his own country; but the face of the ground was dry. God spoke to him again, saying: "Go out of the ark, and take with you your wife, your sons, and your sons' wives, and all the fowl and cattle and the creeping things, and put them back upon the land so that they may breed, and be fruitful, and multiply upon the earth."

Then Noah opened the great door of the ark, through which his strange crew had trooped more than a year before, and each and every pair followed Noah and his family onto the wonderful dry land. At last the world was alive again.

As soon as all were on dry land Noah built an altar of thanksgiving to the Lord to show his gratitude for having been saved. Upon the rough stones he made burnt offerings to the God who loved him, and gave thanks for the new hope in the world.

The Lord smelled the sweet savor of Noah's offerings and was pleased with what was in the good man's heart, and he vowed in his own heart that he would never again curse the ground to punish man or destroy all life on the earth. "While the earth remains," he promised, "seedtime and harvest, and cold and heat, and summer and winter, and day and night shall not cease to be." God then blessed Noah and his sons, and said to them: "The earth is yours. Be fruitful, have many children, and replenish it." He gave to them the earth and every living thing upon it.

Then he caused a great arc of lovely colors to vault the sky. "This is a token of the vow between us," he declared. "I make my promise to you and all the living creatures you have brought with you, and to your off-spring for all time. I do set my rainbow in the sky as a reminder of my covenant with every living thing on earth. When you see it, you will remember what I say to you, and know that I remember. And this is my everlasting vow: The waters shall no more become a flood to wash all living things away. Never again will there be a flood to destroy man from the earth."

The Tower of Babel

****

The three sons of Noah were to be the founders of a new human race, one that would start afresh in a world washed clean by the flood. After leaving the ark and receiving God's blessing, they made new homes for themselves, and it was not long before sons were born to their wives. The family of Noah increased greatly, generation after generation, so that in the course of time the world was indeed replenished through Japheth, Shem, and Ham.

Noah himself lived on for three hundred and fifty years after the flood, his boat-building days over forever. He farmed his lands, worked in his vineyards, and watched his huge family grow. At the age of nine hundred and fifty years, he died, knowing that his sons were the fathers of the nations of the world.

From Japheth's seven sons came the Gentiles, or the non-Jewish nations. Shem's five sons were to be the fathers of the Shemites, or Hebrews; and from his line would spring two upright men called Abram and Lot. Ham's four sons would go forth and people Africa, and would also be the fathers of the non-Hebrew inhabitants of Canaan. Eventually the descendants of Shem, later to be called the Israelites, would be in constant battle against the Canaanite descendants of Ham, but this was not to be for many, many years after the death of Noah.

Thus were the families of the sons of Noah separated into the nations of the world. And the whole earth, with all its nations, was of one language and of one speech.

The descendants of Noah left the region of Mount Ararat and traveled south into the valley of the Euphrates. They found a fertile plain in the land of Shinar, which was part of the country of Babylonia, and settled down to live there.

"Let us make bricks and mortar," they said to each other, "and let us build a city in which we can live together. And let us build a tower, so great and tall that its top will touch the skies. We will make a name for ourselves with our tall tower, and we will be a nation instead of being scattered abroad over the face of the whole earth."

They set to work, and it must be said that they labored with all their strength. They made bricks and more bricks, and carried heavy loads to the building site; they piled brick and mortar higher and higher until the tower grew to be as tall and magnificent as a temple to a pagan god. And still they went on building. They had no need for a tower so elaborate and vast, but they wanted theirs to be the greatest building in the world so that they could point to it with pride in their accomplishment.

And then the Lord came down to see the city and the tower which the children of men were building. He did not like the tower and what it told him of their pride. "The people of the earth are only one people," he thought, "and they have only one language. And even so, they are doing this to keep themselves together. If they can do such a thing as this, surely nothing will keep them from doing anything they dream of doing. But their pride is sufficient sin." For it looked, indeed, as though they had again forgotten all about God and were beginning to worship the creations of their own hands. "Let us go down there and confound their language," said the Lord, "so that they may not understand each other's speech."

And suddenly the builders of the city and the tower could not understand each other. Work stopped at once. It was impossible to go on building when the workmen all spoke different languages. It was the same thing throughout the city. Those who could understand each other came together and moved away to stay together. Soon little pockets of people speaking their own language appeared throughout the earth. Whoever was left in the city gave up building altogether because most of the citizens had scattered far and wide. And that is why the city is named Babel; it was here that the Lord confused the language of all the earth, and from there that the people scattered to the far corners of the earth to form separate nations, each with a language of its own.

The Journey
of Abram and Lot

✢✢✢✢✢✢✢✢✢✢✢✢✢✢✢✢✢✢✢✢✢

One of the descendants of Shem, a man by the name of Terah, made his home not far from Babel in a great city called Ur in the land of the Babylonians, or Chaldeans as they were also called. He had three sons, and their names were Abram, Nahor, and Haran.

Now Ur at this time was a very beautiful and very wealthy city, but its inhabitants did not pray to the God of the Hebrews. Many people in those days bowed down to the sun or the moon or the stars, or even the great rivers and the mountaintops. The people of Ur made idols and worshiped them, believing themselves to be especially favored by the moon-god. Terah himself had forgotten how to pray to the true God of his own people, but he did not feel completely at home in the city of Ur. He was a simple man and a farmer, and city life was not for him. When his sons had grown to manhood he decided to leave Ur and go to the land of

Canaan. By the time he was ready to go, one of his sons, Haran, had died in Ur, so Terah took with him Haran's son Lot, Abram his own son and Abram's wife Sarai, and his second son Nahor and Nahor's wife Milcah.

Together they journeyed up along the course of the river Euphrates in search of a better land. Instead of turning south and going into the land of Canaan, which the people of today call Palestine, they veered north and settled in a place called Haran in the district of Padan-Aram.

Terah had been quite rich in cattle and sheep even before leaving Ur. Now, in Haran, he soon established himself as a wealthy shepherd-farmer and the respected head of a growing family that worked hard and added steadily to the wealth. In time Terah died, and Abram became the head of the family and all the people who had joined their settlement to work in the household or among the flocks.

When Abram was seventy-five years old he heard the voice of the Lord say to him: "Leave your country and your kinsmen and your father's house, and go to a land that I will show you. I will make of you a great nation, and I will bless you and make your name great. Through you shall the families of the earth be blessed."

And Abram, even though he was no longer young and still without a son to help him, listened to the voice of the Lord and gathered his people together. His wife Sarai would of course go with him at his side. Nahor and his family decided to remain at Haran. Lot elected to go with Abram. Abram was glad that Lot chose to make the journey, because it meant that the two of them could share the leadership of the expedition. As soon as all was ready, Abram's caravan of shepherds and cattlemen and household retainers traveled away from the great river Euphrates toward Canaan in the southwest. With them they took all their sheep and cattle and their household goods, and they followed Abram and Lot and Sarai into the land the Lord had spoken of.

They journeyed on until they came to a place called Sichem on the plain of Moreh, which was in the land of Canaan. Here the Lord appeared to Abram and said: "To you and your children shall I give this land." Abram halted his caravan while he built an altar there to thank the Lord, and then went on with all his followers to a mountain on the east of Bethel. Here he pitched his tents so that all might rest a while, and he built another altar in praise of his Lord. Again he moved, journeying steadily toward the south, for he was not a city-dweller who would plant his roots deeply in one place but a tent-dweller and an animal farmer who needed to move where the pastures were rich.

The time came when the rivers dried up and there was a famine in the land. Abram needed water and fresh grass to pasture his herds and also to feed his people, so he and his train of followers went down into the well-watered land of Egypt to live there until the famine should pass. When at last it did he took Sarai and Lot and his whole caravan back into the land of Canaan, back to Bethel where he had pitched his tents before.

Life was good to them in the land the Lord had shown them, and Abram became rich not only in cattle but also in silver and gold from the land of Egypt. His flocks increased greatly, so that as the years passed he needed more pasture for them and more shepherds and herdsmen to look after them. Lot also had done well; he, too, had flocks and herds and tents and many people working for him. In fact, Abram's settlement was now so large that the land could not support all the living things that were upon it. The family and their serving men lived in a cluster of tents as large as a small city, while the sheep and cattle roamed far into the countryside in search of grazing ground.

It became a contest between the men of Abram and the men of Lot to find the best pastures for their herds when there was really only enough for one group or the other in the region of Bethel. The herdsmen began to quarrel among themselves. Abram called Lot aside and spoke to him about the arguments between their men. "Let there be no strife, I pray you," he said, "between the two of us or between our herdsmen. It is true, there is not room for both of us in this one place. But does not the whole land lie before us?" As they spoke they stood high upon the mountainside, and they could see the land below them stretching in all directions. "Let us separate, I beg you," Abram said. "Choose which way you will go. If you will go north, I shall go south; if you choose the east, I shall go west. Choose what you will, but let us not quarrel."

Lot surveyed the land below. Some of it was semi-desert plain and forbidding mountain; some, to the east, was green and fertile, as well-watered and productive as the garden of the Lord or the land of Egypt where they had escaped the famine. It was the plain of Jordan; and he knew that he could do well there with his flocks. He also knew that it was Abram's right to make the choice and take the fertile eastern lands. But Abram had offered that right to him, and so Lot took it.

"I shall go east," he said, and chose for himself all the gentle plain of Jordan.

They separated, then, and Lot journeyed into the eastern plain with his family and flocks. Abram stayed in the land of Canaan, content with whatever lands his nephew Lot had left him. Lot traveled on toward the cities of the plain, and eventually he pitched his tents and pastured his flocks near the city of Sodom. It was a good land for a farmer, and it was also convenient for Lot to be near a city of some size. But the men of Sodom were exceedingly wicked, and they sinned against the Lord continually.

After Lot had made his choice and left, the Lord spoke again to Abram.

"Lift up your eyes, Abram. Look northward from where you stand, and southward and eastward and westward. All the land that you see I will give to you and your children, and your children's children, forever. I will give you many descendants, as many as there are grains of dust upon the earth. Arise, walk through the land, across the length of it and the breadth of it, for I will give it all to you."

Then Abram moved his tents and journeyed through the land to see what God had given him. When he had had enough of travel he halted on a plain called Mamre, and pitched his tents among the tall oaks near the city of Hebron. Here he built another altar to the Lord who had guided him and given him so much. He and his wife Sarai prospered, although they did not yet have any of the children the Lord had promised Abram, and were happy with their simple way of life. But Lot had grown to enjoy the pleasures offered by the cities of the plain, and had moved his family into the city of Sodom.

The Capture of Lot

✦✦✦✦✦✦✦✦✦✦✦✦✦✦✦✦✦✦✦✦

The city of Ur in Babylonia had been a godless place, but Sodom was even worse. Its people thought of nothing but their own pleasures and the pursuit of wealth. Nor was Sodom the only city of its kind; the neighboring town of Gomorrah was equally bad. Both Sodom and Gomorrah were known throughout the land for the evil deeds of their inhabitants.

These two cities and three others lay in the vale of Siddim near an inland sea called the Dead Sea, or the Salt Sea. The five of them were long-time enemies of the mighty king of Elam and his three powerful allies, and in fact had lost in battle to them and were obliged to pay tribute to their conquerors for many years. The tax was a burden to them, but it was not so heavy that they could not still afford to live in luxury. As long as they could go on enjoying themselves, they would rather pay the tribute money than fight to free themselves.

When at last they rebelled against the king of Elam and refused to go on serving him, they were so softened by easy living that they had almost forgotten how to fight. The forces that faced them were smaller than their own but at full fighting strength, and the war went badly for the people of Sodom and Gomorrah. Four kings fought with five in the vale of Siddim, and the five kings fled before the king of Elam and his fighting friends. They turned and ran, with all their soldiers, into the mountains and the valleys, and left their cities open to the mercy of the enemies.

The conquering soldiers swarmed into the cities of Sodom and Gomorrah, looking for the gold and silver they knew were hidden in the houses of the wealthy, and looting everything they could find in the homes and market places. They took goods and food and captives, and went back to their camp with all that they had taken. And with them they took Lot, Abram's brother's son, and all Lot's goods, and they held him in captivity with many other men and women whom they had taken for their slaves.

But one man managed to escape from the enemy camp. He broke loose from his captors and fled across the country to find Abram in the plain of Mamre, and when he had found him he told Abram about the awful battle and the fate of Lot. Abram was a peaceful farmer-shepherd and not a fighting man, but when he heard what had happened to his nephew Lot he knew at once that he must rescue him. With the help of a few friends who lived near him, he gathered together his band of herdsmen and the servants of his household, and he swiftly formed them into a well-armed fighting force. There were three hundred and eighteen of them, all born to his household, and all trained men who knew well how to defend their flocks and pastures from attack. This time they would be the attackers; and

Abram knew that they would fight with him to save his kinsman with all their strength and loyalty.

Abram placed himself at the head of his small army and went off in hot pursuit of the forces who held his nephew Lot. Far to the north, at a place called Dan, he came upon the enemy camp at night and launched a swift attack. It was so sudden and so unexpected that the enemy broke camp and ran. Abram's forces pursued them almost to Damascus, attacking all the way, before letting the remnants of the Elamite forces straggle away into the hills of their homeland.

And Abram rescued all the captives and their stolen possessions, all the men and women and their goods; and his nephew Lot, and all his goods. Lot was a grateful man that day; and grateful, too, were all the people of the ransacked cities. But though Abram could have made himself a very rich man indeed by keeping the goods he had recovered, he would take no reward from their kings for what he had done. Instead, he returned the goods to the people and the people to their cities, accepting nothing in return but the food he needed for the young men of his tiny army. Lot and his family went back into the city of Sodom, which had become no less wicked for having been saved by Abram; and Abram went back to the quiet life of his tent home on the plain of Mamre.

God's Promise
to Abram

✝✝✝✝✝✝✝✝✝✝✝✝✝✝✝✝✝✝✝✝✝✝✝

Thus, although it was the custom for the conqueror to keep the spoils of battle, Abram accepted no reward from man. But soon after the rescue of Lot, Abram heard the voice of the Lord saying: "Fear not, Abram, I will protect you and reward you greatly for your righteousness."

Now Abram had everything he wanted out of life but for one thing; and the lack of that one thing was a cause of sadness to him.

"Lord God, what is my reward?" he asked. "I still have no child of my own. Eliezer of Damascus, who is the steward of my household and watches over everything I own, was born in my house and is a good man. Should he be my heir?"

"He shall not," the Lord told him. "Your own son shall be your heir. Look up at the stars, Abram. See if you can count them. As many stars as there are up in the heavens, so many will be the children of your family. I am the Lord who brought you out of Ur to give you this land to inherit. I give it to you, and the children of your children, and not to someone else born in your house." And Abram, although he was old and still without a son, believed in the Lord's word.

God also told him something of the far-off future, when the Hebrews would suffer hard times but would overcome their sorrows. In a distant time, God told the faithful Abram, the children of his family would be strangers in a strange, unfriendly land for four hundred years. They would be slaves to the people of that nation, but when they left it they would become a great people in their own right and they would possess the land of Canaan for themselves.

And eventually it did happen that the descendants of Abram became slaves in the land of Egypt, and that they left the country of the Pharaohs and journeyed slowly back to the promised land. But it would be many years before this came to pass, and Abram himself was not to see it happen. While he still lived in Mamre near the great oaks of Hebron, not only Abram but his wife Sarai continued to think about the children that they did not have.

Sarai thought about it for a long time, for she wanted children very badly. Even though she knew of God's promise to her husband, time was passing by and she could no longer believe that she would ever have a baby of her own. One day she said to Abram: "The Lord has not let me have a child. Go to my handmaid, Hagar. Take her to yourself; in that way I may have a child through her." Now Hagar was an Egyptian maidservant who had become attached to Abram's household during his journey to Egypt at the time of the famine in Canaan. In those days it was not unusual for a man to have more than one wife, or for a wife to give her handmaid to her husband. Sometimes childless women like Sarai would ask their husbands to produce children through a trusted handmaid, and

then the wife would be thought of as the mother of
the handmaid's children.

Abram agreed to Sarai's request, and Sarai gave the
handmaid Hagar to him so that she might bear a child.

It was not long before Hagar knew that she was
going to have a baby. She was proud of it, and she
began to mock her mistress because Sarai had not been
able to have a child of her own. This was not at all
what Abram's wife had hoped for, and she was most
unhappy. Instead of feeling like a mother herself, she
felt she was a failure as a wife. And Hagar let her
feel it; Hagar despised her openly.

"I was wrong to do what I did," Sarai said sadly to
Abram. "It was a mistake, for now I am despised in
Hagar's eyes. Tell me, what should I do now?"

"She is your maid," Abram replied. "Do with her
what you will."

And Sarai was hard on the mocking Hagar; she
treated her so severely that Hagar could no longer bear
it, and ran away into the wilderness. It was not long
before she tired and was obliged to rest. She stopped by
a fountain of water on the way to Shur, and it was here
that the angel of the Lord found her in the wilderness.

"Hagar, Sarai's maid!" he said. "What are you doing
here, and where are you going?"

"I am running from my mistress Sarai," she replied.

"Return to your mistress," said the angel of the
Lord, "and obey her. God has seen your suffering. You
will have a child, and he will grow up to be a strong
and mighty man who will dwell in the wilderness.
Through him you will have a great family of your own.
But now you must go back, Hagar. The Lord sees you,
and is with you."

Hagar returned to the tents of Abram and Sarai.
When her time came she bore a son to Abram, and
they called him Ishmael. Abram was eighty-six years
old, and proud to have a son even though it was not
Sarai's; but Sarai could never bring herself to forgive
Hagar or to accept Ishmael as her own beloved son.

And it was true that Ishmael was not the child that

God had promised Abram. He grew into a strong, wild lad, loved by Abram and disliked by Sarai; and Abram and Sarai kept on growing older.

When Abram was ninety-nine years old and Sarai herself, though younger, was past the age when she might have a child, the Lord appeared again to Abram and said: "I am the Almighty God, and I shall make a covenant with you. You have been faithful and have served me well; and you will be the father of many nations. From your children, and your children's children, there will come great men and kings, and all the land of Canaan will be theirs forever." And because Abram was to be the father of many nations, the Lord told him that his name would change. Instead of being Abram, which meant "exalted father," he would become Abraham, which meant "father of a multitude." Sarai, too, must change her name. Her new name would be Sarah, meaning "queen," for she would be the mother of nations and from her would come men who would be kings.

Then Abraham, who had believed the Lord all the years of his life, hardly dared to believe what he was hearing now. That he would still have his own child was so incredible to him that he laughed, and in his heart he said: "Shall a child be born to a man who is nearly a hundred years old? And to a woman who is ninety?" And he thought of the one son he did have, and whom he loved even though the boy was not Sarah's child. Abraham wanted good things for him, too. "O Lord, what of Ishmael?" he asked.

And God said: "I have blessed Ishmael. He, too, will have many children. Twelve princes will descend from him, and I will make of him a great nation. But my covenant is not with him but with the son of Sarah. For Sarah shall indeed bear a child, and you will call him Isaac. I say to you now that Sarah shall have a son at this same time next year."

Yet it was still hard for Abraham to believe, and harder still for Sarah.

The Visit
of the Strangers

❋❋❋❋❋❋❋❋❋❋❋❋❋❋❋❋❋❋❋❋❋❋

One day the Lord appeared to Abraham as he sat in the shaded doorway of his tent in the heat of the day. The old man looked up and saw three strangers walking toward him through the tall oak trees that gave cool shade to the camp, and he knew at once that they were from a very far country. In his heart he was sure that the Lord had come to him in the form of three angels from heaven. Whether they were angels or ordinary travelers through the desert, they would be well received by the hospitable Abraham; but somehow he knew that there was nothing ordinary about them.

He ran to meet them from the tent door and bowed low toward the ground. "My Lords," he said, "if I have found favor in your sight, do not travel on. Stay here, I pray you, and I will have water brought to you so that you may wash your feet. Do rest yourselves beneath the shady trees, and I will fetch a morsel of food so that you may refresh yourselves before you go upon your way."

They thanked him and accepted. "Do as you have said," they answered. "We will rest here with you."

So Abraham brought them cool water for their feet, for it was the custom that wayfarers should wash their feet and rest them as they paused upon their way. Then he hurried into the tent to find Sarah, and said: "Quickly, prepare three measures of fine meal, and knead it, and make cakes upon the hearth."

She set to work at once and without question while Abraham ran to the herd and chose a calf, a good young one and tender, which he gave to a young man-servant to prepare and roast. When all was ready he took butter, milk, baked cakes, and roasted calf to the waiting strangers, and placed the food before them under the shade of a large tree. He stood by them beneath the tree while they were eating; and when they were rested and refreshed they talked to him.

"Where is your wife Sarah?" they asked, for their backs were toward his tent and they had not seen her yet.

"She is in the tent," said Abraham.

"The Lord shall bless her," said one, the one whom Abraham thought must be the Lord himself. "Sarah your wife will have a son at the appointed time, as I did promise."

Now Sarah stood hidden within the doorway of the tent, and she heard this, and she laughed. Many times before she had heard about this promise, and now it was much too late for it to come true. Both she and Abraham were very old: he was a hundred years, and she was ninety, well past the age when she could have a child. Therefore Sarah laughed silently within herself.

And the Lord, who was indeed among the strangers, said: "Why did Sarah laugh, and think to herself that she is too old to bear a child? Is anything too hard for the Lord? At the time appointed I will return to you and Sarah, and she will surely have her son."

Sarah heard this, and suddenly she was afraid. How could someone have heard her silent laughter and her innermost thoughts? "I did not laugh," she denied, looking out fearfully from the tent door.

"But you did laugh," said the Lord. Yet he was not angry, for he could understand her doubts.

Then the three men, with the Lord among them, rose from beneath the tree and looked toward Sodom, for it was toward the city that they were making their way. Abraham went with them for a short distance to show them the right road, and as he led them to the road to Sodom he wondered to himself what their business could be in that wicked city. His nephew Lot still lived there, and Abraham had heard many tales about the growing sinfulness among the people of the town. Again it seemed as though the Lord had heard his thoughts.

"Shall I hide from Abraham the thing I am about to do?" said the Lord. "No, because I know you, Abraham. I know that you will become a great and mighty nation, and that you will teach your children and your children's children to be righteous and keep the ways of the Lord. So I will tell you what I am going to have to do. I am going now to Sodom, because the people there are full of sin. The two cities, Sodom and Gomorrah, cry out their evil to the skies. I shall go first to Sodom, to see for myself if they are as bad as the report that has been brought to me, and I shall learn if these cities can really be as wicked as they seem. I shall know when I see them. And I will know what I must do with them."

Abraham stopped in the road and stood before the Lord. He knew what those words meant. He thought of Lot in Sodom, and other men who perhaps did not deserve to die. The two men with the Lord turned away and went on toward the wicked city, but Abraham still stood before the Lord.

"But surely you will not destroy the righteous with

the wicked?" he said anxiously. "Perhaps there are fifty good people within the walls of Sodom. Would you also destroy them with the city, or would you spare the place because of them? It would not be like the Lord to slay the righteous with the wicked. It would not be right. And shall not the Judge of all the earth do right?"

The Lord felt pity for Abraham and all the people of the city. "If I find fifty righteous people in Sodom," God said to Abraham, "I will not destroy the people or the city. All Sodom will be saved because of them."

Abraham thought this over. He felt that he was taking too much upon himself to talk in this way to the Lord of all the earth, but he had to try again. He wondered if the number of fifty was not too much to hope for. "Perhaps there will be a few less than fifty," he suggested. "Perhaps five less. Would you destroy the whole city for the lack of five good men to make up fifty?"

The Lord said, "If I find but forty-five good men, I will not destroy the city."

But Abraham still felt troubled. He did not want any good men to be destroyed along with the bad, but from all accounts that he had heard of Sodom it was not likely that as many as forty-five righteous people could be found there. "Perhaps there will be no more than forty," he said hesitantly.

The Lord was patient with him, for the Lord himself did not want to destroy good men. "For the sake of forty I will not destroy the city," he told Abraham.

Forty seemed rather a lot to expect in a town like Sodom. Abraham went on pleading. "Oh, do not be angry with me, Lord, but what if there are less than forty? No more, perhaps, than thirty?"

"Then I will not do it," the Lord answered. "If I find thirty good souls there, I will not do it."

"Lord," said Abraham, "now that I have taken it upon my humble self to speak to you in this way, I cannot help going on. May I ask what will happen if there are twenty good men found in Sodom?"

"I will spare the city for the sake of twenty."

But perhaps there would be fewer than twenty good men found in Sodom, and one of them his nephew Lot. "Oh, please do not be angry, Lord," Abraham begged him. "This is the last time I will speak. What if there are only ten?"

"If there are ten good men, then for the sake of ten I will not destroy it," the Lord assured him, and went upon his way. Abraham watched him walk off into the distance toward the wicked city, and then returned to the place of his tents to think about the fate of Sodom and his brother's son.

He could only hope that the angels of the Lord would find ten good men in the midst of all that wickedness so that they and their city could be saved.

The Fate of Sodom

✠✠✠✠✠✠✠✠✠✠✠✠✠✠✠✠✠✠✠✠✠✠✠

Of all the five cities in the vale of Siddim near the Salt Sea, the city of Sodom and the neighboring town of Gomorrah were the worst in sinfulness. Yet Lot had freely chosen to make the city of Sodom his home, knowing that he could make a good living by supplying the townspeople with fresh meat from his herds and believing that their wickedness would have no effect upon him. In spite of their evil ways, the people of Sodom had enough respect for Lot to allow him to become a great man in their city, and as time passed they came to regard him as one of their judges or wise men. And as a wise man he became accustomed to sit at the main gate of the city where he could be easily found when people sought his advice in settling their quarrels.

On the evening of the day during which Abraham had been visited by the two angels and the Lord, Lot

was sitting in his usual place near the gate of Sodom
when two strangers approached and entered through
the gate. Lot knew how the people of Sodom were used
to treating strangers; instead of offering friendly greetings they would make sport of newcomers, and instead
of offering food and rest they would offer brutality and
cruel harm. Lot quickly rose to meet the two men,
unaware that they were angels of the Lord come to see
the wickedness of Sodom for themselves, and he bowed
low toward the ground.

"I greet you, my Lords," he said. "Come into my
house, I pray you, and refresh yourselves, and stay the
night. Rise up early if you wish and then go on your
way, but do not try to go further in the city tonight."

"No, we thank you," the two men answered Lot.
"We will spend the night in the street."

"No, my Lords" Lot said firmly, "You shall not stay
here in the street." He was sure that the strangers
would not be safe unless he offered them protection
from the people of Sodom. "I beg you to join me in my
house." As the two men looked around and saw the
filth of the streets and the leering faces of the people
who were crowding around, they began to think that
perhaps they would be better off to accept Lot's invita-
tion. But they were there to see what Sodom was like
and so they hesitated, looking carefully at the people
who stared back curiously and talked excitedly among
themselves about how they might rob and hurt the
strangers.

Lot pressed them. He insisted. They must please
come with him to his house, he said. Finally they
nodded and followed him into his home. As darkness
fell upon the city they went with Lot to wash their
travel-weary feet and rest within his house. Lot made a
feast for them, and they ate gratefully. Soon they
would lie down to sleep.

But before they could lie down there came a loud
knocking at the door. The word of Lot's two visitors
had spread throughout the town, and the people of
Sodom wanted to amuse themselves by tormenting the

two strangers. Young and old, and from every quarter of the city, they swarmed around Lot's house and demanded that he let them in or turn his guests over to them so that they could have their awful fun. "Where are the men who came to your house tonight?" they shouted to Lot as they battered against the doors and windows. "Bring them out to us!"

Lot went out of his house alone and stood with his back against the door.

"I pray you, my brothers," he said quietly "stop your wickedness. Leave these men alone. Do what you like to my family, but spare the strangers in my house. They came under my roof for shelter, and shelter they shall have." But his words did nothing to change the men of Sodom except to make them even more angry and excited. "Stand aside!" they shouted. "You are nothing but a stranger here yourself, and you have made yourself a judge over us. If you do not get out of our way we will deal worse with you than with those other men!" They crowded rudely against him, pushing him brutally and almost succeeding in breaking down the door. But the two men inside quickly reached out their hands and dragged Lot into the house with them and firmly shut the door.

The door shuddered and creaked, and almost splintered inward under the savage battering of the Sodomites. But suddenly the heavy pounding stopped, and instead of howling for the blood of the two strangers the men of Sodom howled with fear. Each one of them, the great ones and the small alike, had been struck blind by a power they could not understand, and they could no longer even find the door to hammer on it. At last Lot realized that he was harboring angels in his house, for it was they who had struck the men outside with blindness.

The heavenly agents had seen for themselves that Lot was a good man who would risk his own life to save theirs, but it was clear to them that it was unlikely they would find as many as nine other good people in this terrible town.

And they said to Lot: "Do you have any other family in this town? Sons, daughters, sons-in-law, or anyone else? If you have, get them out of Sodom, for this place is about to be destroyed. It is evil altogether, and the Lord himself has sent us to destroy it."

Lot hurried off to speak to his sons-in-law, and said to them: "Get up! Get out of this place! Listen to me and go, for the Lord is about to destroy the city." But he could not make them understand that he was serious, and they would not believe that Sodom would be destroyed. They laughed, and made no move to leave.

Very early on the following morning, before the sun had even touched the sky, the angels aroused Lot and begged him to hurry away. "Arise!" they said urgently. "Take your wife and the two daughters who live with you, and go quickly from the city or else you will die with it."

It was hard for Lot to leave. Sodom had been his home for many years. If he fled now, after so little preparation, he would be leaving much behind: his home, his lands, his riches, even part of his family. And so he lingered, casting longing eyes at the things he did not want to leave. But the Lord was merciful to Lot and did not let him stay. As he lingered, the angels of the Lord took hold of Lot, his wife, and their two daughters, and dragged them away by the hand until they were well outside the city walls. "Now you must run for your lives," the Lord said through his angels. "Do not look back, and do not stay here in the plain. Go to higher ground; escape to the mountain, or you will perish with all the people of the plain."

"Not the mountain!" pleaded Lot. "My Lord, you have shown me great mercy by saving my life. I beg you, show me more mercy yet. I cannot escape to the mountain, for some evil might overtake me and I shall die. There is a small city nearby that we may flee to. It is much closer than the mountain, and it is only a little city so it cannot be too bad and it is not much to save. Is it not a little one? Spare that little city, Lord, I beg you, and let us escape to it and go to live there."

He was talking about the city of Zoar, one of the five cities of the plain that lay near the Salt Sea. Although its reputation was not so good as it might have been, the Lord decided to save it and thus make escape easier for Lot.

And through one of his angels he said to Lot: "I will do what you ask, and I will not overthrow the city of Zoar. But you must hurry. Escape to it quickly, and do not waste time by looking back. There is no longer any time to lose."

Lot hurried toward the tiny city. The sun was rising just as he and his daughters entered Zoar, and all at once the earth began to tremble and quake and the sky was red with an ugly light. Behind them, the ground split open with a rumbling sound that was like the loudest thunder, and the plain heaved mightily. Fire and sulphur seemed to pour down from the very heavens themselves, and the waters of the Salt Sea churned and boiled. Buildings shook and flew apart, and the earth crumbled. Hot ash and blazing fire, flying sulphur and streams of scalding water rained down upon Sodom and Gomorrah and the neighboring cities of the plain; and the Lord overthrew those cities and the people in them. The plain itself was swamped with the fire from above and the walls of salty water that were thrown out by the churning sea, so that everything that lived and grew upon it was destroyed. Nothing was left undamaged on the plain of the Salt Sea but the little town of Zoar. Its people were unhurt; Lot and his daughters were safe.

But not Lot's wife! She was behind her husband and daughters as they ran, because she had been slow to tear herself away from the city that had been her home, and when the earth began to quake and roar she was still behind him; and she did look back. She paused for a moment too long. There in the vale of the Salt Sea she was engulfed by the waters that boiled and plunged beneath the fiery heavens, and she was caught there on the plain. And she herself became a pillar of salt.

Early that same morning Abraham left his tent and went to the place where he had stood before the Lord and pleaded for Lot and the people of Sodom. The distant sky was a strange color and the winds brought back to him the smell of sulphur. So there had not been ten good men, he thought.

But God had remembered Abraham, and had sent Lot safely out of the midst of the giant upheaval that was still overthrowing the cities of the plain. As Abraham looked across the plain toward Sodom and Gomorrah he could see the smoke of the country rising like the smoke of a furnace. His heart grieved for all the people, wicked though they had been. He watched in sadness for a while and then went back to his tent beneath the trees near peaceful Hebron.

Lot was not happy in the town of Zoar; somehow he no longer felt safe upon that devastated plain. In his fear he decided to leave town. With his two daughters he went up into the mountain that he had avoided before, and the three of them lived in a cave without any of the comforts they had been used to all their lives. Gone were all the sheep and cattle; gone were all the riches; gone Lot's wife, and gone the sons-in-law; and all because in earlier years Lot had chosen to pitch his tent near Sodom. But at least he was alive.

Years later, Lot's older daughter had a son whom she called Moab, who became the father of the Moabites; and Lot's younger daughter bore a son called Ben-Ammi, whose descendants were the Ammonites. Both the Moabites and the Ammonites were to cross the lives of the Hebrews in the land of Canaan throughout the years to come.

But that was far into the future, and in the meantime Lot lived almost like a hermit in his cave. And Abraham and Sarah were still waiting for their dreamed-of child.

The Sons of Abraham

(The Story of Hagar and Ishmael)

✽✽✽✽✽✽✽✽✽✽✽✽✽✽✽✽✽✽

Abraham was a hundred years old when his son Isaac was born to him and Sarah. For the Lord did visit Sarah as he had said he would, and he did fulfill the long-awaited promise. And thus did Sarah bear Abraham a son in his old age, at the very time of which the Lord had spoken.

Sarah remembered how she had laughed when she had overheard the prophecy of the stranger resting underneath the trees. Then her laughter had held the bitterness of disbelief, but now she could laugh with a heart full of happiness. "God has given me reason to laugh, so that all that hear will laugh with me," she said joyfully. "Who would have thought that Sarah should have given a child to Abraham, and both of us so old?"

The baby Isaac grew and left his mother's arms. When he was barely past babyhood and only just big

57

enough to explore the settlement of large tents and shady trees for himself, Abraham decided that his son was old enough to be shown off to their friends and relatives in the neighboring tent towns. He gave a great feast in celebration; and the two old parents were filled with quiet pride in their young son. It was a wonderfully festive occasion, but something happened to spoil it for the people who had most reason to be happy. Sarah saw the son of Hagar, the Egyptian woman, making fun of little Isaac. Ishmael was a lad of fourteen by this time, and Sarah did not like the way he treated her small boy.

Angrily, she said to Abraham: "Send away this Egyptian woman and her son! My son shall not grow up with that boy, and that woman's son shall not be heir with Isaac. Send them both away from here!"

This was a hard thing to ask of Abraham, who himself asked little of life but that everyone should live in the ways of God and be content. He loved his Sarah deeply and would do anything in his power to make her happy. Yet he also loved his son Ishmael and did not want to send him away, perhaps even into danger, for in those days people who lived or journeyed without protection were almost certain to run into trouble of some kind. Even if there were no question of danger, he did not want to be unfair to Hagar and her boy. And he would miss his firstborn son. Therefore Abraham was exceedingly unhappy.

God saw his sorrow and told him not to grieve. "Listen to Sarah," said the Lord. "Do whatever she says. And do not grieve because of the lad, or because of the woman. It is with Isaac that I have my covenant, and it is through Isaac that your name shall be forever known and your family shall be blessed. As for the son of the Egyptian woman, I will also make a nation of him, because he is your child. Therefore, have no fear for Ishmael and Hagar."

Abraham was still grieving in his heart when he arose very early the next morning to say farewell to Ishmael and the woman from Egypt who had borne him, but his pain was less and he no longer feared for them. He took food from his supplies and gave it to Hagar and placed a bottle of water on her shoulder; and he sent her away with her child.

Hagar took the boy from Abraham's home and walked for many days, heading for her own distant homeland of Egypt through the wilderness of Beersheba. And there in the wilderness the two of them wandered alone and without help, meeting no one on the way to offer them food or a place to rest. The day came when their food ran out and the water bottle was drained of its last drop. They went on walking, more slowly all the time, looking for a well or spring so that they might at least be able to drink. But there was no water in sight; nothing but the hot sun blazing down on them, the burning desert shimmering with the heat, and the low shrubs that gave off scarcely any shade and not a drop of moisture.

Together they stumbled on as long as they could move, still hoping that help would come from somewhere. At last Hagar could go on no longer. She and young Ishmael were faint for the lack of food and water, and tired of the endless walking with nothing to sustain them. Their hope gone and their bodies weak, they stopped where they were and sank down onto the burning sand. Hagar rested for a moment and drew breath for what she had to do. Lovingly, and with a heart that was near to breaking, she laid her son beneath one of the small shrubs so that he would have its scant shade to comfort him if nothing else. Then she turned and walked away as far as she could go; as far as an arrow shot from a bow, but no more, for she was deadly tired and heartsore and could go no further. Yet she could not bring herself to stay beside that small shrub and watch the suffering of Ishmael. She sat down, then, and the tears trickled down her face. "I cannot bear to see the death of the child," she wept, and turned her head away. In her heart she was sure that he would not last long, and that she would follow soon after.

But God had not forgotten her, or his promise to both her and Abraham; and they were not alone and lost in the wilderness. He heard their voices, and he answered.

"Hagar! Do not be afraid, for I have heard the cry of the lad where he lies. Arise! Lift up the boy and take him by the hand, for you shall both be saved and I will make of him a great nation."

And God opened her eyes, and she saw a well of water. With new strength she rose and filled the bottle with water, and gave it to the lad to drink. They went on then, the woman and the boy, but not as far as Egypt. Hagar made an end to their wanderings when they came to the Wilderness of Paran, and made a home for the two of them in the wild country. God watched over them in their lonely home and saw that no harm came to them. The boy grew tall and strong, and became a man skilled in hunting with the bow and arrow. His mother took him a wife out of the land of Egypt, and soon Ishmael had children of his own. His sons were strong, rough men of the outdoors even as he; and *their* sons counted among them twelve princes and twelve mighty tribes. And thus, out of Ishmael, there came a nation.

The Sacrifice
of Isaac

❦❦❦❦❦❦❦❦❦❦❦❦❦❦❦❦❦❦❦❦❦

As the years passed Isaac grew into a fine young lad who loved his father as much as Abraham loved him. Just as Abraham obeyed the Lord, so did Isaac trust and obey his father Abraham in every way. God watched over them both, never forgetting his promise that Abraham would become the father of a multitude through his son Isaac.

Yet God had one more test for Abraham, and it was a very difficult one. The Lord had taught his people that he required their complete faith and love, even their lives, and that they should be willing to offer everything to him. And yet at the same time he had said that no man should shed another's blood. A burnt offering from a man's flocks, given freely and with all his heart, was enough to show a man's desire to offer all he had. The sacrifice of a man himself, or of a beloved child, was wrong in the eyes of God. And the

Lord wanted to be sure that Abraham understood this even while he proved his love and faith.

And so he tested Abraham, the founder of the Hebrew race from which the Savior of the world would come.

"Abraham!" he called.

"I am here, Lord," Abraham answered.

And God gave him a terrible command that would require a special kind of obedience and trust from Abraham.

"Take your son," said God, "Isaac, your only son, and bring him with you into the land of Moriah. There you will give him up to me as a burnt offering upon a mountain that I will show to you."

Abraham did not question God. He, too, remembered God's promise that his family, through Isaac, would be great and blessed. If he wondered at all at God's command, he wondered how the promise could possibly come true if he gave up Isaac as an offering. And yet he did believe the promise. He had faith, and he obeyed.

He rose early in the morning and made ready to go. It was a long way to the land of Moriah and he could not walk the whole way with the boy's hand held in his. So he called two of his young manservants to him, saddled his donkey, and cut wood for the fire he would build upon the mountain. When the donkey was laden with the wood he sent for Isaac; and then they left on their long journey.

On the third day he saw the place from afar, the place that God had told him of. As they drew near Abraham said to the young men: "Stay here with the donkey while the boy and I go up into the mountain and worship. Wait, and we will come back to you when we have made the offering." For his love was so great and his faith was so strong that even while he was prepared to give up Isaac to his Lord he was sure in his heart that God would somehow return his son to him.

He took the wood for the burnt offering and laid it on Isaac's shoulder to carry, and he himself took the fire and a knife. Father and son went off together to climb the mountain where the offering would be made. As they climbed Isaac began to wonder why they had not brought anything to offer on the altar.

"Father?" he asked, looking at the things Abraham carried in his hands.

"I am here, my son."

"I see the wood and I see the fire, but where is the lamb for the offering?"

"My son," said Abraham, "God will provide himself a lamb for a burnt offering." That was enough for Isaac, for he trusted in his father and his father's God. They went on climbing together.

When they came to the place on top of the mountain that God had told him of, Abraham built an altar of stones and laid the wood upon it. Isaac looked around; he still could see no lamb.

Abraham reached gently for his son and bound his hands and feet. This time Isaac asked no question. Then Abraham laid his son upon the wood of the altar and reached out his hand for the knife. He raised it slowly, still willing to give everything to God and still believing that God would not take his son from him forever.

He brought the knife up high, ready for the downward plunge.

"Abraham! Abraham!" a voice called out. He stopped. It was the angel of the Lord calling to him out of heaven. Abraham turned the knife aside and listened. "Here I am," he said.

"Do not lay your hand upon the lad," said the angel of the Lord. "Do no harm to Isaac. Now I know that your love for God is deep and true and that you are obedient, seeing that you did not withhold your son, Isaac your only son, from him. Lift up your eyes!"

And Abraham lifted up his eyes and looked around him. As he turned he saw behind him a ram caught in the bushes by its horns. Quickly, he untied his son, rejoicing in his heart. He went and took the ram from the thicket, and offered it up on the altar for a burnt offering in the place of his beloved son. It was all that God required; Abraham had already proved not only his obedience but his trust.

When he and the boy had worshiped God and completed the offering, Abraham gave a name to the place where he had been prepared to give up Isaac, and where he had told his son that God would provide himself a lamb. He called it Jehovah-jireh, meaning "The Lord will provide." Now he knew even better than before that God would provide for those who truly loved him. And he also knew that God did not want his people offered to him as gifts on blazing altars, for those whose faith and love was strong already belonged to God with their hearts and souls.

Father and son walked together down the mountainside and returned, as Abraham had said they would, to the young men who were waiting.

Rebekah at the Well

✛✛✛✛✛✛✛✛✛✛✛✛✛✛✛✛✛✛✛✛✛✛✛

Sarah died when she was a hundred and twenty-seven years old. Abraham wept for her and mourned his loss; but their life together had been long and good and she had given him a son to comfort him. Because the land of their forefathers was so far away, Abraham bought a burial plot from one of his neighbors, one Ephron of the Hittite tribe. Ephron's field was called Machpelah, and on it there were many trees and a cave that would serve well as a burial place. Therefore Abraham laid his wife to rest in the cave of Machpelah, close to the plain of Mamre where they had lived together for so many years. Thus Sarah became the first of all the Hebrew people to die and be buried in the land of Canaan, the land that God had promised to the descendants of Abraham.

Isaac was a grown man and Abraham was very old; but the Lord had blessed him in all things. When the loss of Sarah had become less painful to him he began to think of Isaac's loneliness, for it was time that Isaac should take a wife. Now, though Abraham was friendly with his neighbors and respected by them, he did not wish his tribe to merge with theirs. It was necessary, he felt, to find a Hebrew maiden for his son to marry. And he remembered that his brother Nahor and his wife Milcah had remained, years earlier, at Haran in the district of Padan-Aram, and he had heard that their family now was large with children and their children's children. It would be most desirable, Abraham believed, if Isaac were to marry a cousin from Padan-Aram. But he did not want Isaac to leave Canaan himself and go back into the land the Lord had commanded him to leave.

Therefore he called to him one day the oldest steward of his house, the one who ruled over everything he had, and gave to him the task of finding a suitable wife for Isaac. "Give me your hand and swear to me," he said, "by the Lord who is the God of heaven and earth, that you will not take a wife for my son from the daughters of the Canaanites among whom I dwell, but that you will go back into my old country to look among my kinsmen for a wife for Isaac."

The steward felt that this would be no easy task. "Perhaps," he said, "the woman I choose will not be willing to come with me from her land to ours. And perhaps your son Isaac will not approve my choice. Should I not take him back into the land from which you came so that he might make his own choice?"

But that was not what Abraham wanted. And he said: "No, you shall not take my son with you into that land. The Lord God of heaven, who took me from my father's house and promised this land to me, will surely send you his angel to guide you, and you shall choose a wife for Isaac according to his guidance. Give me your oath that you will do as I ask. If the woman is not willing to follow you, then I shall free you from the oath and not blame you. Only do not take my son back to that place. Now swear to me.

"I do swear it," the trusted servant said, and gave his hand to Abraham. "I shall go and so as you say."

He took ten of his master's camels and loaded them with goods for gifts. Then he departed, taking with him several of Abraham's men to help him with the camels, and traveled for many days across the plains and deserts to the land of Mesopotamia where Abraham's brother had made his home. At last he stopped at a well outside the city of Haran in the district of Padan-Aram and waited for the guidance that would lead him to the family of Nahor and a wife for Isaac.

It was evening when he arrived, and it was the time when the women of the town came out to draw water from the well. The steward watched them as they drew near, and he made his camels kneel beside the well. He did not know what he could do but put his trust in God. Therefore he prayed within his heart. "O Lord God of my master Abraham, I pray you, help me this day and show kindness to my master Abraham. Behold, I stand here by the well, where the daughters of the men of the city come out to draw water for their houses. Give me, I pray, a sign. Let it be that the young woman I shall ask for water to drink from her pitcher will say to me, 'Drink, and I will give your camels drink also.' Let her be the one whom you have chosen for your servant Isaac. By this sign shall I know her, and know that you are showing kindness to my master."

Even before he had finished speaking in his heart, a young woman came down to the well with her pitcher on her shoulder. The maiden's name was Rebekah, and she was very fair to look upon and not yet married. She lowered her pitcher into the well and brought it up brimming with cool water. The steward watched her, wondering if she might be the one. He went to meet her, and asked the question he had planned to ask. "Let me, I pray you, drink a little water from your pitcher."

And she said, "Drink, my lord." And although he was a stranger she was courteous to him, lowering her pitcher at once into her hand and offering it to him so that he might drink. When his thirst was quenched she said: "I will draw water for your camels also, until they have had enough to drink." As she spoke she emptied the pitcher into the drinking trough, and hurried to the well to draw more water so that all the camels might drink their fill. The man wondered at her, but he held his peace. It was the sign that he had been praying for, yet he still could not know for certain whether the Lord had made his journey a success or not. He would know only when he had found out who this kindly maiden was.

When the camels had finished drinking, the man took from a satchel a golden earring and two gold bracelets as a gift of thanks. He gave them to the girl and asked: "Whose daughter are you? And tell me, I beg of you, is there room in your father's house for us to lodge in?"

And she said to him: "I am the daughter of Bethuel, who is the son of Milcah and Nahor. There is room for you to lodge in, and both straw and feed enough for all the camels. I will tell my father that you are here."

She smiled and turned away. Abraham's steward bowed his head and worshiped God. The granddaughter, her very self, of Abraham's brother Nahor! "Blessed be the Lord God of my master Abraham," the man prayed thankfully. "You have been merciful to my master and answered my prayer, for you have led me to the house of my master's brother."

Rebekah ran to her family's house to tell them about the friendly stranger at the well. Now Rebekah had a brother named Laban, and when he heard Rebekah's story and saw the golden gifts in his sister's hands, Laban went out to meet the man who was standing with his camels at the well.

"Come in, you blessed of the Lord," he said, with welcome in his voice. "Why do you stand outside? For the house is ready for you, and there is room for the camels. Come!"

So Abraham's servant and the men who had come

with him went into the house of Bethuel the son of
Nahor, Abraham's brother, and they were received
with kindness even though the family did not yet
know who this stranger was. Laban brought water for
the travelers' feet and himself attended to the camels,
unharnessing them and giving them their feed and
straw. When that was done he saw to it that food was
set before his visitors to eat; but Abraham's head
servant would not eat until he had explained his er-
rand. "First let me tell why I have come to you," he
said.

"Very well, speak on," said Laban. He and his
father listened courteously and with growing interest
while the steward spoke.

"I am Abraham's servant," he began. "The Lord has
blessed my master greatly, so that he has become great
himself. God has given him flocks and herds, and silver
and gold, and menservants and maidservants, and
camels and donkeys. Sarah, my master's wife, bore him
a son when she was old, and that son Isaac is heir to
everything that Abraham has. But Isaac is not yet
married, so my master sent me to find a wife for him
among his own people, for he would not have Isaac
marry a daughter of the Canaanites." Then Abraham's
servant explained how his master had made him swear
an oath and sent him off with a promise that an angel
would guide his choice at the proper time; and how
Rebekah, in answer to his prayer, had offered water not
only to him but to his thirsty camels. "Now tell me," he
finished, "if you will deal kindly and truly with my
master, or if you will not, so that I will know which
way to turn and what is right."

Then Laban and his father Bethuel answered: "This
has come to us from the Lord, and it is not for us to
say whether it is good or bad. See, Rebekah is here.
Take her and go, and let her be the wife of your
master's son, as the Lord has spoken." For they truly
believed that it was the Lord who had sent them Abraham's servant, and that the Lord desired Rebekah to
go.

When Abraham's servant heard their words he was deeply thankful to the Lord who had guided him to the family of Nahor. He bowed down to the earth and worshiped, with a grateful heart, the God who had helped him in his task. Afterward he brought forth from his satchels the riches he had brought from Abraham: jewels of silver and of gold, earrings, bracelets, goblets, cloth, and beautiful clothes from the far-off land of Canaan; and he gave them to Rebekah. He also gave her brother Laban and their mother many precious things that pleased them and showed to all that Abraham and Isaac were men of wealth and standing.

When he had told his story and given to all the rich gifts from Abraham, he at last consented to eat. He and the men who had come with him on the journey ate and drank, and spent the night resting at the house of Bethuel, the father of Rebekah.

When they rose in the morning the steward said: "Now I must return to my master with the girl Rebekah."

But his visit had been so unexpected that the family of the girl had had no time to get used to the idea of saying goodbye to her and watching her go far off into a strange land. Laban and his mother did not want her to leave so suddenly, so soon. "Let her stay with us for a few days, ten days at least," they asked the steward. "After that time she shall go with you."

Yet the steward had completed his mission and was eager to be on his way. "No, do not hinder me," he said. "The Lord has made my journey a success, and now I must go back to my master with the maiden!"

They hesitated still, for they did not know how Rebekah felt about hurrying off with scarcely time to catch her breath. "We will call the girl and ask her what she has to say," they said. They called her and she came at once. "Will you go with this man?" they asked her. For they loved her and wanted to be sure that she was doing what she wished.

"I will go," Rebekah said.

So they blessed her lovingly, and helped her to

prepare the things she needed for her journey. And they sent her away, Rebekah their sister and her nurse and several handmaidens, with Abraham's head servant and his men. The steward rode ahead to lead the way, and behind him rode his men and all the women of Rebekah's party. Bethuel and his family watched them ride off on their camels until they were no more than dots upon the desert.

They rode for many days, following much the same route as that taken by Abraham a long, long time before when he had left his brother Nahor in Haran to venture, with Lot, into the promised land of Canaan. Rebekah traveled with her face uncovered, looking at the new country from her camel's back and wondering all the time what manner of man her husband would turn out to be.

At last they reached the south country where Isaac lived with Abraham. It was evening, and Isaac was walking in the fields and meditating as the sun dipped low over the land that belonged to him and Abraham. He lifted up his eyes and saw the caravan of camels coming from a distance, and he started walking toward the distant dust.

Rebekah also lifted up her eyes. When she saw the man in the distance she got down from her camel, for she felt who the man might be and wanted to meet him on foot.

"Who is that man who is walking in the field to meet us?" she asked the steward.

"It is my master Isaac," he told her.

Thereupon Rebekah took a veil and covered her face, as was the custom among the women of her people. Later, when they had properly met, she would unveil and he could see her. But it was not yet time for that.

Isaac and the camel caravan came together near his dwelling place, and both halted. The servant told Isaac everything that he had done, and how the Lord had guided him to the daughter of Bethuel; and Isaac was well pleased.

A while later he took Rebekah into his mother Sarah's tent and made it into a home for her. She became his wife, and they loved each other deeply. And thus was Isaac comforted after his mother's death.

Esau Loses
His Birthright

****

Abraham himself was not too old to require comfort. He took another wife, whose name was Keturah, and she bore him six fine sons. The old man was fond of them and gave them many gifts, but he still remembered that God's promise would come true through Isaac and he was determined that Isaac should be his only heir. He sent his young sons away to live in the east country, while he and Isaac remained in the southland, and apart from the gifts that he had given the six boys he gave all he had to Isaac.

Then Abraham died at a good ripe age, a man full of years. He was one hundred and seventy-five years old when he was gathered to his people. Ishmael, the son of Hagar, came from the wilderness to say farewell, and he and Isaac buried the old man in the cave of Machpelah near Mamre, where Abraham's wife Sarah had been laid to rest more than forty years before.

Isaac and Rebekah made their home at Beersheba, where Abraham had once dug a well of water and planted a grove of trees. Years passed, and it began to look as though Rebekah would not have a child. Then Isaac prayed to the Lord for his wife, and the Lord granted his prayer. There was something that troubled Rebekah, though, and she inquired of the Lord why she felt as she did.

And the Lord said to Rebekah: "Two nations are within you, and two kinds of people. The one shall be stronger than the other, and the elder shall serve the younger."

When her time came Rebekah gave birth to twin sons. The first to be born was redheaded and hairy, and they named him Esau; the second was smooth-skinned and more slight of build, and they called him Jacob.

And the boys grew.

Esau was the rough and hearty one. He was strong and swift of foot, a wily hunter and man of the outdoors who lived among the birds and beasts of the field. Jacob, the younger by little more than seconds, was a plain man and a quiet one who dwelled in the tents and preferred to stay close to home minding his father's flocks. Isaac loved both his sons, but he loved Esau the more because he was so very strong and manly, and because when he came from the hunt he brought venison that he prepared in just the way to delight his father. But Rebekah loved Jacob, the quiet man of dignity. Isaac's family was rich, important in the district and destined to be great, and Rebekah's feeling was that Esau was not the proper man to be Isaac's heir.

Because of Rebekah, Jacob came more and more to think about his misfortune in being born after his brother. As the elder son, Esau had the birthright. That meant, among the people of those lands and those times, that when Isaac died Esau would inherit a double portion of whatever his father left. It also meant that he would become the head of the family with all the patriarch's rights and responsibilities, and with certain

priestly privileges and duties. In the case of the family
of Abraham and Isaac, the birthright was even more
than usually important: Esau, as the oldest son of Abraham's son, was in line to receive great blessings from
the Lord who had made the promise of greatness to
Abraham and Isaac. But Esau did not seem interested
in the honor of having such a precious birthright. He
was in love with the outdoors and the simple things of
life, and he gave not a thought to the question of his
birthright and his future as the head of the family. He
knew he was the elder son. Why should he spend his
days thinking about it?

But Jacob and Rebekah thought about the birthright. Many times did Rebekah recall the words of the
Lord, spoken before her children were born. Certainly
they were different, and one was surely stronger than
the other, at least in terms of physical strength. Possibly
Jacob would turn out to be the stronger in other ways.
But the last part of the prophecy was especially puz-
zling. "The elder shall serve the younger." What could
it mean? Rebekah wondered.

Jacob went on thinking about the birthright, and
Esau went on forgetting about it.

One day, much like so many other days, Esau was
out in the woods and fields and Jacob was among the
tents. But this day Esau's hunt was long and unsuccess-
ful, and he came home ravenous after his hard and
useless work. The first thing he noticed was a delicious
aroma of food. Jacob had been making a tasty lentil
soup; and Esau had not found a deer all day. Esau
sniffed hungrily. He was tired, and he was as hungry as
a bear. He had been hunting all day for nothing, and
he needed food.

"Feed me, I pray you," he begged his brother Jacob.
"Give me some of that pottage, for I am faint with
hunger."

Jacob turned and looked at him thoughtfully. "I will,
if you sell me your birthright this day."

"I am starving to death!" said Esau, in his rough

way. "What good will a birthright do me if I die of hunger?"

"Swear it to me!" said Jacob. "Swear that you will sell it to me if I give you food this day."

"I swear, I swear! The birthright is yours. Only give me the food before I drop."

And he sold his birthright to Jacob, and Jacob gave his brother Esau bread and lentil soup in exchange for all the rights of an elder son. Esau ate and drank and went upon his way, satisfied with his meal; and not until long afterward did he give any thought to the bargain he had made.

And thus did Esau throw away his birthright.

Jacob Tricks
His Father

++++++++++++++++++++++++++

Isaac continued to prosper as he grew to old age. The Lord blessed him with great riches: abundant lands that gave forth plentiful crops; huge flocks and herds; and a multitude of servants. Some of his neighbors among the people of Canaan were envious of his wealth and alarmed because of his growing power in the land, yet they could not succeed in making war with him. The most unfriendly of his rivals were the Philistines who lived in the coastal lands of Canaan and repeatedly made trouble for Isaac as he dug wells in the desert in times of drought and famine, for they thought he was trespassing on their property and they feared his power. The more wells he dug the more anxious they became. They envied him his great wealth and his many servants, and because they themselves were accustomed to fighting for what they wanted to take they were afraid that he, with his ever-growing strength, would do the same to them. But Isaac was a man of peace, and eventually he managed to persuade even the Philistines that he had no wish to steal their lands or harm their people. He became known among all his neighbors as a peaceful, God-loving man blessed by the Lord.

After Isaac came to his understanding with the Philistines, life at Beersheba was peaceful and without event for several years. And then, without consulting his father, Esau took two wives. Rebekah and Isaac were deeply distressed, not because their elder son had taken two wives but because the women were Hittites and not acceptable to a Hebrew family. But Isaac was forgiving, and his love for Esau did not lessen.

It came to pass that, when Isaac was old and his eyes were dim so that he could not see, he began to think of the day of his death and of the blessing that he must give his firstborn son before he died. The blessing would confirm the birthright and grant rights and riches to the blessed one, and was thus of great importance to the elder son. Isaac therefore called to Esau. "Come to me, my son," he said. And Esau came to him, saying, "I am here, my father."

"Look now, I am old," said Isaac. "I do not know when I shall die; it may be soon. Take your weapons, your quiver of arrows and your bow, and go out into the fields. Hunt the deer for me once more. Bring me some venison and prepare for me the savory meat such as I love. Give it to me then that I may eat; so that my soul may bless you before thy Lord before I die."

Esau left at once and went into the woods and fields to hunt for deer so that he might bring his father the tasty venison of which the old man was so fond.

But Rebekah had heard Isaac speaking to Esau, and she did not want the elder son to receive the blessing that was his right. She called her favorite son, Jacob, and told him what she had overheard and how Isaac wanted to bless Esau before he died. And then she said: "Now therefore, my son, obey my voice and do as I command you. Go to the flock and get me two young goats, kid goats that are good and tender, and I will prepare them in such a way that the meat will taste like the savory venison that Esau prepares. Then you will take it to your father so that he may eat the meat he loves, for he will not know the difference, and he will bless you before he dies. He will not see that you are Jacob, for his eyes are dim."

But Jacob was afraid that Isaac would not be so easily deceived. "Yes, but my brother Esau is a hairy man," he told his mother, "and I am smooth. What if my father reaches out and touches me? Then he will feel that I am not hairy, and I shall seem to him as a deceiver. I will bring a curse down upon myself, and not a blessing."

"The curse will be on me, my son, not you," Rebekah said. "Only obey my voice and bring me the young kids."

Jacob went to the flock and picked out two tender young goats and brought them back to his mother. Skillfully she prepared the meat with herbs and spices so that it tasted like the venison Isaac enjoyed so much, and set the skins aside for later use. When the food was ready she took some of Esau's clothes and put them upon her younger son. Next, she covered Jacob's hairless hands and the smoothness of his neck with the soft, hairy skins of the young kids, and she gave to him the savory meat and bread that she had prepared. "Go to your father," Rebekah said.

And Jacob, in his borrowed skins and clothes, took the savory food to his father Isaac.

"I am here now, my father," he said, trying to sound like Esau.

"Who are you, my son?" said Isaac, uncertain of that voice.

"I am Esau, your firstborn," answered Jacob, "and I have done what you asked. Arise, I beg of you; sit up and eat the venison I have prepared for you, so that your soul may bless me."

Isaac was puzzled by the voice and by his son's

unusually swift return from the hunt. "How is it that you found the meat so quickly, my son?" he asked.

"The Lord your God led me to it," answered Jacob.

Isaac was still not completely satisfied. "Come near to me, I pray you," he said to this son he could not see. "Let me touch you, my son, so that I may know for certain that you are Esau."

Jacob went close to the old man and let him feel the false hairiness of his body. Blind Isaac touched the goat-skin-covered hands and neck of his younger son and wonderingly said: "The voice is Jacob's voice, but the hands are the hands of Esau." And Isaac did not discover the deception, for Jacob's hands felt as hairy as his brother Esau's hands.

Isaac said again, "Are you truly my son Esau?"

"I am," said Jacob.

"Then bring the food to me," the old man said. "Bring, and I will eat of my son's venison, so that my soul shall bless you."

And Jacob brought it to him. Isaac ate the meat, and found it savory and delicious, and Jacob brought him wine to drink with it.

When Isaac had eaten the meal which he had asked from Esau and received from Jacob, he was ready to pronounce the precious blessing.

"Come near now and kiss me, my son," he said. Jacob drew close and leaned down for the kiss that went with the blessing. Isaac smelled the good smell of Esau's clothes, that carried with them the fragrance of the out-of-doors, the tang of the hunter and man of the soil, and the clean smell of the woods and fields. And Isaac blessed the younger son, saying: "See, the smell of my son is as the smell of a field which the Lord has blessed. Therefore, God give you of the dew of heaven, and the fatness of the earth, and plenty of corn and wine. Let people serve you, and nations bow down to you; be lord over your brothers, and let your mother's sons bow down to you. Cursed be every one that curses you, and blessed be every one that blesses you."

It was done. Jacob had deceived his father and once again tricked his brother Esau.

Now it happened, as soon as Isaac had finished blessing Jacob, and Jacob had scarcely left the presence of his father, that Esau returned from the hunt with venison. And he also made savory meat and brought it to his father.

"Rise up, my father and eat of your son's venison," said Esau, "and then let your soul bless me as you have said."

Isaac sat up in great surprise. "Bless you? Who are you, then?"

"I am your firstborn son, Esau," said the hairy man.

And Isaac's old body started trembling all over. Something here was very wrong, and his distress was great.

"Who? Esau? Then who was it that prepared the venison and brought it to me before you came? For I have already eaten, and I have blessed the one who brought it. And the blessing remains his; blessed he shall be."

When Esau heard the words of his father he cried out with a great and bitter cry, for he knew at once that it was Jacob who had received the blessing meant for him. "Bless me, too, my father!" he pleaded.

Isaac was sorely troubled, for blessings were not given lightly and could not be taken away. "Your brother came to me with subtlety," he said sorrowfully, "and he has taken away your blessing."

Esau groaned with deep dismay. "My brother! Is he not rightly named Jacob, 'the supplanter'? Twice he has taken my place; twice he has used trickery to take something that is mine. He took away my birthright; and now he has taken away my blessing. Oh, my father! Have you not saved any blessing for me?"

And Isaac answered, saying: "How can that be? I have made him lord over you, and I have given all his brothers to him as his servants so that they will all serve him. With corn and wine in plenty have I provided him; and I have given to him all the blessing that is

mine to give. What can be left that I may now do for
you, my son?"

"One blessing only!" Esau begged. "Have you only
the one to give? Oh, bless me, too, my father!" And
Esau lifted up his voice and wept, for his loss was very
great.

And Isaac his father, grieving, answered and said to
him: "A blessing I shall give you, but it cannot be what
I have already given Jacob of my own. Your dwelling
shall be the richness of the earth and of the woods and
fields you love, and of the dew of heaven from above.
You will live by toil and by the sword, and you will
serve your brother. But the day will come when power
shall be yours, and then you will break his yoke from
off your neck."

It was not so much a blessing as a promise for the
future; and Esau hated Jacob because of the lost blessing. In his heart he swore that he would have revenge.
"Not yet," he told himself. "Not while my father lives.
But he is old and soon will die. When the days of
mourning are over, I will surely kill my brother
Jacob."

Jacob's Ladder

✛✛✛✛✛✛✛✛✛✛✛✛✛✛✛✛✛✛✛✛✛✛✛✛

Esau did not speak of his rage and hatred to his father, but neither did he keep it to himself. The news of his great anger spread, and his vengeful words soon came to the ears of Rebekah his mother.

She sent at once for Jacob and warned him of his danger. "Hear me, my son," she said. "Your brother Esau has sworn that he will kill you. Therefore obey my voice and go away from here. Flee to my brother Laban at Haran. Stay with him for a few days, until your brother's fury turns away and he forgets what you have done to him. Then I will send for you and bring you back, for I do not want to lose you."

Then she went to Isaac. Instead of telling him that she was afraid for Jacob's life she brought up a question that she knew was close to Isaac's heart. "I am weary of my life," she said, "because of the daughters of the Hittites. Esau has already married among them, and that is not the way of our people. If Jacob also takes a wife from those Hittite daughters of the land, what good is my life to me?"

Neither did her husband wish their second son to marry one of the women of Canaan. Isaac called Jacob to him and blessed him. "You shall not take a wife of the daughters of Canaan," he told his younger son. "Go to Padan-Aram, to the house of Bethuel from which your mother came, and find a wife among the daughters of your mother's brother Laban. May God Almighty bless you and give to you the blessing of Abraham, so that you will have many children and inherit this land that God has given us."

And thus did Isaac send Jacob away; and Jacob left his home in Beersheba and began his long and lonely journey to Haran. He did not know then that he was to be away for far longer than a few days, and that he would never see his mother again.

When Esau saw that Isaac had again blessed Jacob and sent him away to Padan-Aram to find a wife instead of marrying one of the daughters of the Hittites, he realized that his marriages to the women of Canaan did not please his father. He therefore took another wife; and this time he chose a daughter of his father's half-brother Ishmael, son of Abraham and Hagar.

In the meantime, Jacob was making his way across the hills and plains of Canaan, feeling unhappy and afraid. At last he came to a certain place where there were rocks for shelter, and because the sun had set he decided to stay there for the night. He took one of the stones of the place for a pillow, and lay down to sleep on his hard bed. As he slept, he dreamed.

In his dream he saw a ladder with its feet set upon the earth and the top of it reaching to the heavens, and the angels of God were going up and down upon it. And he saw the Lord God standing there above it, and the Lord spoke to him and said: "I am the Lord God of Abraham, and the God of Isaac. The land on which you are lying, this will I give to you and to your children. Your descendants shall be as many as there is dust upon the earth; and they will spread to the west, to the east, to the north, and to the south, and through them shall all the families of the earth be blessed. Behold, I am with you, and I will be with you wherever you may go, and I will bring you back again into this land. For I will not leave you until I have done what I have promised."

Jacob awoke from his sleep. He looked about him in the starlit night and he saw that he was alone; but he did not feel alone. And he said, "Surely the Lord is with me in this place, and I did not know it."

And he felt great awe. "How wonderful is this place!" he said reverently. "It is none other than the House of God, and this is the gate of heaven."

He rose early the following morning and took the stone he had used for a pillow and set it upright as if it were a pillar in monument to something holy. Then he anointed it with oil as an offering to God, and now indeed it was a holy monument. Though the name of the place was Luz, he renamed it Bethel, or "The House of God." And he made a vow, saying, "If God will be with me and watch over me as I go, and give me bread to eat and clothes to wear, and let me come again to my father's house in peace, then I shall know that the Lord is truly my God. And this stone, which I have set here for a pillar of worship, shall be God's house. And of all that God gives me I will surely give back to him a tenth."

Then Jacob left the place that he had dedicated to the Lord, and went on with his journey to Haran.

Rachel and Leah

✚✚✚✚✚✚✚✚✚✚✚✚✚✚✚✚✚✚✚✚✚✚✚

Though Jacob traveled alone he was not lonely, for the Lord watched over him as he went along his way. After several days in the desert he came into the land of the people of the east, where Rebekah's family dwelled, and he saw a sight that was a welcome change from the miles of rugged rock and desert sand that he had covered on his journey. It was a fertile field, such as herds and flocks use for their grazing; and Jacob knew that he had come again into the company of men.

He looked about him and saw a well in the field, and there were three flocks of sheep lying near it while their shepherds talked idly among themselves. This was the well out of which all the flocks in the neighborhood were watered, and a great stone covered its mouth while it was not in use. The stone was very heavy, so that it was only when all the flocks were gathered together that the shepherds would roll the stone from the well's mouth, give water to their sheep, and then put the stone back into place over the mouth of the well.

Jacob greeted the men. "Where are you from, my brothers?" he asked of them.

"We are from Haran," they answered, "and this is Haran's well."

Jacob's heart was full of joy, for he was at his journey's end and soon he would see his mother's family.

"Do you know Laban, of the family of Nahor?" he asked.

And they said, "We know him."

"Is he well?" asked Jacob.

"He is well," replied the shepherds. "Look yonder; there comes his daughter Rachel with the sheep."

Jacob looked and saw her coming, and he noticed again that the well was covered even though the flocks were lying nearby.

"What are you waiting for?" he asked. "It is high noon. Why do you not give water to your sheep, and then take them to the field and let them feed?"

"We cannot," they answered, "until all the flocks are gathered together and the stone is rolled away from the mouth of the well. Then we water the sheep. But they are not all here yet."

And while Jacob was still talking to them, Rachel came to the well with her father's sheep, for it was she who tended them. When Jacob looked at Rachel, the daughter of his mother's brother Laban, he decided that so comely a girl should not be kept waiting until all the flocks were there. He went quickly to the mouth of the well and rolled the heavy stone away without the help of any other man, and afterward he himself watered the flock of Laban his mother's brother. Then he turned to the lovely girl and saw that she was looking at him with surprise, for she was not used to such special treatment from her neighboring shepherds.

"You are my cousin Rachel," he told her, "for I am Jacob, the son of Rebekah, who is your father's sister."

And then Jacob kissed Rachel and wept tears of joy, so glad was he to see a member of his family after his long journey. He was glad, too, to meet such a lovely relative so soon after arriving at Haran.

Rachel hurried home to tell her father of the meeting at the well. And when Laban heard that Jacob, his own sister's son, had come to visit them, he ran to meet him. The two men embraced warmly, and Laban welcomed Jacob into his house. Jacob told him again what he had told Rachel, and gave his uncle news of Rebekah and her home in Canaan. "Surely you are my flesh and bone," said Laban, "and you shall stay with us and be welcome."

Jacob stayed with him, working in the fields and helping Laban with his flocks and cattle. During his youth in Canaan among his father's flocks Jacob had become a skillful shepherd-farmer and his knowledge of farming with animals was much greater than that of his uncle Laban. And Laban saw that he was very useful to him in the fields. He said to Jacob, "Because you are my sister's son, should you therefore work for me for nothing? No, you shall be paid for your services. Tell me, what should your wages be?"

Now Laban had two daughters. Leah, the older of the two, was plain-looking and undesirable in Jacob's eyes. But Rachel, the younger, was beautiful and pleasing to look upon. And Jacob had loved her from the start. He said to Laban, "I will serve seven years for your younger daughter Rachel."

Laban nodded agreeably. "It is better that I give her to you than to any other man. It is agreed, then. Stay with me, and my daughter shall be yours."

At the end of his term of service Jacob approached his uncle Laban. "Give me my wife," he said, "because I have fulfilled our agreement and the days are ended."

Again, Laban agreed. He gathered together all the men of the place and prepared a wedding feast. The men feasted long and heartily, and when it was late evening Laban called his daughter to him with her handmaid Zilpah. But the daughter whom he called to him was Leah, not Rachel, and it was Leah in a thick wedding veil that he took to Jacob in the darkness of the night.

And thus did Jacob marry Laban's daughter after seven years of service.

In the light of morning Jacob looked and saw the face of his bride; and he saw that instead of his beloved Rachel, it was Leah. He did not love her and he had not wanted her, and he was outraged at Laban's trick.

"What have you done to me?" he said to Laban angrily. "Did I not serve seven years with you so that I might marry Rachel? Why have you deceived me?"

Laban managed to look surprised, and came out with the excuse that he had prepared years before when he had made his promise to Jacob. "It is not the custom in our country," he said smoothly, "to give the younger in marriage before the firstborn. Surely you knew that?" He might have added that he had taken the only course he could think of to find a husband for his homely elder daugher, and that he wanted Jacob to stay there because he needed him; but it was not his way to say the honest thing and deal fairly with a man when he could gain by tricking him. "But you have no reason to be angry," he went on. "Spend a week with Leah, then marry Rachel also as soon as the week is out. Many men have more than one wife; so shall you have Leah and Rachel. Or you shall if you agree to serve me yet another seven years."

Laban drove a hard bargain. Fourteen years of work for Jacob for the sake of one woman whom he loved, and one woman whom he loved not! But Jacob agreed, for he loved Rachel very deeply and wanted more than anything in the world that she should be his wife. He spent his week with Leah, as required by custom, and then he married Rachel. Laban gave Rachel his hand-maid Bilhah to wait upon her and obey her; and thus did Jacob's household increase.

It increased a great deal more as the years went by and Jacob continued to work hard and well for his scheming uncle Laban, but the increase was largely through the woman he had not intended to marry rather than through the woman that he loved more than any other.

He was husband to them both, but he loved Rachel far more than he could ever think of loving plain Leah; and Leah could not help knowing that she had not been wanted. She felt as though both Rachel and Jacob hated her, and her life was exceedingly unhappy.

But when the Lord saw that Leah was sorrowful, he gave her his own love and mercy so that she had children by Jacob while Rachel could not and did not have a child.

In a short space of time Leah had four sons, whom she named Reuben, Simeon, Levi, and Judah. And then, for a while, she had no more children.

But her younger sister Rachel had no children at all, beautiful and beloved though she was. And envy ate into her heart.

Jacob and Laban

It was a shame and a disgrace for a Hebrew woman not to have a child, or so Rachel thought. Childless Sarah had felt bitter and ashamed for many years; Rebekah had been unhappy for a long time before her twins were born; and now Rachel was suffering in the same way. She envied her sister Leah with a bitterness that was close to hatred, and she turned to Jacob with her reproaches.

"Give me children, or else I die!" she begged.

Jacob's anger roused against her, because it was not his fault that she had no children. "Do you think that I am God, to have withheld a child from you?" he said wrathfully.

And Rachel knew that he was not to blame. But, like Sarah, she was almost desperate to give her husband a child that she could call her own, whether she herself bore it or not, so she thought of a way to do it. "Take my handmaid then," she said to Jacob. "Go to Bilhah, that I may also have children by her."

Jacob did as his wife asked him, and Bilhah had first one son and then another. Rachel was pleased and grateful to the Lord, for at least it was her own handmaid who had had the children and not the envied Leah. And then Leah, who had stopped bearing children for a while, decided to follow Rachel's course and give her own handmaid to her husband. So she gave Zilpah to Jacob; and in time Zilpah had two sons on behalf of Leah. Thereupon Leah herself had two more sons, followed by a daughter. Rachel's offspring by this time were hopelessly outnumbered, and she still did not have a child whom she could truly say was her very own.

And then at long last Rachel bore a son, and she felt that she must surely be the happiest mother alive. "God has taken away my shame and given me a child!" she said joyfully, and she called him Joseph. Jacob was just as pleased as Rachel, for he still loved her more than Leah; and so he loved his youngest baby Joseph more than all the rest. Now he had twelve children altogether: one girl, whose name was Dinah, and eleven boys.

It was not long after Joseph was born that the fourteen years of Jacob's promised service to Laban came to an end. During all that time Jacob had had no news of his parents, and he wanted to go home again. He went to Laban and said to him, "Send me away, so that I may go back to my own country. Give me my wives and my children, for whom I have served you through all these years, and let me take them with me; for you know that I have given you the service that I promised."

Laban knew it very well. He also knew that Jacob was a very skilled shepherd and herdsman who had added much to Laban's wealth by his knowledge of animal farming. What was more, Jacob's expert services had cost Laban nothing but two daughters for whom he would have had to find husbands anyway. He had given low wages indeed for the work of fourteen years.

"I pray you," Laban said earnestly, "if I have found
favor in your eyes, then do not leave me. While you
have been with me I have done well, so I beg you to
stay. I have learned by experience that the Lord has
blessed me because of you. Stay here; tell me what
wage you want, and I will give it to you."

Jacob answered carefully, for he had realized in the
course of the years that Laban was cunning enough to
cheat him again if he should have the chance. And
Jacob himself still had some of the craftiness he had
used on his brother Esau. "You know how I have
served you," he began, "and how your flocks and cattle
have improved under my care. For what you had was
little when I came, and now it has increased into a
multitude. It is true that the Lord has blessed you since
my coming. But what do I have? All these possessions
are yours and I have nothing. When shall I provide for
my own home?"

"What shall I give you, then?" Laban asked again.

Jacob's answer was a surprise to him. "You shall
not give me anything," he answered. "If you will do
one thing for me, then I will stay to tend your sheep
and cattle and make my wage in my own way. I will
go through your flocks and herds today and remove all
the sheep and cattle that are speckled and spotted, and
all the brown sheep as well; and also the spotted and
speckled and striped among the goats. Whatever flocks
and herds I may build up from these will be my price
of hire. And when the time comes for me to receive
my wage from you, you will be able to tell at once
that I have taken no animal into my flock that does
not belong to me. For I will have nothing in my flocks
or herds that is not marked as I have said, nor any
sheep that is not brown, or you will know that I
have stolen from you. And I will not steal."

Laban quickly agreed to Jacob's proposition. There
were not, he knew, more than one or two brown sheep,
nor more than a very few animals that were spotted or
speckled or striped. "It will be as you say," he said,
with a friendly smile.

But just to make sure that he had the better end of the bargain, Laban went to the flocks and herds before Jacob could get to them and removed every animal that was spotted or speckled or striped, every one that had the smallest patch of white in it, and all the brown among the sheep. Then he turned them over to his own sons and sent them all to a far-off pasture three days' journey away from the flock that Jacob was to tend for him.

Jacob looked at what was left of Laban's flock and saw that he had again been cheated, but he had been expecting it and his plans were ready. He was a far better farmer than Laban or any of his uncle's sons and it was not long before he succeeded in breeding several healthy animals that were brown or otherwise marked in the unusual manner he had specified. From these first few he bred others; and then he separated them from Laban's flock and kept them apart from all the other animals. Carefully, and with great skill, he fed and watered his own flock so that his animals thrived and became strong, and then he bred the strongest ones together until his own flock of oddly colored but healthy beasts was far bigger than Laban's.

So cleverly did he work among the animals that eventually Laban's flock was not only reduced in size but contained only the weaker of the cattle and sheep, while Jacob himself continued increasing his possessions and his riches. In time he became very rich in flocks and herds, maidservants and menservants, camels and asses, and all manner of household goods.

By this time he had worked for Laban for twenty years, and he had earned his riches through his hard work and his skill. But Laban's own sons were jealous, for now they had much less than Jacob. They began to mutter among themselves about this foreign relative of theirs.

Jacob heard the things that they were saying about him. "Jacob has taken away all that was our father's," they said angrily. "From what was once our father's he has made all these riches for himself. By trickery, he has obtained what should have been ours." He had, it was true, outwitted them, but in whatever he had done he had stayed strictly within the terms of his bargain with Laban. But they were no longer interested in bargains. They had lost their wealth to Jacob, and that was all they cared about.

Then Jacob saw how Laban himself was beginning to look at him; and the look was nowhere near as friendly as it had been in the earlier years when Jacob was working only to make Laban rich. Indeed, Laban's face was very far from friendly.

It was time, thought Jacob, for him to be on his way. And the Lord said to him: "I am the God of Bethel, where you anointed the pillar and made a vow to me, and I have seen all that Laban has done to you. Arise, now, from this place. Return to the land of your fathers and to your kindred, and I will be with you."

Jacob called Rachel and Leah to him secretly and told them how God had helped him in his dealings with Laban, and how it was that he had managed to obtain so many sheep and cattle. "And now I see that your father does not feel toward me as before," he said, "because he no longer has all the riches that he had before. But the God of my father has been with me, and it was God who took away the cattle of your father and gave them to me. You know that I have done everything in my power to serve your father, while he has done nothing but deceive me. He has changed my wages ten times, always saying one thing and then doing the other, and promising me falsely; but God did not permit him to hurt me. The riches that I now have and share with you are ours by right, and God has said to me that I must arise and go. I did deal honestly with Laban, yet he is angry with me. Therefore let us leave, for the Lord my God has told me that I must return to the land of my own kindred."

Rachel and Leah listened to him and both answered, saying, "There is nothing left for us in our father's house. You must do whatever God has said to you, and we will go with you."

Jacob went about his arrangements very quietly, for he was sure that Laban would again try to delay him or even prevent him altogether from leaving with his family and possessions. He chose a time for his departure when Laban was in his distant pastures shearing sheep, and then he quickly gathered together everything he had. He did not know that Rachel was taking something that did not belong to her; for while he organized his servants and his flocks, Rachel stole from her father's household certain gods, or images of gods, that Laban valued highly.

So Jacob set his wives and children upon camels and left Padan-Aram without Laban knowing anything about it. He took with him all his flocks and cattle and possessions, and the servants he had gained, and made for his home in the land of Canaan. He and his caravan crossed the river Euphrates and turned toward Mount Gilead.

It was not until three days later that Laban heard that they had gone. Rapidly he took stock of what was left and what had been taken, and he was very angry. With his sons and a band of fighting men, he hurried in pursuit. After seven days' journey they saw signs of their quarry ahead, for Jacob had stopped on the slopes of Mount Gilead to make camp and let his great flocks and herds out to pasture.

Laban himself pitched his camp before going on to Gilead. And he had a dream by night in which God came to him and warned him that he was neither to harm Jacob nor deceive him with soft words.

In the morning Laban overtook Jacob and pitched his tents near him on the mountain slope. His anger had cooled, but not completely, so he went to Jacob and rebuked him harshly. "What have you done, that you have stolen away without my knowledge and carried off my daughters as if they were captives taken by the sword? Why did you flee away secretly and with such stealth? Why did you not tell me that you were going, so that I might have sent you away with merry-making, and with songs and taborin and harp? You did not even allow me to kiss my daughters and grandsons before taking them away! That was a foolish thing for you to do. It is in my power to do you harm, but the God of your father spoke to me last night, saying: 'Take heed that you do not speak to Jacob, either good or bad.' And yet you have done wrong, and you have angered me. Even though you wanted to be gone because you were longing to return to your father's house, why did you have to steal my household gods?"

"What gods?" said Jacob. "I left secretly because I was afraid, for I said to myself, 'Perhaps Laban will take his daughters away from me by force.' But as for your images, your gods, I know nothing of them. Search my tents yourself; take anything you find that belongs to you. And if anyone has taken your gods, let him not live." For Jacob had no idea that Rachel had taken them.

Laban went into the tents and searched them one after the other, but he did not find the missing gods. They were not in Jacob's tent, not in the maidservants', not in Leah's. Then he went to Rachel's tent. Rachel was resting, and she watched her father as he searched. "Do not be displeased, my father," she said to him, "that I cannot rise in your presence, for I am not feeling well."

And Laban allowed her to remain seated, and he did not find the images. For Rachel had hidden the images in her camel's saddle, and she was sitting on them.

When Laban left the tents with empty hands, Jacob was angry for having been accused falsely of stealing. "What have I done wrong?" he chided Laban. "What is my sin, that you have so hotly pursued me? Now that you have searched through all my possessions, what have you found of your household gods? Set it here, whatever you have found, in front of your brothers and my brothers, so that they may judge between us." And there was nothing for Laban to set down, for Rachel still sat in her tent upon the stolen images.

"These twenty years I have been with you," Jacob went on angrily, "And in all that time I have stolen nothing from you of your flocks or household goods. Your ewes and she-goats have been well and healthy, for I tended them with care, and of the rams of your flock I have not eaten. When wild beasts took any of your flock either by night or day I bore the loss of it. I worked long and hard; in the day I endured the heat and drought, and at night the chilling frost, and I did not sleep for taking care of what was yours. I served you fourteen years for your two daughters and six years for your cattle, and during those years you have changed my wages ten times. If the God of my father, the God of Abraham, had not been with me, then surely you would have sent me away now empty-handed. But God has seen my suffering and the labor of my hands, and when he spoke to you last night he was rebuking you."

Laban answered and said to Jacob, "These daughters are my daughters, and these children are my children, and these cattle are my cattle, and all that you see is mine. And what can I do this day to my own daughters, or to the children they have borne? Come, therefore, and let us make a covenant, and let it be as a witness between you and me."

So Jacob took a stone and set it up for a pillar, and his men gathered stones into a heap. "This heap is a witness between us," Laban said. "May the Lord watch over us when we are absent from each other, so that you will not harm my daughters. God is witness between you and me. Behold, this heap and this pillar shall be witness that I will not pass beyond this point to come after you, and you shall not pass beyond this heap and pillar toward me to do me harm. May the God of Abraham and Nahor judge between us."

Thus did they make their vows to one another. They called the heap of stones Mizpah, meaning "watchtower," because the Lord himself would be watching over Laban and Jacob to see that each man would fulfill his vow.

Jacob offered up a sacrifice upon the mountain, and called his family and his men together to break bread and eat with him; and after they had eaten they spent all night on the mountain.

Early in the morning Laban rose, kissed his grandsons and his daughters and gave his blessing to them, and departed on the return journey to his own land. Jacob also went his way.

And this was the final parting between the family of Abraham, the Hebrews of Canaan, and the people of the old country. For neither Jacob nor Laban nor their sons would pass that pillar or the heap of stones and meet again. By the vow of Jacob and Laban, the descendants of Abraham were freed of their ties with their forefathers in the land of Babylonia; and from that time on they were a nation in themselves.

The Meeting
of Jacob and Esau

✠✠✠✠✠✠✠✠✠✠✠✠✠✠✠✠✠✠✠✠✠✠✠

While Laban traveled north to his home in Haran, Jacob journeyed west and south with his huge company of flocks and family and menservants. He was not entirely easy in his mind as he led his caravan toward the fields of home, for though it was twenty years since he had last seen Esau he was still afraid of his brother's temper. Esau had promised revenge; would he still take it? Or would he have mellowed with the passing of the years and forgive Jacob for his deceptions?

Jacob wanted to see his brother, and yet he did not want to. By this time Esau had left Canaan and made his home in the land of Edom, south of the Dead Sea and some distance from Jacob's destination, yet Jacob realized that a meeting, some time, would be inevitable. And so he felt worried and uncertain, even though he had trained serving men to defend him in case of trouble. But even as he worried a band of angels met

100

him on his way, and Jacob drew courage from his meeting with these messengers of God. He himself sent messengers then, to go ahead of his party and tell Esau of his coming.

"Go to my brother in the country of Edom," he commanded them. "And when you speak to my lord Esau, tell him this: 'Your servant Jacob says that he has been these many years with his uncle Laban, and that he now has oxen, asses, flocks, menservants and womenservants of his own.' Say also that I am sending word of my coming so that I may find grace in his sight."

The messengers hurried off, and Jacob waited for them on the north bank of the river Jabbok. His men came back quickly with alarming news. First, Esau was coming to meet Jacob. That in itself was good; but there was more. "We saw your brother Esau," the messengers said, "and he is coming to meet you—and four hundred men with him."

Then Jacob was greatly afraid and distressed. A company of four hundred men sounded ominous. It surely looked as though Esau planned to attack him with his fighting force. Jacob therefore called all his followers together and divided them, with the flocks and herds and camels, into two groups. "If Esau should attack one company, then at least the other will escape," he explained to them.

And then he prayed. "O God of Abraham and Isaac, the Lord who said to me, 'Return to your country and your kindred, and I will deal well with you.' Lord, deliver me, I pray you, from the hand of my brother, from the hand of Esau. For I fear him, that he will come and kill me, and the mothers with the children. Yet you did say to me that you would surely be good to me, and make my descendants as many as the sands of the sea, which cannot be counted, so great is their number. Help me, God; I pray you."

Jacob spent the night by the river. In the morning he took from his vast possessions a lavish present for his brother Esau: two hundred she-goats and twenty he-goats; two hundred ewes and twenty rams; thirty milk-giving camels with their colts; forty cows and ten bulls; twenty she-asses and ten foals. He divided these into droves and gave each drove to a servant, with instructions to keep the droves separate and drive them one ahead of the other. "Put a space between drove and drove," he told them. "Cross the river before me and travel on ahead." Then, to each of the servants in turn, he said: "When my brother Esau meets you and asks, 'Whom do you serve? Where are you going? And who owns these beasts that you are driving?' you shall say, 'They are your servant Jacob's. It is a present sent to my lord Esau, and Jacob himself follows behind us.'"

He sent them off, hoping that his gifts could appease his brother's anger. "This present that goes ahead of me shall be my peace-offering," he said to himself. "After Esau receives it I will meet him face to face and see what his feelings are toward me. Perhaps he will have forgiven me; perhaps he will accept me."

With the present on its way, Jacob rested in the camp with the remaining company, wondering if he would receive an answering message from Esau or a sign from God that he had not been abandoned. During the night he rose up restlessly and sent his two wives, his two womenservants, and his children across the river Jabbok by the ford. When they were safely across the river he sent after them everything he owned and had with him; and then he was left alone on the north bank of the river.

Yet, as before at Bethel, he was not really alone. An odd thing happened to him, and yet he was not frightened. In the darkness a strange and shadowy figure appeared in front of him and without a word laid hands on Jacob and fought with all his strength. All night long Jacob wrestled with the stranger, and neither of them said a single word. It was only when the first light of dawn gently touched the sky that the stranger finally spoke. "Let me go, for it is daybreak," he said.

And then Jacob was sure of what he had already

half-believed: that this man was no ordinary mortal but a heavenly visitor, the hope and help that he had asked of God.

"I will not let you go unless you bless me," Jacob said.

"What is your name?" asked the other man.

"Jacob."

"You shall no longer be called Jacob," said the stranger. "You shall be called Israel, for you are a prince of power with God and men." And in the language of those days the name 'Israel' meant 'soldier of God' or 'a prince of God.' "You are God's soldier, and you have won your battle," the stranger finished, and tried again to leave.

Jacob held him back. "Tell me your name, I pray you," he asked the wrestler of the night.

"Why should you want to know my name?" the other answered. "You have the blessing that you asked." And the stranger blessed him there beside the river, and then was gone.

And Jacob felt that the blessing had come to him from God. He named the place Peniel, which means 'the face of God'; for, as he said to himself, "I have seen God face to face, and my life is saved." He crossed the river Jabbok by the ford, leaving his fears behind him at Peniel as the sun rose and shone down upon him. On the other side he halted and lifted up his eyes and looked into the distance. In a cloud of dust he saw Esau coming toward him with four hundred men as rough and hairy as Esau himself. But Jacob was no longer afraid. He felt as though he had already won the hardest of his battles. Calmly, he arranged his band of people so that, if there should be a fight against the forces of his brother, he would be ready. He divided the children between Leah, Rachel, and the handmaids; and then he put the handmaids and their children in front, Leah and her children next, and Rachel and Joseph last. He himself strode to the head of the column and watched his brother Esau advancing toward him with his rough four hundred.

Jacob bowed as he walked forward, seven times with his head low toward the ground, until he came near to his brother. Esau ran to meet him with open arms that held no weapons in them, for all thoughts of vengeance had long since passed away, and he embraced Jacob with a heart full of warmth and friendship. Each man fell on the other's neck and wept tears of happiness and welcome after the long years of parting. From one side Jacob's people stood back and looked on; and from the other, Esau's men saw their master greet a beloved brother. No one had come to fight.

At last Esau looked up and saw all the women and children behind his brother. "But who are all those people with you?" he asked.

"The family and children which God has graciously given to your servant Jacob," answered the younger brother. And Jacob made them all draw close, his handmaids and his wives and children, and lovingly presented them to his rough-looking but forgiving brother. They bowed, all of them, and greeted the gruff and hairy man whom Jacob had feared so needlessly throughout the years. Then Esau had another question.

"And what did you mean by those droves of beasts which I met along the way?" he asked.

"They were a present for you," Jacob answered, "so that I might find favor in your sight."

Esau shook his head. "There is no need for that, my brother. I have enough. Keep what you have for yourself."

"No, I beg you; if I have found grace in your sight, then accept the present that I offer you. I have seen your face at last and my pleasure is great, and I know that you are not displeased with me. I pray you, take the blessing I have brought to you, because God has dealt graciously with me and I have enough."

Jacob went on urging him until Esau finally took his gift and said: "Let us start upon our journey. I will go ahead of you."

"I cannot leave here yet," said Jacob. "You know that the children are young and tender and cannot travel without rest, and that I also have with me flocks and herds with young of their own. If they should be overdriven for only one day all the flock will die. Go on ahead, I pray you, and I will follow at a slower pace, according to what the children and the cattle are able to endure."

"Then let me leave some of my men with you," Esau said.

"Why? There is no need of that," said Jacob. "As long as I have found grace in your sight, that is all I want."

They made their farewells, then, and Esau started back to his home in Edom. Jacob slowly made his way into the land of Canaan, halting whenever it was needed to rest his family and pasture his flocks. He stopped for some time at Shechem to spread his tents and worship God, and there God said to him: "Arise, go up to Bethel and dwell there, and make an altar there unto the God who appeared to you when you were fleeing from your brother Esau."

So Jacob gathered his household together and traveled south to Bethel. There he built an altar, and God appeared to him again to repeat the promise made to Abraham and Isaac that from them and from Jacob would come a race to whom the land of Canaan would belong. And he said again the words that Jacob had heard beside the river Jabbok: "Your name is Jacob, but that is no longer your only name, for your name shall be called Israel."

And in later years the descendants of Jacob came to be known as the children of Israel.

At last Jacob felt it was time to move on. But they had not traveled long when Rachel became ill, for she was about to have a child and the heavy traveling sapped her strength. Jacob called a halt again so that she could rest and be cared for. It was too late. The baby was born, and Jacob called him Benjamin; but Rachel his beloved wife died in giving birth. Jacob buried her in Bethlehem and set a pillar upon her grave so that it would always be remembered. Grieving, he turned south to Hebron and his home, to find that his mother Rebekah was long dead and that his father Isaac was a tired and feeble old man of one hundred and eighty years. He died not long after welcoming his son and all the new grandchildren; and Esau came from Edom to help Jacob bury him in the family cave of Machpelah.

Jacob and his family settled down in the land of Canaan, sure that it would be his home and his family's home for many years to come. He now had thirteen children; one daughter Dinah, and twelve sons from whom the tribes of Israel were to spring: Reuben, Simeon, Levi, Judah, Issachar, and Zebulun by Leah; Gad, Asher, Dan, and Naphtali by the two handmaids; and Joseph and Benjamin by Rachel. Of them all, Joseph was still his favorite. And because Joseph was loved more than the rest, his brothers came to hate him.

The Coat
of Many Colors

✝✝✝✝✝✝✝✝✝✝✝✝✝✝✝✝✝✝✝✝✝✝✝✝

Old Israel, still known as Jacob to his family, made much of Rachel's firstborn. Benjamin was still far too young to be a companion to him, especially since he did not even remember his own mother, and the ten older brothers were rough and ready men who did many thoughtless and sometimes evil things without regret. Joseph, on the other hand, was a good and faithful boy, although a little too anxious to tell his father about the wrongdoings of his brothers. Jacob was so fond of the lad that he made for him a wonderful coat of many colors as a special token of his favor. The older brothers had no such fine robes to wear, and they muttered sourly among themselves. The very sight of the coat enraged them, for they saw it as a sign of Jacob's great love for the boy and his lesser love for them. In their jealousy they hated Joseph, so much that they could not even speak to him without being rude and angry.

One night, when Joseph was about seventeen, he had a dream; and in the morning he told it to his brothers, little realizing how they would feel about it. "Listen to my dream," he said eagerly, quite sure that they would be as interested as he. "In this dream we were binding sheaves in the field, and all at once my sheaf stood upright in the center. And then all your sheaves stood round about and bowed down to my sheaf!"

"Ah, is that the way of it!" his brothers sneered, for they could sense the meaning of the dream. "Will you indeed reign over us, and we bow down to you? Do you really think that you will be our ruler?" And they hated him even more for his dreams and for his words. Yet when he dreamed another dream he told that one of them, too, and said; "I have dreamed again; and in my dream I saw the sun, the moon, and the eleven stars bowing down to me." This time even his father showed a trace of anger, and rebuked him. "What is this that you have dreamed?" he said. "Shall I and your mother and your brothers indeed bow down to the earth before you, as if you were a king?"

Yet Jacob thought about the dream and wondered if it could really mean that some day Joseph would be greater than all his family. The same thought came to the brothers, and it made their hate and envy grow.

The pastures around the family home were not large enough to feed Jacob's growing flocks, and when the fields were grazed clean of grass he would send his sons off to drive the animals as far away as they needed to find fresh pasturage and water. On one occasion Jacob sent his ten older sons to Shechem with the flocks, for he needed Joseph's help at home, and the men stayed away for such a long time that Jacob began to worry and wonder about their welfare.

He called Joseph to him and said, "Your brothers are in Shechem with the flocks, and I wish to send you to them."

"I am here to do as you say, and will gladly go," said

Joseph, although it was quite a distance for a young man to travel alone.

"Go, then," said Jacob, "and see if all is well with your brothers and the flocks, and bring back news of them."

Joseph put on his fine coat and set forth on his journey from the vale of Hebron, and he came at last to Shechem. But when he got there, there was no sign of his brothers or their flocks. A man of Shechem saw him wandering in the fields and asked him, "What are you looking for?"

"I am looking for my brothers from Hebron," Joseph said. "Can you tell me where they might be feeding their flocks?"

"Oh, they have left here," the man replied. "I heard them say, 'Let us go to Dothan.' So at Dothan you should find them."

So Joseph headed north through the hills toward Dothan with the message from his father. After many hours of hard travel he could see the flocks with their shepherds, his brothers, in the distance, and they themselves saw him coming from afar wearing the hated coat of many colors. At the sight of him and his fine clothes, their old dislike and envy burned within them. They watched him approach with his youthful, light-hearted step, and they began to plot against him.

"Behold, here comes the dreamer," they said to one another. "Let us kill him and cast him into some pit, and we can say to our father that some wild beast must have eaten him. Then we shall see what becomes of his dreams!"

But Reuben, the oldest of the brothers, had more mercy than the rest. "Let us not kill him ourselves," he said. "There is no need to shed his blood. Instead, let us throw him into this pit in the wilderness and leave him there, and lay no hand upon him." For Reuben wanted to save the boy from them, and planned to come back later to free him from the pit and return him to their father.

Joseph came to them without any thought but that

they would welcome him and gladly give him a return message for their father in Hebron. To his great surprise, they seized him roughly and ripped off his coat of many colors and threw him into a pit. The pit was deep and empty, without even a drop of water in it to quench his thirst or attract other desert wanderers who might come in search of water. And there they let him stay and cry for help while they sat down on the nearby grass to eat.

When they had finished their meal, some of the brothers went back to the pastures to care for the flocks, and Reuben went farther off than any of them to make his plans and wait for an opportunity to help his brother Joseph. The others stayed near the pit and talked. As they idled at the pit they saw a caravan of merchants and their camels approaching across the wilderness. They knew the men to be Ishmaelites, those who were descended from Ishmael of the wild lands; and they were coming from Gilead with their camels laden with spices and balm and myrrh to take to the markets of Egypt. And brother Judah was struck with a new and interesting thought.

"What profit is it to us if we kill our brother?" he said. "Would it not be better to sell him to these Ishmaelites for money? We should not let him die, for after all he is our brother and our flesh."

The others agreed to Judah's suggestion. In this way they would be rid of Joseph at a profit to themselves.

When the caravan of Ishmaelite merchantmen drew close enough so that the brothers could hail them to come closer yet, Judah and his brothers pulled the struggling Joseph from the pit and sold him to the merchants for twenty pieces of silver. The Ishmaelites took him willingly, for they knew they could easily sell a strong young man to some wealthy householder in Egypt for much more than he had cost them. And the Ishmaelites went off with him, toward the land of Egypt.

Shortly afterward Reuben came back, hoping to find that his brothers were no longer near the pit so that he could rescue Joseph. His brothers were indeed out of sight, but when he looked into the pit he saw that Joseph was no longer there. He stared down into the empty pit and called out hopelessly, but he could see that there would be no answer. The boy had gone. And he could not have climbed out by himself. Reuben tore his clothes with fright and grief. He ran into the pastures and cried out to his brothers: "The child has gone! And I, what shall I do, where shall I go?" For as the oldest son he felt the blame on his own shoulders, and he could not bear to think what he would have to tell his father.

The brothers told him what they had done, and he listened in horror. There was no undoing it; even Reuben could see that. So then they took the coat of many colors, which they had stripped from Joseph when he came to them, and killed one of the young goats of their flock. While Reuben looked on in shame they dipped the lovely coat into the blood, and they took it back with them to their father in Hebron.

They handed Jacob the once-beautiful coat, now so horribly stained. "This we found in the wilderness," they said. "It is torn and bloodied, but we think we recognize it. See, Father! Do you know whether this is your son's coat?"

Jacob took it from them and knew it at once. "It is my son's coat!" he cried out bitterly. "Some wild beast has devoured him. Without doubt my son Joseph has been torn to pieces!"

And Jacob tore his clothes in the agony of his grief, and dressed himself in mourning sackcloth. All his family tried to comfort him, even those who had caused his terrible sorrow, but Jacob could not be comforted. Only little Benjamin could ease his pain; yet he was not his brother, and could not make up for the loss of Joseph. Jacob's heart was broken. "I will go down into my grave mourning for my son," he moaned sorrowfully.

Thus did Jacob mourn for his lost son. He had no reason to believe that his beloved Joseph had not been torn apart by some wild animal on his lonely journey. Ten brothers knew that no animal had taken him, but they dared not to say what they had done. In fact, they did not know what had become of the brother they had sold.

Joseph was on a slave block in the land of Egypt.

Joseph
a Captive in Egypt

✚✚✚✚✚✚✚✚✚✚✚✚✚✚✚✚✚✚✚✚✚✚

The slave buyers of the Egyptian market place prodded and peered at Joseph with critical interest. He was a strong and handsome lad and would surely make a useful servant. Joseph in his turn looked around and saw wonders he had never seen before in his short life on the plains of Canaan: splendid temples to strange gods; odd, massive structures he had heard called pyramids; busy city streets thronged with swarthy men, some important in their rich robes and some surly in the rags of beggars; and goods of all kinds up for auction in the market.

And he himself was one of the goods, an object sold for silver by the brothers who hated him, and brought to this foreign place to be sold again.

The Ishmaelite merchants quickly found a buyer for their captive. A man named Potiphar, himself an Egyptian and captain of the Pharaoh's guard, bought Joseph

113

to be his slave and took him into his own house. And
the Lord was with Joseph, for Potiphar was not only a
wealthy man but upright, a man of honor as well as
rank. He soon saw that Joseph was no ordinary slave.
The boy learned quickly, and he was honest. Everything he did seemed to prosper at his hands. In a very
short time he became a favored servant, and after a
while Potiphar made him overseer over his house and
all his wealth. So thoroughly did the captain of the
guard trust Joseph that he put all his business and
household affairs into the young man's hands, no longer
troubling himself about any of his possessions except
the food he ate. Potiphar needed a man like Joseph to
take charge of such matters for him, because as a
high-ranking military officer he was often away from
home and unable to attend personally to his business.

The years went by; Joseph worked hard and Potiphar's wealth increased. Even though he was a slave,
Joseph was treated well in the Egyptian's household,
almost as though he were a free man and an equal; and
he was not unhappy. But his comfortable state could
not last forever. Joseph was a good-looking young man,
and as he added years he became even more handsome
and good to look upon. His master's wife began to cast
her eyes upon him in a way that was a great embarrass-
ment to Joseph. Time after time she tried to make him
love her, but Joseph would not be persuaded.

"My master trusts me with everything he has," he
told her, "I am responsible for everything in this house,
so that he does not even question what I may be doing.
He has been kind and generous, keeping back nothing
from me but yourself, because you are his wife. How,
then, can I betray him? How can I do this great wickedness to him, and also sin against God?"

Nevertheless, Potiphar's wife kept on trying to win
Joseph's love. And still he would not let her have her
way. She grew more and more determined. One day,
when Potiphar was away and all the other people of the
house were about their business, she tricked Joseph into
coming into her room. Still he refused to love her, and

ran from her in great dismay. This time she became so angry that she screamed for help and pretended that Joseph had tried to do her wrong. To her husband, when he came home, she told a wicked lie. "That Hebrew servant of yours!" she cried, full of false rage. "While you were gone he tried to force himself upon me, and only when I lifted up my voice and cried out for help did he run away."

When Joseph's master heard his wife's words he was surprised and angry. He took Joseph from his house and thrust him into the prison where the king's own prisoners were kept. There Joseph stayed, innocent of any crime.

But the Lord was still with him. Even in prison Joseph did well, because he remained as cheerful and intelligent and honest as he had always been in Potiphar's house. The Lord was merciful to him and gave him favor in the eyes of the keeper of the prison. After a time, the keeper placed so much reliance upon Joseph that he felt safe in putting all the prisoners in Joseph's care. The keeper himself, like Potiphar before him, questioned nothing that Joseph did. As far as he was concerned, Joseph was in charge, and Joseph could be trusted.

A while later it happened that the chief butler and chief baker of the king's household offended their lord the Pharaoh, king of Egypt, and Pharaoh angrily threw them into the prison where Joseph was held. They, too, came under Joseph's charge, and he looked after them. They were exceedingly unhappy, for their ranks in the king's household had been high, and now they were prisoners with no idea of what the future held for them.

One night these two men dreamed a dream, each a slightly different one, and the strange dreams puzzled them. The next morning Joseph came to them and saw that they were sad. And he asked these one-time officers of the Pharaoh: "Why do you look so sad today?"

And they said to him, "We each have dreamed a dream, and we have no one here to tell us what they mean." For they took dreams very seriously, believing that they were prophecies. In Pharaoh's court there were wise men who were supposed to be able to interpret dreams, but in prison there was no one to explain the meaning. Or so they thought.

But Joseph was an experienced dreamer himself; and also he believed in God.

"Do not interpretations come from God?" said Joseph. "I am God's servant. Surely he will reveal his meaning through me. Tell me your dreams."

The chief butler, whose duty it had been to serve Pharaoh with wine, spoke first. "In my dream," he said to Joseph, "there was a grapevine in front of me, and on the vine there were three branches. Before my eyes the branches seemed to bud; then the blossoms opened and became clusters of ripe grapes. Pharaoh's wine cup was in my hand; and I took the grapes and squeezed them into Pharaoh's cup. And then I took the cup and gave it into Pharaoh's hand, even as I used to do when I served wine at my master's table."

And Joseph said to him, "This is the interpretation of your dream. The three branches are three days. Within three days Pharaoh will raise your head high and restore you to your place. You will serve him just as you used to when you were his butler. All shall go well with you. But think of me, I beg you, when you leave here and prosper once again. Show kindness to me and mention me to Pharaoh that I may be released, for I have been imprisoned unjustly. Indeed, I was stolen away out of the land of the Hebrews; and here also I have done nothing to deserve being put into this dungeon."

The butler was pleased with Joseph's explanation of his dream and readily promised to speak to Pharaoh about Joseph. And when the chief baker saw that the first interpretation was good he was encouraged, and he said to Joseph: "I also dreamed, and in my dream there were three white baskets on my head, one above the other, and in the topmost basket there were all manner of baked foods for Pharaoh. And the birds flew down and ate the food out of the basket on my head. What does this dream mean?"

Joseph did not like what he had to say, but he answered the baker: "This is the meaning of your dream. The three baskets are three days. Within three days Pharaoh will raise your head high—and hang you from a tree. And the birds will eat your flesh."

On the third day, which was Pharaoh's birthday, the king held a great feast for all who served him. It was the custom on such festive occasions for Pharaoh to review the sentences of those he had cast into the royal prison. Some would be pardoned; others would not. Pharaoh therefore sent his men to take his chief butler and chief baker from the prison. And he restored the chief butler to his old place beside the king's table; and once again the man offered the wine cup to his Pharaoh. But Pharaoh hanged his chief baker from a tree, as Joseph had said he would.

The butler was impressed with Joseph's interpretation, but he was so overjoyed with his good fortune at being restored to his former place that he did not remember his promise to Joseph. He forgot all about him. Joseph remained a captive in Pharaoh's prison while the weeks and months dragged into years.

Joseph's Brothers Bow

✦✦✦✦✦✦✦✦✦✦✦✦✦✦✦✦✦✦✦✦✦✦

If Pharaoh had not dreamed of cows and corn, Joseph might have been a captive even longer than he was. As it was, two full years passed while he waited for release; and then Pharaoh dreamed first one strange dream, then another. While the king of Egypt slept he saw fat cows and lean ones at the riverside; and after this he saw full, luxuriant ears of corn and thin ones in a field of grain.

In the morning he was greatly troubled. He sent for all the wise men and magicians of Egypt and told them what he had dreamed. But none of them could explain the dreams to Pharaoh. And then, all at once, the chief butler thought of the dream he had had while in prison.

"I do remember my faults this day!" he told his king. "Pharaoh once was angry with his servants, both the chief baker and me, and put us into prison. Each of us dreamed a dream one night, which we could not understand. There was a young man in the prison, a Hebrew, who was servant to the captain of the guard. We told him our dreams and he told us what they meant; and within three days we saw that he was right. I was restored to office, and the other hanged."

In haste, then, Pharaoh sent for Joseph. The young Hebrew shaved quickly and changed his clothes; and the king's men took him out of his dungeon and led him into the presence of Pharaoh.

The king of Egypt looked at him, this foreigner from Canaan, and wondered how he could help where all the old wise men had failed. Nevertheless, the Hebrew had been right before. Perhaps he would be right again.

"I have dreamed a dream," he said to Joseph, "and there is no one here who can tell me what it means. I have heard it said of you that you can understand dreams and explain their meanings. Is it indeed so?"

"The understanding is not in me," said Joseph. "But God will give Pharaoh an answer through me so that your mind shall be at peace."

"In my dream, then," Pharaoh said, "I stood upon the river bank. And as I watched, there came out of the river seven cows that were fat and healthy, and they went to graze in the meadow grass. Then seven other cows came up after them; and these were poor, bony, and very lean, such meager and unsightly cattle as I have never seen in the land of Egypt. And the lean, ill-favored cows ate up the first seven cows, those that were good and fat; but the thin ones were still as thin as ever! Then I awoke, and some time later slept again."

Joseph listened carefully to the troubled man in the regal robes. Whether he would be rewarded for his help he did not even think. But he did know that God would give him understanding.

"And now I dreamed," Pharaoh went on, "that I saw a stalk of corn with seven rich, good ears upon it. Then seven other ears sprang up after the good ones, and they were withered, thin, and blasted by the east wind. As I watched, the thin ears ate the seven good ears; and again I woke. But when I told these dreams to my magicians, they could not explain them to me."

"It is but one dream," Joseph said. "God has shown to Pharaoh what he is about to do. The seven fat cows are seven good years, and the seven good ears of corn are also seven years: the dream is one. The seven thin and ill-favored cows that followed the first are seven poor years; and the seven empty ears blasted by the east wind shall be seven lean years of famine. In this way God is showing to Pharaoh that there will be seven years of great plenty throughout all the land of Egypt, which will be followed by seven years of famine."

All Pharaoh's court was silent as Joseph explained the dream, dismayed by his interpretation but believing in it.

Joseph went on to tell them more. "The famine shall consume the land," he said, "and cause such desolation that the years of plenty will soon be forgotten, and there will be no food at all to eat. God sent Pharaoh a double dream to show that these things are certain to come to pass and that they will happen soon. It is a warning, so that Pharaoh may prepare for the bad years that will follow the good. Therefore, let Pharaoh find a man both discreet and wise and put him in charge of preparing for the years of need. And let that man appoint officers to make sure that a fifth part of the harvest is gathered up and set aside during the seven good years; and let them lay up corn and keep supplies of food in all the cities. Have them see that the food is stored as a supply for the people to draw against when the seven years of famine shall be in the land of Egypt. If this is done, then the people and the land will not perish from the famine."

The plan was good in the eyes of Pharaoh, and in the eyes of his men at court. "Can we find such a man as this?" he said to his attendants. "A man with the Spirit of God in him? Surely there can be no man more wise, more suitable, than the very man to whom God has shown all this." And the king of Egypt turned to Joseph. "You yourself shall be put in charge," he said.

"My people shall be ruled according to your word. Only on the throne shall I be greater than you. In everything else, I am setting you over all the land of Egypt to do as you have said."

And Pharaoh took from his own hand the ring with his kingly seal upon it, and himself put it onto Joseph's finger. Then he dressed Joseph in royal robes of finest linen, and put a gold chain about his neck, and gave Joseph a chariot to ride in that was second only to his own. "Without you," Pharaoh said to Joseph, "no man shall lift his hand or foot in all the land of Egypt."

Thus did Joseph of Canaan, he that was sold at seventeen by his ten older brothers, become ruler over all of Egypt at the age of thirty. In his royal robes he rode in his glorious chariot, in front of which the people cried: "Bow down! Bow low the knee!" and he was a mighty man in the eyes of all Egyptians. In time he married an Egyptian girl, daughter of an honored priest, a girl given to him as his wife by Pharaoh himself.

In the seven plentiful years that followed, the earth brought forth abundant food. Joseph traveled throughout the land of Egypt, showing the people how to make the best use of their soil and how to conserve what they grew. He and his officers gathered up corn wherever they went, until it seemed as though they had saved as much corn as there were sands of the sea. Joseph gave up counting his supplies, for they were well past counting. From the grainfields around each city he gathered corn for that city's storehouses, so that throughout the land the cities were supplied with stocks of grain from their own nearby fields. Wherever he went he made sure that every fifth part of every harvest was taken from the whole and stored against the day when there would be no harvest. And when that happened, he himself would give out food as needed. Those seven years were good and happy years for the people of Egypt; and they were happy, too, for Joseph. His wife bore him two sons, Manasseh and Ephraim; and Joseph was grateful to the Lord for having caused so much good to come out of his earlier afflictions.

Then the drought fell upon the land. The soil no longer yielded fat corn nor even empty ears; the cattle became lean and miserable for want of food and water. At first the famine was less severe in Egypt than in the neighboring lands, for the waters of the Nile still trickled through the fields. But it was very bad in other countries that had never been well-watered, and their fields dried up and their cattle slowly died. After a while even the people of Egypt used up the small stocks they had kept in their own homes. And when all the land of Egypt was famished, the people cried out to their king for food.

Pharaoh said to them: "Go to Joseph. Do what he tells you to do." They went to Joseph. He opened all the storehouses and supplied the Egyptians from the stores gathered in the years of plenty. Soon the people of the neighboring countries came into Egypt to buy corn from Joseph, for he had conserved so well that there was food to spare.

And the famine was over all the face of the land. Soon it reached the land of Canaan, even as it had during the time of Abraham when it had driven him into Egypt with his flocks. Joseph's own family began to suffer badly in their parched and sunburnt land.

Now when Jacob heard that there was corn in Egypt, he called his sons to him and said: "Why do you look at one another, asking where you may find food to eat? I have heard that there is corn in Egypt. Go down there and buy food for us so that we may eat and live."

So the ten older brothers gathered up their empty grain sacks, saddled their donkeys, and departed to buy corn in the land of Egypt. But Benjamin, the youngest brother, stayed home with his father, for Jacob had never given up sorrowing for his one lost son and was afraid that some mishap would take Benjamin from him as well.

The ten men traveled through the starving land of

Canaan and other lands that were as dry and famished
as their own. At last they came to Egypt, not knowing
that their own brother Joseph was the governor of the
land and that it was he who sold the grain to all the
people that came from the hungry lands.

Even when they saw him they did not realize who he
was, for it was more than twenty years since they had
seen him last. Then he had been a lad, and now he was
a man; then he had been stripped of his coat of many
colors and sold from a pit in Canaan to a group of
passing merchants, and now he wore fine robes and sat
upon a throne in Egypt.

They went toward his throne and bowed low.

But Joseph knew them at once. And as he saw them
bow down to the earth in front of him, he remembered
his old dreams. His brothers were indeed bowing down
to him; the same brothers who had sold him into
slavery. There was no thought of vengeance in his
heart, but he did wonder if his brothers were as harsh
and cruel as they had been in the old days. He spoke to
them in the language of Egypt through an interpreter,
and he pretended that he did not know or trust them.

"Who are you?" he asked roughly. "Where do you
come from?"

"We are from the land of Canaan," they replied,
"and we have come here to buy food."

"You are spies!" Joseph said sharply. "You have
come to see the famine and weakness of the land, and
then you will send an army to make war against us."

"No, no, my lord," they protested. "We are not spies.
It is only to buy food that we, your servants, have
come. We are twelve brothers, sons of one man in the
land of Canaan. Our youngest brother is with our father, and one brother has been lost to us."

"You are spies," Joseph said firmly, determined to
test them to the limit. "And you will not leave here
until I see this younger brother that you talk about.
When he comes here, only then will I know that you are
telling me the truth." For he wanted very much to see

his brother Benjamin, and yet he also hoped that they would not forfeit the youth to save themselves.

They gave him no further answer, except to repeat that they were honest men in search of food. Joseph hardened his heart, although he was a kindly man and wished no harm to them, and put them all into prison for three days. Only by their words and actions under hardship would he know if they had changed.

On the third day he released them from the prison.

"Do as I say and you shall live," he said, "for I am a God-fearing man and will not hurt you if you are what you say. If you are honest men, nine of you shall return home with corn for the famine of your houses, and one shall stay here, bound in the place where you have been imprisoned. And he shall stay here until you return with your youngest brother, for only by bringing him back to me will you prove your words. Then none of you shall die. But if you do not do what I ask, then I will know that you are spies."

Deeply disturbed and very much afraid, they talked among themselves in their own language. They did not know that Joseph could understand their every word.

"This has come upon us because of our own guilt," they whispered to each other. "We saw the anguish of our brother Joseph, and when he pleaded with us we would not hear his cries. That is why we suffer now, and it is right that we should suffer."

"Did I not beg you then not to harm the boy?" said Reuben. "And you would not listen to me! God requires us to answer for the shedding of our brother Joseph's blood. We did wrong, my brothers, and that is why this punishment is on us."

Joseph heard them and his heart was touched by their repentance. He turned away from them and wept. But he was still not sure that they had fully learned their lesson, nor did he yet know what they would do about his brother Benjamin.

He turned back to them and spoke again through his interpreter, and in front of their eyes he took their

brother Simeon and had him bound for his return to
prison. Then he ordered the other nine to go.

They left for Canaan with their grain sacks full of
corn, not knowing that he had commanded his steward
to put each man's money back into his sack. Their
donkeys were laden with corn and they had good provisions for their journey, yet they were sad and troubled
as they traveled home. Joseph had been lost to Jacob
many years before; now their brother Simeon was a
prisoner in Egypt and must stay there until they came
back with Benjamin. If they did not return with their
youngest brother, then Simeon would surely die.

But worse fears were still to come. When at last they
reached home and their waiting father, they emptied
their grain sacks and found that each man's bundle of
money—the money they thought they had paid to the
cruel governor of Egypt—was still there in each sack.
Haltingly, they told their story to their father, and all
were much afraid. Now the Egyptian would not only
think that they were spies, but thieves as well!

"I will go back!" said Reuben. "If the man sees
Benjamin, he will know we did not lie. And I will take
the money back with me."

"No, you shall not!" cried Jacob. "I have already
lost both Joseph and Simeon. You will not take Benjamin away from me. All these things are against me!"

"I must go back with the money," said Reuben.
"And I must take Benjamin. I swear that if you let me
take him, I will bring him back to you. I swear it by
my own two sons."

"I will never let you take him," Jacob said. "His
brother is already dead; must I lose him as well? No, if
any harm should come to Benjamin through what you
do, then you will bring my gray hairs down into the
grave with sorrow."

And there the matter stayed.

But the corn brought from Egypt did not last long,
and the famine lasted for as many years as Joseph had
predicted. Still there was no rain in Canaan. Still there

was no fodder for the starving flocks. Still the fields
were bare of corn to feed the family of Jacob, who was
also Israel.

It was impossible for the brothers to go back to
Egypt. Surely they would lose their brother Benjamin.
And yet—what else was there to do?

Joseph's
Family in Egypt

****

The children and grandchildren of Israel who lived in Canaan numbered sixty-six, and with them in their home were many workers of the fields. The food from Egypt was soon gone. The bare land could not feed them all, and all of them were hungry. When the time came that they had eaten up the corn from Egypt they knew they had, somehow, to find more food, or die.

Jacob called his sons together. "You will have to go again," he said. "Go back to Egypt, and buy more food for us."

"We can only go if we take Benjamin," Judah reminded him. "The man who rules there told us that he would not see us again unless we take our youngest brother with us. If you let us take him, we will go. Otherwise, there is no use in going."

Jacob groaned bitterly, remembering. "Why did you

tell the man you had another brother?" he asked
reproachfully.

"Because he asked us," Judah answered. "He asked
about our family, and wanted to know if our father was
still alive and if we had another brother. There seemed
no reason not to answer him. How could we know that
he would say, 'Bring your brother to me'? But he *must*
go, my father. Send the lad with me, so that we may see
the man and buy the food. Or else all of us shall die of
hunger—you, we, and all the little ones. I myself will
be the guarantee for Benjamin. If I do not bring him
back to you, then all blame shall be on me forever."

They argued more, the brothers and the old man,
and at last Jacob agreed to let them go with his beloved
Benjamin. "If it must be so," he sighed, "then it must
be. Take your brother and go. But do this, too: take
with you the best fruits of the land. Carry a good
present to the man; a little balm, some wild honey, rich
spices and perfumes, nuts and almonds, the best of
everything we have. And take double money with you
also, so that you may pay for what you buy and return
what you found in your sacks. Perhaps it was an over-
sight, that it was given back to you. Go now, and look
after Benjamin, and may that man be kind. Pray that
God Almighty will show you mercy before the man in
Egypt so that he will send back both Simeon and
Benjamin. But if it is God's will that I should lose my
children, then . . . it is God's will."

The brothers took the presents and the double money, and young Benjamin journeyed with them to the
land of Egypt. Once again, ten brothers stood before
Joseph, ruler in a foreign land. But this time Rachel's
younger son stood with them.

When Joseph saw Benjamin he was deeply moved.
"Take the men from Canaan to my house," he told his
steward, "and prepare a feast, for these men shall dine
with me at noon."

Joseph's servant led the brothers away. And the
brothers were very much afraid when they saw that
they were being taken to the ruler's house, for they

thought that some terrible punishment was in store for them. "It is because of the money put back in our sacks," they told each other. "He thinks we stole it, and now he will throw us into prison with Simeon and we shall all be slaves." When they reached the door of Joseph's house they could contain their fears no longer.

"About the money in our sacks," they said to Joseph's steward. "We did not steal it; we do not know how it came to be put back in the sacks. But we have brought other money to replace it if you think we stole it."

"Why, no," the steward said, as he showed them into Joseph's home. "Peace be to you; do not be afraid. It must have been your God that gave you treasure in your sacks. I received your money, and you owe us nothing." So saying, he left them and came back with Simeon. Then he made all of them comfortable in Joseph's house, washing their feet according to the custom and providing fodder for their donkeys. "My master will be here at noon," he explained to Joseph's brothers, "and he has asked that you should eat with him."

Joseph came home at noon and welcomed them kindly to his house. They bowed low in front of him, grateful for his kindness and for Simeon's release, and they gave him the presents they had brought from Canaan. Joseph accepted their gifts cordially and inquired about their welfare, "And is your father well?" he asked, with far more interest than they could know. "The old man of whom you spoke, is he still alive?"

"He is alive and well," they answered, bowing low again.

Then Joseph looked at his brother Benjamin, son of Rachel his own mother. "Is this your younger brother, of whom you spoke to me?" They nodded. "That is he," they said.

"God be gracious to you, my son," said Joseph, scarcely able to hide his powerful emotions, for he yearned to greet the youth and show his love. Yet he was not ready to reveal himself. Alone for a moment, he wept, then washed away his tears and went back to his brothers.

They all sat down to dine. Joseph, as ruler, had a table to himself, and his Egyptian officers sat apart. And the eleven men from Canaan sat at a table by themselves, marveling and wondering how Joseph could possibly have known their ages—for he had seated them himself, in order, from the firstborn to the youngest. And Joseph sent dishes from his own royal table to his honored visitors, offering Benjamin five times as much as all the others.

They dined and drank, and all were merry. The strange man who was ruler seemed to be their friend, and he had brought them all together again. Simeon was free, and Benjamin had not been taken in his place. All fears were forgotten.

The brothers set forth again on the following morning, their hearts full of relief and their sacks full of the grain so badly needed by Jacob and his family. But again they did not know that Joseph had given his steward special instructions that would put them to a further test.

"Fill the men's sacks with food," Joseph had said, "as much as they can carry, and put each man's money back into his sack. But to the youngest one you shall not only return the corn money, but also take my silver drinking cup and put it into his sack."

The steward did as Joseph had commanded him. And the brothers traveled cheerfully toward the land of Canaan.

They had not gone far when Joseph gave his steward fresh instructions. "Hurry, now!" he said. "Go after those men, and when you overtake them, you must say: 'Why have you returned evil for good? You have stolen my lord's drinking cup, and in this you have done evil!' "

The steward hurried off. Soon he overtook the brothers, and he said to them what Joseph had commanded him to say.

"We did steal a silver cup?" The brothers were

shocked. "How can you say such a thing? God forbid that your servants should have stolen anything. Did we not bring back the money we found in our sacks when we last traveled up to Canaan? Is it likely that we should steal from your lord's house either gold or silver? Search us, if you like. If the cup is found with any of us, then let that man die, and the rest of us will be slaves to your lord of Egypt."

"I will look," said Joseph's steward. "And he with whom the cup is found shall be my servant, but only he. The rest of you shall not be blamed."

The brothers took their sacks down from their donkeys and confidently opened them. They were very sure that the cup would not be found, for each man knew that he had not been the one who had taken it.

The steward searched each sack, beginning with that of the oldest son Reuben and ending with the sack of Benjamin, the youngest. And there, in Benjamin's sack, the steward found the silver cup that he had put there himself.

The brothers were astounded and dismayed. They tore their clothes in fear and sorrow, but they loaded up their donkeys once again and returned to the city where Joseph awaited them with a stern, accusing face.

Joseph saw that they had all come back; not only Benjamin, but all of them. His heart rejoiced that the younger brother had not been abandoned. "What deed is this that you have done?" Joseph demanded, pretending an anger that he did not feel. "Did you think that I would not find you out?"

And then Judah, the one who had been most responsible for selling Joseph into slavery, showed that he was a changed man indeed. He said: "What can we say to you? How shall we clear ourselves? We know not how the cup came into our brother's sack, but we do know that God has seen the sins of our younger years and is punishing us. If one of us is guilty, then all of us are guilty, and all of us shall be your slaves."

"God forbid that I should keep you all as slaves," Joseph replied. "Only one of you is guilty. The man who took my silver cup shall be my slave, and only he. The rest of you shall go in peace to your father's land."

Here was their opportunity to escape and leave Benjamin behind in slavery. But the brothers would not take their chance to go. Judah, once so hard of heart and selfish, came forward once again and spoke to Egypt's ruler.

"Oh, my lord, let me speak, I beg you," he said, "and do not let your anger burn against us. You remember that you asked us once before about our father, and if we had another brother. And we answered you. Then you wanted us to bring our brother to you, but we knew it would break our father's heart if we did so. If our father loses Benjamin, he will die of sorrow. Yet all of us would have died of famine if we had not come to you again; so we came again to Egypt and brought with us our younger brother as you said we must. And now, if we return without this lad who is everything to Jacob since the loss of his son Joseph, our father will surely die of sorrow. My lord, I promised my father that no harm would come to Benjamin, that he would return in safety. Therefore, my lord, I pray you, let me stay here in his place to be your slave, and let my brothers take the lad home to his father. For I could not bear the sadness that would come upon my father if his beloved youngest son were taken from him."

Now Joseph could not restrain himself, for he could see that his brothers were no longer the cruel men they had been.

"I am your brother Joseph!" he cried out. "Tell me again that my father is still alive!"

His brothers were thunderstruck, and could not answer him. For the first time this hard Egyptian ruler had spoken in their own language, and he had said this incredible thing! In their astonishment and fear they hung back, and said nothing.

"Come near me, I beg you!" Joseph said, and held his arms out to them.

At last, and slowly, they went close to him.

"I am Joseph, your brother, whom you sold into Egypt," this powerful ruler said; and now they shook and trembled. "But do not be grieved or angry with yourselves because you sold me, for it was God who sent me here ahead of you to save our people's lives. God brought me here and made me ruler throughout the land of Egypt; God, not you; so that you might be preserved upon this earth. For two years now there has been famine in the land, and there will be five years more without a harvest. Therefore hurry to your home, and speak to our father. Tell him: 'God has made your son Joseph lord of all Egypt.' Tell him that he is to come at once with all his family and live near me in the part of Egypt called the land of Goshen. Say that he must bring his children, and all his children's children, and all his flocks and herds and everything he has, for I will look after all of you in this time of poverty. Make haste, tell my father, and bring him here to me!"

And then Joseph took his brother Benjamin into his arms and wept tears of joy after the many years of parting. Afterward he embraced his other brothers, too, as proof that all had been forgiven and that he loved them also; and then they talked together as they had never talked before.

Pharaoh soon heard that Joseph's brothers had come, and he himself insisted that their father and all their family should come to live in Egypt where there was food in plenty.

Eleven brothers, guilt-free and happy at last, took the rich gifts given to them by Pharaoh and his governor Joseph, and went back into the land of Canaan to tell the good news to their father. With the gifts they took provisions for their journey, and wagons from the king so that they might bring back to Egypt all their family and their goods.

When Jacob saw that not only Benjamin but Simeon as well had come back with all the others, his relief and joy were great. But greater still was his happiness when they told him: "Joseph is alive! Your son is governor over the land of Egypt! And we have come to take you and all our family back with us to be near him."

At first the old man could not believe his ears, and his heart was faint because of what he heard. But when they told him everything his son had said, he believed them and rejoiced. Yet he was not sure that God meant him to go into the land of Egypt, for Canaan was his promised land. Then the Lord God spoke to him and said: "I am God, the God of your fathers. Do not be afraid to go to Egypt, for I will be with you and make of you a mighty nation. You shall see your son Joseph again, and in time I will bring your family out of Egypt back into the land of Canaan."

Then Jacob, father of all the people whom the Egyptians called the Israelites, took his family into Egypt and once again saw his beloved, long-lost son. Joseph greeted him with tears of joy, and Pharaoh himself accepted the children of Israel as honored friends.

Thus did the children of Israel settle in the land of Goshen, a rich and fertile district that was part of Egypt, and there they lived for many years. Pharaoh was kind to them, and the people of Egypt loved and respected the children of Israel because they were the family of Joseph who had saved them all from famine and starvation.

No more than seventy Israelites, including Joseph and his children, settled in the land of Goshen. But in time the family grew, became great in numbers, and prospered among their Egyptian friends. For several hundreds of years the children of Israel were happy in the alien land.

Moses
in the Bulrushes

++++++++++++++++++++++

The Hebrews in the land of Goshen grew rich and multiplied exceedingly. Each of Jacob's twelve sons became the father of a tribe of Israel, and all the tribes but one were named after Joseph's brothers. Joseph's own tribe became two, which were named after Joseph's two sons, Manasseh and Ephraim.

Old Jacob, father of all Israel, died, and was mourned by Egyptians and Israelites alike. Then Joseph died, and those of his generation. But still the children of Israel were fruitful, and increased to hundreds of thousands. The land was filled with them, and they were mighty.

Then there arose a new king over Egypt, one who had not known Joseph and his brothers. And this Pharaoh was afraid of all these foreign people in his land, for it seemed to him that soon there would be more Israelites than Egyptians in the land of Egypt. They

worked hard and he needed them, but he did not want
their numbers to increase. He said to his people: "Behold, the people of the children of Israel are more and
mightier than we. Come, let us deal wisely with them so
that they no longer multiply. For what if there is war,
and they should join our enemies and fight against us,
and then leave this land? They must not go from
Goshen, nor become too powerful. I shall make their
lives a burden to them; I shall make them slaves."

Therefore the Egyptians set taskmasters over the
children of Israel to make them work as hard as men
can work. Pharaoh wanted treasure cities built; the
slave drivers made the Hebrews build them. But the
harder they worked and the more rigorous their lives,
the stronger the Israelites grew and the more they multiplied.

"Work them harder yet!" Pharaoh commanded. "Increase their burdens, double their labors. Make each
man work until he drops and then flog him until he
works again."

The Egyptian overseers did as they were ordered. In
every way they made life bitter for the children of
Israel, driving each man to work to the very limit of his
strength. The Hebrews carried great loads of bricks and
mortar, and they built from morn to night; they slaved
in the fields with the crops and the cattle; they dug and
they dragged and they carried to the sound of the whip
and the shout; and they were beaten savagely if their
masters thought they were not working hard or fast
enough. And yet, in spite of the misery of their lives,
the Israelites continued to thrive.

Then the king of Egypt spoke to the Hebrew midwives and ordered them to destroy all boy babies when
they were born to the women of Israel. But the midwives
believed in the God of Israel and could not bring
themselves to obey the king. Instead, they saved the
boy children, and told Pharaoh that Hebrew women
were not in the habit of waiting for midwives before
having their babies, and that therefore they had been
unable to follow his orders.

Pharaoh thereupon devised another plan. He gave his people a cruel command. "Every son that is born to the Israelites from this day on, you shall cast into the river. Only the daughters shall you save alive."

Now there was a man of the house of Levi who had married a woman of his tribe. They already had a three-year-old son named Aaron and a daughter, Miriam. And now the woman bore another boy. When she saw what a lovely, sturdy child he was she could not bear to part with him, least of all in the terrible way commanded by the king, and she kept him hidden so that the king's men would not find him. For three months she managed to keep his birth a secret, but then she found that she could no longer hide him. Pharaoh's men were coming too close to her home in their search for Hebrew babies. So she wove for him a basket out of bulrushes, shaping it like a tiny, covered ark and plastering it with pitch and clay to keep the water out. She laid the child inside it and set the basket down among the tall reeds at the river's edge. Sadly, she turned away and went back to her house. But her little daughter Miriam stayed hidden among the reeds a short distance away to see what would become of her baby brother.

A group of women in fine clothes came into view. They were maidens of Pharaoh's household, come down to the river with the daughter of Pharaoh; for Pharaoh's daughter meant to bathe in this quiet stream with its concealing bulrushes. The women walked together along the river bank while Miriam watched. And then Pharaoh's daughter saw the strange little woven boat lying among the reeds. At once, she sent a maid to bring it to her.

And she opened it and saw the child, and the baby began to cry. Pharaoh's daughter picked him up tenderly and with compassion in her heart, for she knew about her father's cruel decree. "This is one of the Hebrew children," she said gently. And she could not think of letting the lovely, innocent baby die.

Sister Miriam watched from the tall reeds and saw the look of love and pity on the princess' face. She left her hiding place and went to Pharaoh's daughter, who was holding the child as if he were her own.

"Shall I go and bring you a nurse from among the Hebrew women?" the girl asked eagerly. "So that she may nurse the child for you?"

"Yes, go," Pharaoh's daughter said to her.

And the baby's sister ran off to find her mother. The woman of Levi came quickly and saw the princess holding the tiny baby she herself had placed so lovingly in the bulrush basket.

"Take this child away," Pharaoh's daughter said softly to its mother, "and nurse him for me. I will give you wages for your work."

Then the woman, with a happy heart, took back her own child and nursed him with a mother's love and care. No longer was she afraid that harm would come to him, for Pharaoh's daughter was the boy's protection.

When the child was old enough to leave his mother she took him to the palace and gave him to Pharaoh's daughter, knowing that he would be well looked after. Pharaoh's daughter called him Moses, "because," she said, "I drew him out of the water." And the boy became her son.

Moses, the Hebrew boy, grew up in the palace of the Pharaoh who feared and hated Hebrews, but Pharaoh's daughter cherished him and saw to it that he was educated as if he were a royal prince. From the Egyptians he learned much of the arts and sciences unknown to his own people; and from his mother's early training he learned that he was one of the children of Israel, whose God was the one true God.

As he grew to manhood he would often leave the royal palace and go out among his own people. He would see their sufferings and their heavy burdens, and the taskmasters who drove and struck them. And it happened, on one of those days that he walked among his fellow men, that he saw an Egyptian overseer reach out his hand against a Hebrew slave and strike the man unmercifully. Moses suddenly forgot himself, forgot that he was a noble in the court of Pharaoh. All he could think was that a brutal slave driver had struck a brother Hebrew. He swiftly looked this way and that, and when he saw that there was no one watching him he hit out savagely and killed the Egyptian. Carefully, he hid the body in the sand and quietly went away. He knew that he had been wrong to kill the man, but he had seen much oppression and his anger had been great.

The next day he went out again. This time he saw two men of the Hebrews fighting one another, and he said to the one who was in the wrong: "Why do you strike your fellow Hebrew?"

The man stared back at him with hatred in his eyes, not knowing that Moses loved his people and only wished them well.

"Who made you a prince and a judge over us?" the man said bitterly. "Do you intend to kill me, as you killed the Egyptian yesterday?"

Fear struck at Moses' heart. So the deed was known; it was being talked about! Word of his crime would surely come to Pharaoh, and the punishment would be terrible. He turned away from the two men and walked off rapidly. He would have to flee at once.

It was not long before the king heard about the murder of his overseer and gave commands that Moses be found and put to death. But Moses had already gone. He left the land of Egypt and traveled deep into the wilderness, looking for a place where he might be safe from Pharaoh's wrath and live in peace. Somewhere he would find a new home and forget the past and the riches and the tyranny of Egypt.

He came eventually, tired and footsore, to the land of Midian. And he sat down by a well.

Now Jethro, the priest of Midian, had seven daughters. While Moses was resting at the well they came there with their father's flock to draw water and fill the troughs so that the sheep might drink. But as they tried to water their flocks, other shepherds came with flocks and tried to drive the women away. It was not the first time this had happened, for there were few wells in the wilderness; the flocks were many, and the daughters of Jethro were no match for the rough, discourteous men. But this time there was a stranger at the well, a man who looked like an Egyptian, and for once the women had a man to help them. Moses stood up and firmly held the shepherds back while he helped the seven sisters draw their water, and he filled the troughs until the thirsty sheep had drunk their fill.

When the women came home their father was surprised to see them, for they were earlier than usual. "How is it that you have come so soon today?" he asked.

"There was an Egyptian at the well," they said. "He defended us from the rough shepherds, and he drew water for us, and he watered our flock himself."

"Well, where is he?" demanded Jethro. "Why did you not bring the stranger with you? Go and call him, that he may eat with us."

And so they did. The family of Jethro welcomed Moses to their home, and a friendship quickly grew between them.

Moses was happy with his new friends. When Jethro asked him to stay with them, Moses was grateful and content to live in Midian. He soon took charge of the family flocks and spared the women from their work.

In time, Jethro gave his daughter Zipporah to Moses for his wife. She bore him two sons, and they all lived a peaceful life together in the land of Midian. The man who had learned so much from the wise teachers of Egypt had now become a simple shepherd in a wilderness far from the land of Pharaoh and the captive Hebrews. He could not forget the sadness and slavery of his own people; but he was an outcast and a murderer who could find no way to help them.

And then the king of Egypt died. At first there was rejoicing among the Israelites, for they thought his cruelty might die with him and that their lot would change.

Their hopes were quickly shattered. The new Pharaoh was even more cruel than the old, and the children of Israel were forced into a state of slavery and misery worse than they had ever known. they cried to heaven with the anguish of their bondage; and their cries went up to God. *

The Lord heard the agony of their voices and saw their dreadful burden. In his great pity he remembered his convenant with Abraham, with Isaac, and with Jacob, and he resolved to set their children free.

A man would have to be found who was capable of leading the Israelites to freedom. Moses, a man of the tribe of Levi and a man who knew both Hebrews and Egyptians well, might be such a leader. Yet he was far away in exile, hiding from a king, knowing nothing of recent happenings in Egypt.

The Burning Bush

****

For many days and months and years Moses tended the flock of Jethro his father-in-law, priest of Midian. As time went by he thought less and less of faraway Egypt, although he never quite forgot. So far as he knew he would be nothing but a shepherd all his life, caring for another man's sheep.

One day he led the flock to the far side of the desert in search of greener pastures, and he came to the foot of Mount Horeb, also known as Sinai, which was the mountain of God. As he grazed his flock he saw, some distance from him, a most unusual sight. A flame sprang suddenly from the middle of a bush, and as he watched, the bush kept burning brightly with the fire until it seemed that it would surely turn to ashes and die. But the flames kept on blazing through the dry desert shrub and yet the bush was not destroyed.

"This is strange indeed!" said Moses to himself. "I

must turn aside and look more closely at this great sight, to see why the bush does not burn through and die."

It was the angel of the Lord in the flame of fire, though Moses did not know it yet. He left his flock and slowly came toward the burning bush. When the Lord saw that he had turned aside to see, he called out to Moses from the midst of the miraculous fire and said: "Moses, Moses!"

Moses looked about him in astonishment. "Here I am," he answered.

God's voice came again from the burning bush. "Do not come closer. Take off your shoes, for this is holy ground. I am the God of your father, the God of Abraham, the God of Isaac, and the God of Jacob; the God of all your people."

Moses took off his shoes as he was bidden and hid his face, for now he knew why the bush was not consumed by the fire and he was afraid to look upon his God.

The heavenly voice went on. "I have seen the sufferings of my people in Egypt and I have heard the cries wrought from them by their Egyptian taskmasters; I do know their oppressions and their sorrows. And I have come down to deliver them from the Egyptians. I will bring them out of that land into another, a good land and large, flowing with milk and honey; the land of Canaan. Come now, therefore, and I will send you to Pharaoh, so that you may lead forth my people the children of Israel out of Egypt to the promised land."

Moses was astounded by these words. "*I*, lead them out of Egypt?" he thought to himself in wonderment; for he had no notion of how he would set about such a difficult task.

He said to God: "Who am I, that I should go to Pharaoh, and lead the children of Israel out of Egypt? I do not know how I shall do it."

"Fear not," said the Lord. "I will be with you, and this shall be a token to show that I have sent you: I tell you now that when you have brought my people out of

Egypt, you will worship me upon this mountain of Sinai."

"But when I go to the children of Israel and say to them that the God of their fathers has sent me to them, what if they no longer know their God?" Moses protested, for he knew how easy it was for people to turn to idols and forget the one true God. "If they say to me, 'What is his name?' what shall I say to them?"

And God said to Moses, "You shall tell them that I am Jehovah, he who exists that you may exist. You shall say that you have been sent by the God who made all mankind. And this also shall you say to the children of Israel: 'The Lord God of your fathers, the God of Abraham, the God of Isaac, and the God of Jacob, has sent me to you.' This is my name forever, and by it shall I be remembered through all generations."

And then God described to Moses how he should free the Israelites.

"Go and gather the elders of Israel together, and say to them that I, the Lord God of your fathers, have appeared to you. Tell them that I have seen what is being done to my people in Egypt and that I will lead them out of their bondage into a land flowing with milk and honey. They will listen to your voice. And then you and the elders of Israel shall go to the king of Egypt and say to him: 'The Lord God of the Hebrews has appeared to us. Now let us go, we beg you, three days' journey into the wilderness, so that we may make offerings to the Lord our God.' And I am sure that the king of Egypt will not let you go even for these three days; no, he shall refuse completely. And then I will stretch out and strike Egypt with the wonders I will do in the midst of them. After that, the king will let you go. And you shall not go empty-handed, for the Egyptians will give your people fine clothes, and jewels of gold and silver, and you will take these things with you."

"But they will not believe me or listen to my voice," Moses protested. "They will say, 'The Lord has not appeared to you; who are you to say that he has done so?' How shall I make them believe?"

"They will believe," God answered. "What is that in your hand?"

"It is my shepherd's rod," said Moses.

And God said, "Cast it on the ground."

Moses obeyed. He threw his shepherd's crook down on the ground and started back in horror, for it had turned into a wriggling snake.

"Do not be afraid of it," said God. "Reach out your hand and take it by the tail."

So Moses reached out his hand unwillingly and grasped the tail, and at once the snake became a harmless rod in his hand.

"That is so they may believe that the Lord God of their fathers has appeared to you," God said. "Now reach your hand beneath your cloak and place it against your chest."

Moses did so, and when he drew his hand out from beneath his cloak he saw that it was white as snow and diseased as if with leprosy.

"Again," said God. "Put your hand once more against your chest."

And Moses once again reached beneath his cloak and placed his hand against himself. This time, when he drew it out, it had turned again into healthy flesh.

"If they do not believe these signs," said the Lord, "there will be other signs that they will believe. After these signs you will take water from their river and pour it onto the dry land. And the water from the river will turn at once to blood."

But Moses was still not convinced that he was the man to set his people free.

"O my Lord," he said, "I am not an eloquent speaker. My tongue is slow, my words are halting. I know not how to use my speech so that men may be persuaded."

"Who made man's mouth?" said God. "Was it not I? Who makes the dumb, or deaf, or the seeing, or the blind? Is it not I, the Lord? Therefore, go now, and give no more thought to your halting speech. I will be with your mouth, and I will teach you what to say."

"O my Lord, I pray you," Moses pleaded, "send another man, not me."

Then the Lord was angry with him. "Is not Aaron the Levite your brother?" he said sternly. "I know that he speaks well. I know, too, that he is coming out to meet you, and when he sees you he will be glad of heart. Therefore let him be your spokesman. I will teach you what to do and say; and you will speak to him and put the right words in his mouth. He shall be your mouth, and you will instruct him in what he has to do. And you will take that rod in your hands and do signs with it as I have shown you."

Then Moses had nothing more to say. He left the holy mountain and the bush that would not burn to ash, and he returned to Jethro his father-in-law. The story that he told was strange. But Jethro was a good man and a priest, and he believed that Moses truly had been given a mission. It was right, he said, for Moses to return to Egypt and see if his people were still living.

"Go in peace," said Jethro.

Yet Moses was still uneasy about returning to the place from which he had fled in haste so many years before.

God spoke again to Moses in the land of Midian. "Go, return to Egypt," said the Lord, "for all the men who sought your life are dead."

So Moses saddled up his donkeys and took his wife and sons with him on his journey into Egypt, and all the while he held the rod of God firmly in his hand.

The Lord said to Moses: "When you return to Egypt, see that you do before Pharaoh all the wonders that I have put into your hand. His heart will be hard against you, and at first he shall not let the people go. But the harder his heart, the greater shall be his punishment, and my people shall be freed."

And he said to Moses' brother Aaron in Egypt: "Go out into the wilderness and meet your brother Moses."

So Aaron went out from Egypt and met Moses at the

mountain of God, and he greeted his brother with love.
Moses told Aaron everything the Lord had said to him,
and all about the signs he was to show to the people in
the land of Egypt.

Aaron's faith and great enthusiasm gave Moses the
extra strength he needed. Together, the two brothers of
the tribe of Levi traveled back to Egypt with the woman Zipporah and her two sons riding on the donkeys;
and as soon as they arrived they gathered together all
the elders of the chidren of Israel and told them that
God had sent Moses to deliver them from the unfriendly land.

Aaron spoke as one inspired. Eloquently, persuasive-
ly, he told the elders everything the Lord had said to
Moses and he showed them the signs that proved that
Moses had indeed seen God. And when the people
heard his words and saw the signs, they believed with
all their hearts that the Lord had truly visited them and
seen their suffering. For the first time in many years
they felt real hope that they would be freed from
slavery. And they bowed their heads and worshiped
God.

"Let My People Go"

✻✻✻✻✻✻✻✻✻✻✻✻✻✻✻✻✻✻✻

Pharaoh was not impressed with the two bearded Hebrews who stood before him and told him a strange tale of a voice from a burning bush and its heavenly command.

Moses and Aaron asked little of him to begin with. "These are the words of the Lord God of Israel," they explained to Pharaoh. "He said: 'Let my people go so that they may hold a feast to me in the wilderness.' Therefore we ask that you let the children of Israel go forth to make offerings to their God."

"Who is this Lord, that I should obey his voice to let Israel go?" said Pharaoh haughtily. "I do not know him, nor will I let the people go."

"He is the God of the Hebrews and he has appeared to us," said Aaron. "We ask only that you let us go three days' journey into the desert to make sacrifices, or the Lord our God may punish us with death or pestilence."

"Sacrifices!" Pharaoh said contemptuously. "All you want is to take the people away from their work. Get back to your own work, Aaron and Moses, and interfere no more. I will not have my slaves resting from their burdens."

That same day Pharaoh issued new commands to the taskmasters of the Israelites. "The people are lazy," he complained. "They do not have enough to do. You shall no longer give them straw to make brick, as you have been doing. Let them go and gather the straw for themselves. But at the same time you will make sure that they make as many bricks as before. It is because they are idle that they cry out, saying, 'Let us go and sacrifice to our God.' Give them more work so that they may labor longer and not have time to listen to the empty words of Moses and Aaron."

His taskmasters went out and relayed their new orders. "Go, get straw wherever you can find it," they told the Israelites. "But do not let your work fall behind. No matter how long it takes you to gather the straw, you will still produce your daily number of bricks."

So the people were forced to go all over the land to gather their own material for making bricks. And all the while the taskmasters were hurrying them and driving them relentlessly. If they were slow, or fell behind with their quota of new bricks, the taskmasters would lash at them with harsh words and whips. "Why have you not fulfilled your task of making bricks? Why is the number short, both today and yesterday? You are idle, idle!" And the cruel whiplash sang down against bare backs.

The children of Israel turned their hatred against Moses and Aaron.

"Is this how you help us?" they demanded. "May the Lord judge you! You have caused us to be loathesome in the eyes of Pharaoh and his servants, and given him

yet another weapon against us. We will die from this!
Why could you not leave us alone?"

Their faith, so easily kindled by their hope, died just
as easily in the face of this new torment.

Moses was troubled, too. He returned to the Lord
and said: "Lord, why have you dealt so harshly with
our people? Why did you send me here? For since I
came to Pharaoh to speak in your name, he has been
even more cruel than before. Lord, you have not delivered your people at all!"

"I have heard the groaning of the children of Israel,"
said the Lord, "and I have remembered my covenant.
Go to them and tell them I will surely free them from
their slavery and bring my judgments against Egypt.
You shall see what I will do to Pharaoh now. He will
not let the children of Israel go; he will be glad to drive
them out. But first I have signs to show to him that I
am God. Go to your people; tell them that I am the
Lord and I will save them, for I will take them out of
Egypt into the land of Canaan, which will be their land
and their heritage."

Moses went to the children of Israel and told them
what the Lord had said, believing that they would be
encouraged by his words of hope. But they were so
disheartened by their sufferings that they would not
listen to him.

The Lord spoke again to Moses and to Aaron. "Go
to Pharaoh," he commanded. "When he asks you to
show him a miracle to prove that I have sent you, tell
Aaron to take your rod and cast it down at Pharaoh's
feet, and it shall become a serpent. For I will show my
wonders in the land of Egypt; and though the Pharaoh's heart may harden, he must some day see that I
am the Lord who will bring forth my people and punish the Egyptians who have made them slaves."

The two brothers went to Pharaoh for the second
time. Again they asked that their people be allowed to
leave the land; and Pharaoh's heart was hard. Aaron
cast the rod down in front of Pharaoh and his servants,
and the rod became a serpent. But Pharaoh had seen

such tricks before, or so he thought, and this was nothing to him. He called in his own wise men, the sorcerers and magicians of his court who could use enchantments of their own to do such things, and ordered them to do the same. Each of them cast down a rod, and each of their rods also turned into a snake. Pharaoh smiled with pleasure. But he no longer smiled when Aaron's rod-snake swallowed up the other rods. Then he was angry, and he refused to listen any more to Aaron.

The Lord instructed Moses to show another sign. "Go to Pharaoh in the morning," he commanded. "You will find him bathing in the waters of the Nile. Take your rod and stretch it over all the waters of the land. Say to him that the Lord God of the Hebrews has empowered you to turn the water to blood because he, Pharaoh, will not listen to you and let my people go."

Moses and Aaron did as the Lord commanded. They went to the river and found Pharaoh bathing; and Aaron, in the sight of Pharaoh, lifted up the rod and held it over the waters of the Nile. At once the river turned to blood. The fish died, the river smelled of blood and death, and all the waters of the land were foul and bloody. Even the water in the drinking vessels was turned to blood, and throughout the land there was only blood in the pools and springs and wells. There was water in the land of Goshen, where the children of Israel lived; but there was no water anywhere for the people of Egypt to drink.

Yet this, too, was a feat the magicians of Egypt could achieve with their enchantments, and Pharaoh was not moved.

After seven days the waters cleared.

God spoke again to Moses. "Tell Aaron to stretch his rod again over the waters of the land, over all the streams and rivers and over all the ponds."

Aaron stretched his rod out over the waters of Egypt and a plague of frogs came up and covered the land. They went into the houses and into the bedchamber of the king; they hopped into his bed and scurried through his kitchen; they jumped into the ovens, into the cooking pots, into the freshly kneaded dough; they swarmed over nobleman and servant, and they were everywhere.

Again Pharaoh's magicians could do the same thing with their enchantments. They did so, and brought even more frogs into the land of Egypt.

Pharaoh could not stand it. He called for Moses and Aaron. "Speak to your Lord!" he begged them. "Make him take the frogs away from me and from my people and I will let your people go so that they may make their offerings to their Lord."

Moses did not believe him, but he said: "When shall this be done? Tell me when, and it shall be done at the time you say."

"Tomorrow!" answered Pharaoh, outraged yet desperate.

"Tomorrow it will be," said Moses, "and then you will know that there is no God like the Lord our God."

The next day the frogs died in the houses, in the villages, and in the fields, until all were gone but those that still lived in the river.

But when Pharaoh saw that the plague was over he hardened his heart again. "Certainly your people shall not go into the desert to make offerings," he said harshly, and drove Moses from his presence.

The Lord gave instructions for another plague.

Aaron raised his rod over the dust of the land, and all the particles of dust became lice that settled on man and beast alike, each and every one. Pharaoh's magicians tried with their enchantments to equal what Aaron had done, but they could not bring forth lice. Neither could they rid the Egyptians of the plague sent by the Lord.

Then the magicians knew that the things wrought by Aaron with his rod were more than magic tricks. "This is the work of God!" they said to Pharaoh. But the king, instead of being humbled, further hardened his heart; and he listened neither to Aaron and Moses nor to his magicians with their small enchantments.

So God sent to him another plague. Great swarms of

dirt-bearing flies filled the house of Pharaoh and the houses of his servants, buzzing through the homes and fields and spreading their diseases everywhere except into the land of Goshen, where the Israelites lived. The very land was made filthy by the flying swarms.

"Stop!" screamed Pharaoh, flailing at the buzzing flies around his head. "Make your sacrifices! Make them in the land of Goshen, where your people live." For he thought that he could bargain with Moses; but he could not.

Moses shook his head. "No, we shall not worship our God before the eyes of the Egyptians. Their customs are not the same as ours, and they will surely stone us. We will go three days' journey into the wilderness and worship there, as we have been commanded by our Lord."

"Then go into the wilderness," Pharaoh said wearily. "Only do not go far away. And pray to your God to remove this swarm of flies!"

"I will pray," said Moses. "The flies will go tomorrow. But you, Pharaoh, may no longer deal deceitfully by promising and then not letting the people go to make their sacrifices. This time you must let them go."

"Yes, yes, they shall go. But make this swarm of flies go first!"

On the next day God removed the plague. All at once the flies disappeared from Pharaoh's palace, from his servants, from his people; there remained not a single one to anger Pharaoh.

And Pharaoh broke his promise. As soon as the plague of flies was over, he refused to let the people go. And he was deaf to Moses' warnings.

God sent another plague. This time a deadly disease swept through the Egyptians' herds. Their bulls and cows sickened and died; horses, asses, camels, oxen fell in the fields and never rose again; sheep in the pastures died off by the hundreds until the flocks had dwindled to almost nothing. None of the cattle of the Israelites was dead; and Pharaoh knew it from his messengers.

Yet he hardened his heart, and he did not let the people go.

And then the Lord said to Moses and Aaron: "Take handfuls of ashes from the furnace, and sprinkle them toward the heavens in the sight of Pharaoh."

Moses went to Pharaoh and cast the ashes into the air. They drifted off in tiny specks of dust and settled over Egypt. And wherever the fine dust settled on man or animal it caused a painful sore: open boils broke out on every Egyptian beast and human being. The magicians could do nothing. Their own boils were so bad that they could not come to see Moses nor even stand before their king.

But Pharaoh did not relent. Moses warned him once again; it was no use. "The people shall not go!"

And the heavens resounded with thunder. Hailstones, of a size and quantity never before seen in the land of Egypt, slammed down from above and ravaged the fields. Unprotected cattle, ripening crops, men hurrying home to safety—all were killed. Lightning flashed across the sky, came down to earth mingled with the heavy rain of hail, and ran along the ground in tongues of fire. Trees fell, their limbs broken and trunks uprooted; flax and barley crops were flattened against the soil, and the fields were devastated. But the children of Israel in the land of Goshen were untouched by the terrible storm.

This was still not enough for Pharaoh. He pleaded for an end of it and made his promises, but when the hailstones ceased to fall his heart was harder than ever.

The Lord spoke to Moses.

Moses stretched forth his rod over the land of Egypt, and there was another plague. An east wind blew across the land and brought with it a cloud of locusts that covered the face of the earth, stripping it of every fruit and blade of grass and every young crop which the hail had left untouched. The land was dark with locusts, and not a green thing lived in all of Egypt. The king's own elders turned on him and said: "How long will you let this man bring suffering to us? Do you not see that Egypt is destroyed?"

In his terror Pharaoh called for Moses. "Forgive my sin once more!" he begged. "Be merciful, and take away this death. Only this I ask you!"

Moses spoke to the Lord. And the Lord sent a mighty west wind to blow across the land and sweep the swarms of locusts from the earth and into the Red Sea. But with the passing of the plague, Pharaoh again went back upon his word and would not let the people go.

And again Moses stretched his rod toward the heavens. A dreadful darkness settled over Egypt for three long days and nights. Sun, moon, and stars all ceased to give their light. The children of Israel had light in their homes, but the Egyptians could not even see each other, much less go about their business.

Pharaoh, desperate, called Moses to him. "Take your people and go!" he said. "All of them, the men and women and children. Only leave your flocks and herds behind."

"No," said Moses. "We will take everything with us, everything we have."

"Then you take nothing!" Pharaoh growled. "You shall not leave at all. Get out of my presence and never let me see your face, for on the day I see you, you shall die."

Moses left him and listened once more to the voice of God.

"I will bring one more plague on Pharaoh," said the Lord, "and he will let you go, he will thrust you out of Egypt altogether. Warn him, and then prepare yourself and your people for the thing I am about to do."

Moses listened. The next, and last, would be the most terrible plague of all, and it would strike at the heart of Pharaoh himself.

It was almost too horrible a thing to think about; but Pharaoh in his cruelty had brought it down upon himself.

The Night of Passover

++++++++++++++++++++++++

Moses called together all the elders of Israel to tell them what was going to happen and what they had to do.

"This time we shall leave," said Moses. "First, every man and woman among us will go to his Egyptian neighbor and ask for jewels of silver and gold so that we are not empty-handed. Then you must prepare yourselves to leave with these gifts, and with your children, and with your cattle and all your goods."

The Egyptians gave freely when they were asked for gifts that would enable the Israelites to trade with merchants while they traveled. Even though their Pharaoh had refused to listen to Moses, they had come to regard the Hebrew leader as a great man in the land. They had seen his prophecies come true, and they had respect for him and the wonders he could do.

"And now," said Moses to the elders, "you must

listen to me closely and do exactly as I say. The Lord has spoken to me, and this is what he said: 'At midnight I will go out into the midst of Egypt. And all the first born in the land shall die, from the oldest child of Pharaoh who sits upon the throne to the oldest child of the maidservant working at the mill, and every first born of the cattle. And there shall be a great cry throughout the land of Egypt because of this, such an outcry as there never was before nor ever will be afterward. But against the children of Israel, not even a dog will so much as bark.' That is what the Lord has told me, and that is what I have said to Pharaoh. And when this thing happens, as it must because Pharaoh's heart is hard against us, then the people of Egypt will come to us and beg us to go quickly from their land. And we will go."

And that was to be God's last and most terrible sign to the cruel king of Egypt.

"What you must do," Moses continued, "is take a lamb, a young male lamb that is strong and perfect, one for every household of the Hebrews. The size of it will depend upon the household, for in the meal that you make of this lamb there must be nothing left over. Therefore, if the family is small, let it share its lamb with a neighboring family that is also small. The head of your households must kill the lamb himself and collect its blood in a basin, and then take a bunch of the herbs called hyssop and dip it into the blood. With the hyssop each man is to smear the blood over the lintel and side posts of the door so that every house in which a Hebrew family lives is marked with the blood of the lamb. After marking the doors you shall roast the lamb and eat it with unleavened bread and bitter herbs; but even while you eat you must be dressed and ready for travel, for it is likely that we will have to leave in haste.

"Also," Moses said, "when you have finished sprinkling the blood you are to remain inside your houses until early morning, for during the night the Lord will pass this way to strike his punishment at the

Egyptians. When he sees the blood on the lintels and the doorposts of your houses, the Lord will pass over your doors and not permit death to enter in to harm you. And you shall observe this same day as a memorial every year from this day on, and keep it as a feast to the Lord forever in memory of this night of the passover."

The people of Israel bowed their heads and worshiped, for now they fully believed that Moses and the Lord their God would deliver them not only from the dreadful sorrow that was to fall upon the Egyptians but also from their slavery in the land of Egypt. When they had prayed they hurried home and made the preparations commanded of them by the Lord through his spokesmen, Moses and Aaron; and they roasted lamb, prepared their dough, and painted blood around the doorways of their houses.

That night at midnight the Lord passed through the land of Egypt, and death struck at the homes of the Egyptians. In each household the oldest child died suddenly: from Pharaoh's own firstborn to the firstborn of the lowliest captive in the dungeon and the firstborn of the cattle in the fields, all died. There was not a house of the Egyptians that was spared this tragedy. But wherever the blood of the lamb marked the doorway of an Israelite household, the Lord passed over the house and the people within it were spared.

There was a great cry of anguish throughout Egypt on that night. Pharaoh arose from his bed in the dark hours and saw his terrible loss; his servants and his subjects rose and found their eldest dead; and in every house of the Egyptians there was dreadful sorrow.

Pharaoh called for Moses and Aaron. "Leave!" he cried. "Go! Get away from among my people, you and all the children of Israel! Go, serve your Lord as you have said. Take your flocks, your families, your herds, take everything—be gone!"

His people were no less anxious to be rid of the Israelites, for they knew that they were plagued because of them. "We are dead, unless you go from us," they cried. "Go, and go quickly. Take what you want from us, only leave our land."

The Israelites were ready for travel. They had gathered their goods and flocks; they had eaten their passover meal; and they were dressed to leave even though the hour was late and the night still dark. But the dough they had prepared had not yet risen in its pans, so they bound up the pans of unleavened bread in their bundles of clothes and carried them away upon their shoulders. The Egyptians speeded them their way with gifts of fine clothes and jewels of gold and silver, giving them whatever they required of Egypt's riches. Thus the Israelites did not leave the land of their slavery with empty hands.

It was a great procession that departed the land of Egypt in the early dawn. Four hundred and thirty years before, at the time of Joseph, seventy Hebrews had settled in the land; now six hundred thousand of them— not even counting the many little ones—journeyed away from the Egyptians and took their first steps toward the promised land.

There was war among the people of the north so that it was not wise to travel there. Instead, God led the children of Israel through the way of the wilderness of the Red Sea, going before them by day in a pillar of cloud to show them the way and by night in a pillar of fire to give them light for their journeying.

They traveled on for several days, putting more and more distance between themselves and the cruel king of Egypt, until it was time for them to make camp and rest themselves before going further. Then they pitched their tents beside the Red Sea, which they would some-how have to cross, and gathered strength for further journeying.

But Pharaoh heard through his messengers that they had stopped to camp, and he thought to himself that they would surely be trapped there in the wilderness beside the sea. Now that there were no more plagues to trouble Egypt, Pharaoh and his court attendants were sorry that they had let the Israelites go. Once again their hearts were hardened. "Why did we do it?" they asked each other angrily. "Why should we have let them go from serving us? Now we no longer have the Israelites as slaves to make our bricks and carry them, to build our buildings and work long hours in the fields. How foolish of us, to have let them go!"

And Pharaoh, cruel and hard as ever, readied his chariot and took his forces with him. With six hundred other chariots and an army of men mounted on horseback, he drove his warriors and their captains in swift pursuit of his one-time slaves. It was not long before he came close to overtaking them in their encampment by the sea.

The Israelites saw the clouds of whirling sand churned up by the approaching chariots and horses, and they were terrified.

"Were there no graves in Egypt that you had to bring us out here into the wilderness to die?" they cried out to Moses. "Did we not beg you to let us alone so that we might serve the Egyptians as before? It would have been far better for us to go on being slaves than to die here in the desert!"

Their hearts were faint, but Moses still had faith. "Fear not," he said to them. "Stand still and see the salvation of the Lord, which he will show you today. After this day you will never see these Egyptians again, for the Lord will fight for you. Hold your peace, and see what happens."

They waited and they trembled as the thunder of the horses' hooves and chariot wheels grew close.

Now the pillar of cloud that had led them by day to the wilderness moved and went behind them so that it hung heavy in the air like some great screen of smoke between the Israelites and the forces of Egyptians. On the one side it plunged the army of Egypt into darkness, and on the other it gave light to the camp of Israel. All the night it stayed there so that no one from either camp could cross into the other.

And while the cloud protected the children of Israel, Moses lifted up his rod and stretched his hand out

across the waters of the Red Sea as the Lord had
bidden him. A wind sprang up from the east and grew
strong and wild throughout the night, until its force
became so great that the waters of the sea were parted
and there was a path of land between them.

"Now cross the sea!" commanded Moses.

The children of Israel saw the path that had opened
before them and quickly gathered their possessions.
They hurried and stumbled along the path left by the
windblown waters, and on each side of them there was a
wall of sea held back only by the power of the God-
sent wind.

The cloud screen lifted in the early hours before
dawn, and Pharaoh in his camp saw the last of the
great band of Israelites reaching the far side of the sea.
"After them!" he shouted. He plunged after them with
his galloping horses and his speeding chariots until he
and his huge army were well along the path leading
through the sea. The Lord looked down on them then
as the chariot wheels dug deep into the wet sand and
lumbered heavily and slowly between the walls of
water.

"Stretch out your hand," said the Lord to Moses.

Moses held his rod out over the waters of the sea.
Slowly, as early dawn became full morning light, the
strong wind softened to a breeze. Water lapped at the
horses' legs and chariot wheels. The horses fell,
throwing their Egyptian riders, and chariots overturned
and spilled out the charioteers. While they struggled to
right themselves and turn back across the flooding
path, the walls of water broke against them. Men,
horses, chariots, and the king himself were plunged
deep into the midst of the returning sea. When the
waters quieted down into their accustomed tide there
was not a live man to be seen among the armies of
Egypt.

The Israelites stood on the far side of the Red Sea
and watched the closing waters, and they saw the Egyptians dead upon the seashore. They were saved! Moses
had said they would be saved; the Lord had given his

children their salvation; the Lord had delivered them that day from the hand of the Egyptians!

All fear went from their hearts, and the children of Israel saw the great work of their Lord and they believed in him. Their groans turned into great shouts of gratitude and triumph, and on the safe shore of the Red Sea they joined with Moses in a song of thanksgiving to their God:

> "I will sing unto the Lord, for he has triumphed gloriously,
> The horse and his rider has he thrown into the sea.
> The Lord is my strength and song,
> And he is my salvation:
> He is my God, and I will prepare for him a temple;
> He is my father's God, and I will exalt him!"

And as they sang their song of love and praise, Miriam, the sister of Moses who had watched him from the bulrushes, took a timbrel in her hand and led the women in a rapturous dance of relief and joy. With their own tambourines they danced and followed her, answering the song of Moses with his same words in their own joyous voices:

> "Sing unto the Lord, for he has triumphed gloriously,
> The horse and his rider has he thrown into the sea. . . ."

Thus did Moses bring his people safely across the Red Sea away from Egypt into another land.

Into the Wilderness

++++++++++++++++++++++++

Many generations of slavery in the cities of Egypt had changed the children of Israel from a self-reliant tribe of hardy shepherd-farmers into a timid, downtrodden people accustomed to being told exactly what to do and how to do it. And although they had been able to keep their own flocks and herds in the well-watered land of Goshen, they had long since forgotten what it was like to take care of their flocks or even themselves under the hard conditions of life in the desert. They had hated the cities of Egypt but they were used to them. The world outside was very different.

They journeyed to the south, following Moses into the Wilderness of Shur. It was hot and very dry, and their progress was slow because of their great numbers and the plodding pace of their cattle and sheep. For three long, tiring days they were without water in the wilderness, and their relief was great when they came to a place called Marah. Here at last was water. This, they thought, would save their very lives, for they could go on no longer without drinking.

But when they tasted it they found the water bitter and not fit to drink. Moses was to blame, they told each other; in Egypt they had never had this kind of hardship. They turned on him at once. "What are we supposed to drink?" they demanded of their leader. Only three days in the wilderness after many years of slavery, and already they were losing heart!

"What shall I do, Lord?" Moses cried. The Lord showed him a tree whose wood was sweet, and told him what to do. Moses cast the young tree into the bitter waters of Marah, and the waters became sweet. The people drank deeply and gave water to their herds.

"If you will believe in me," said the Lord, "and do what is right in my sight, I will always be with you. Listen to my voice and obey the things I ask of you, and I will bring upon you none of the diseases which I brought upon the Egyptians. For I am the Lord who helps and heals you."

When the children of Israel were refreshed they traveled on again, now a little more confident that they would find green oases in the desert where they might rest and draw fresh water. The cloud of the Lord moved on ahead and led them to a lovely place called Elim where there was a large, cool grove of palm trees and twelve wells of fresh, sweet water. Here beside the waters they pitched their camp and stayed for several days. It was so pleasant a place that they would just as soon have stayed there longer.

But the cloud moved on again, and they moved with it.

On the fifteenth day of the second month after leaving Egypt, the children of Israel entered the Wilderness of Sin, a vast desert country which lay between Elim and the mount of Sinai where God had spoken to Moses through the burning bush.

The Israelites looked around them and did not like the land at all. The flat plain stretched out for what seemed endless miles, unbroken anywhere by the shapes of tall green palms. Wells there might be, somewhere in that expanse of wilderness, but clearly no food would be found to eat. The children of Israel looked at Moses doubtfully. He led them on.

They plodded on through the dust and heat, seeing no sign of life other than the low shrubs of the desert and once in a while a lizard basking in the sun, and as the days passed they found no food and the pangs of hunger gnawed inside them.

The whole congregation of the children of Israel began to murmur against Moses and Aaron in the wilderness until their murmurs became loud words of anger. "Far better for us to have died by the hand of the Lord in Egypt instead of in the desert! There at least we had pots full of meat and we could eat our fill of bread. But you made us leave and brought us into this wilderness, and now all of us will die of hunger."

God heard their outcry and spoke to Moses. "They will not die of hunger. You shall see that I will rain bread down from heaven for you, every day from this time forth until you end your journey. The people must go out and gather a certain amount, but only what they need, each morning after it has fallen; in this way shall I test them to see whether they obey my words or not. On the sixth day they are to collect twice as much as on the other days, for there must be no work on the seventh day. This evening I will send them meat, and from tomorrow morning forth I will send them their daily bread."

Moses and Aaron relayed these words to the complaining people. "Now you shall see the glory of the Lord," they said, not without some anger. "He has heard your murmurings, and he will send you meat and bread to eat. But remember this: When you complain, you are murmuring not against us—for what are we?— but against the Lord who sends you all his glories."

That evening a flight of quails flew into the camp. The people caught them easily, great quantities of them, and for the first time in many days they had plenty of meat to eat. And in the morning, when the dew had disappeared from the ground around the camp, a strange substance was left behind on the face of the wilderness. A closer look showed that it was a mass of small round things that looked like beads of frost. "What is it?" the children of Israel asked each other.

Moses answered them. "It is the bread sent by the Lord for you to eat," he said. "Go and gather it, each man for the members of his tent. Take no more than you will need for this day, according to the numbers you must feed."

The children of Israel took their food vessels from their tents and collected the Lord's bread eagerly. Some gathered too much, some too little; but when each man measured out how much he had collected, all found to their surprise that they each had exactly as much as they needed. They ate with pleasure. The new food was white like coriander seed, and the taste of it was like wafers made with honey. They called it Manna, meaning 'what is this?', for they did not know what they were eating except that it was good.

"Do not leave any until morning," Moses said. "Eat what you have, for what you keep will spoil. There will be more tomorrow, and every morning except on the seventh day."

But some of the people did not listen to Moses, and they kept some of the manna from one day to the next. It did them not the slightest good, for it turned bad overnight and smelled foul in the morning. And there was fresh manna outside on the ground for them to gather. After that they made sure to collect only what they needed every day, and they did not try to put a store aside. They filled their pots, and when the sun grew hot the remaining manna melted on the ground.

On the sixth day they gathered twice as much as usual for, as Moses said, "Tomorrow is the day of rest, the holy sabbath of the Lord. Therefore bake what you want to bake today and boil what you want to boil, and keep the rest until tomorrow."

They did so, nearly all of them, and in the morning the manna they had put aside was still fresh and good to eat. But some had disobeyed again, and had failed to gather enough for both the sixth and seventh days. When they went out on the sabbath day to gather manna, there was none to gather.

Thereafter they collected manna in the way the Lord had told them, for six days out of every week that they spent wandering through the wilderness.

The cloud moved on. The great caravan of Israelites, with all their goods and sheep and cattle, continued on their journey south. The pillar of cloud led them out of the Wilderness of Sin toward the distant mountain of the Lord.

Then the cloud stopped. The caravan halted with it, and the children of Israel pitched their camp at Rephidim to rest there and refresh themselves.

Again they found cause for complaint. The Lord had commanded them to stop, and yet there was no water for the people to drink. They were burned brown and dry by the blazing heat, parched for want of water, and filled with new despair. Even though God had led them across the Red Sea, made sweet water for them to drink at Marah, and provided them with their daily bread, they still did not have faith enough to know that God would help them now.

"Moses!" As before, they turned their anger against Moses, and this time they were so enraged that they seemed about to kill him. "Give us water!" they demanded hotly. "Why did you bring us out of Egypt— so that you could kill us and our children and our cattle with thirst? Is the Lord with us, or is he not?"

Moses cried out to the Lord. "What shall I do for these people?" he begged. "They are almost ready to stone me!"

The Lord answered, saying: "Take the elders of Israel and go on before your people with your rod in hand. I will show you a certain rock in Horeb, and you shall strike that rock with the rod. Out of it there will come water so that the people may drink."

Moses and the elders went ahead and came to the place of which the Lord had spoken. There was no stream in sight among the mountains, nor any place that looked as though it might yield a spring of water, but Moses did not waver in his faith. The Lord showed him the rock, and Moses struck it before the eyes of the astonished elders. They saw what happened: a stream of water gushed out from beneath the stone and ran in rivulets down the mountainside.

Then fear and anger were forgotten. The children of Israel ran to the water with their pitchers and drank gratefully, and when their thirst was satisfied they watered their flocks and filled their drinking vessels for their tents. For a little while they would again trust Moses and their Lord, until some new thing made them cry out their regrets at ever having left the land of Egypt.

And something happened very soon. In the land where they had pitched their camp there lived a fierce tribe of people called Amalekites after their leader Amalek, who was descended from Esau. Amalek saw the goods and cattle in the Israelite camp, and he launched a series of raids to secure them for himself. The Israelites were not good fighters and they were easily disheartened by Amalek's swift and daring attacks, but Moses could not permit those wild men of the desert to steal from his people and harass them on their journey. He looked over his ranks and called out a stalwart young man by the name of Joshua.

"Choose the best men you can find," he ordered, "and go out and fight with Amalek. We will attack tomorrow. You shall lead the army, and I will stand on top of the hill with the rod of God in my hand so that victory will be ours."

Joshua went among the men and quickly organized a force of the strongest and most courageous of the children of Israel. The next day he went out with his chosen warriors and clashed against the forces of Amalek. Moses, Aaron, and a trusted friend named Hur went up to the top of the hill to watch the course of battle and inspire their people. The Amalekites were powerful and cunning, practiced in fighting and plundering people less warlike than themselves, and Joshua's men were untrained in the arts of war. It was not an even battle; but Moses, on the hilltop, held the rod in his hand and put his faith in God. Whenever he held up his hands the forces of Joshua gained and drove the Amalekites back; and whenever he lowered his hands to rest them the forces of Amalek surged forward and drove back Joshua's men.

It was plain to Moses that he would have to keep his hands raised all the time or Amalek would win the victory. But his hands were heavy and his shoulders tired, so that he had to rest every once in a while and see the Amalekites cut down the children of Israel. Then Aaron and Hur found a large stone for him to sit on, and they placed themselves at either side. One of them raised his left hand and the other his right, and between the two of them they kept Moses' arms upright and stretched toward the heavens until the end of the day.

The Amalekites no longer advanced. Slowly, steadily, they started their retreat, and as the day grew late they fell back in confusion. As they weakened, the Israelites gained strength, and went after them with swords.

Moses' hands were steady until the sun went down. In the dim light of early evening the Amalekites broke ranks and fled, utterly defeated by Joshua's fighting forces and this man upon the mountain. When Moses saw that his people were victorious he lowered his tired arms and offered up a heartfelt prayer of thanksgiving to God.

Now they could travel on from Rephidim untroubled by marauding tribes, and soon they would reach the mountain of God where great things were to happen to them.

The Ten Commandments

✣✣✣✣✣✣✣✣✣✣✣✣✣✣✣✣✣✣✣

In the third month after the children of Israel had gone forth out of the land of Egypt, they came into the Wilderness of Sinai and pitched their camp near the holy mountain.

It was familiar territory to Moses, for while he had been living with Jethro in the land of Midian he had often come here to the far side of the desert to find green pastures for his flocks. He left his people in their camp at the foot of the mountain and climbed the slope where once he had seen a thorn bush blazing with unearthly fire.

"I will be with you," the Lord had told him then, "and I tell you now that when you have brought my people out of Egypt, you will worship me upon this mountain of Sinai."

And now, here he was, climbing the mountain of God; and God was speaking to him from the mountain:

"You have seen what I did to the Egyptians, and how I carried you on eagles' wings and brought you back to me. Now say this to the house of Jacob, to the children of Israel: 'If you obey the voice of the Lord and keep his covenant, then shall you be a special treasure to him above all other people. And you shall be to him a kingdom of priests, and a holy nation.' Say this to the children of Israel, and then return to me."

Moses called his people together and repeated the Lord's words. They answered as one man. "All that the Lord has asked us, we will do," they promised. "Surely we will obey and keep his covenant." And Moses went back to the Lord and told him what the people had said.

Then the Lord was glad, and said to Moses: "From the top of the mountain will I come to you in a thick cloud, so that the people may hear for themselves when I speak to you and will forever believe you. Now go to them; have them wash their clothes and purify themselves today and tomorrow, and be ready by the third day. For on that day I will come down in their sight upon Mount Sinai. Only be sure that none of them sets foot upon the mountain, for it is holy ground. When the voice of the trumpet sounds long and loud, they shall approach the mountain and I will come near."

Moses went back to the camp and prepared his people.

Dawn of the third day broke with thunder and lightning, and a thick cloud covered the peak of the mount. The blare of a trumpet resounded across the camp, and the people trembled with fear. And Moses brought them out of the camp to meet with God. They stood at the foot of the mountain watching it quake and shake in a terrifying manner. It seemed to be covered with smoke, for the Lord had descended upon it in a great flame and the smoke from the flame reached into the heavens like the fiery red smoke of a gigantic furnace.

Then the voice of the trumpet sounded again, and its blasts grew louder and louder. Moses called out to the Lord, and the Lord answered in a voice that could be heard by all the people. And they all heard the thunder rolling across the valley, and saw the shaking, smoking mountain. They stared at it in awe and fear and stumbled back away from it. "Speak to us!" they said to Moses. "Speak, and we will hear. But do not let God speak to us or we will surely die."

"Do not be afraid," Moses answered them, "for God has come to show his greatness to you so that you will believe in him and will not sin."

And the people stood as far back as they could from the frightening scene as the Lord came down upon the mountain in his cloud and called to Moses.

Moses went up to the top of the mountain into the thick cloud of darkness where the Lord was, and he listened to the words of God. "This shall you say to my people," said the Lord.

"I am the Lord your God, who brought you out of the land of Egypt, out of the house of bondage.

"You shall have no other gods before me.

"You shall make no graven images nor any likeness of anything that is in heaven above, or that is in the earth beneath, or that is in the water under the earth. You shall not bow down yourself to them or worship them, for I the Lord your God am a jealous God.

"You shall not take the name of the Lord your God in vain.

"Remember the sabbath day, to keep it holy. Six days shall you labor and do all your work. But on the seventh day is the sabbath of the Lord your God, and on it you shall not do any work, neither you nor those who are with you. For in six days the Lord made heaven and earth and sea, and all that is in them, and rested the seventh day. Therefore the Lord has blessed the sabbath day and made it holy. ·

"Honor your father and your mother, that your days may be long upon the land which the Lord your God has given you.

"You shall not kill.

"You shall not commit adultery.

"You shall not steal.

"You shall not bear false witness against your neighbor.

"You shall not covet your neighbor's house, nor your neighbor's wife, nor his servants, nor his cattle, nor anything that is his.

"All this," said the Lord, "shall you tell the children of Israel. Yet there is more to tell. Now these are the judgments you shall set before them." And God spoke further to Moses, giving him a code of justice by which his people might live and describing the rules and laws that would govern their conduct in the course of their daily lives and in the observance of religious ceremonies. "These things shall you tell them," said the Lord, "so that they will know what is right and what is wrong in everything they do. Say also that I will lead them into Canaan and make their enemies flee before them; not all at once, but little by little, until you inherit the land. Now return to the people and tell them what I have said. Tomorrow I will call you back to speak more upon the mountain."

Moses went back to his awe-struck followers. He told them everything the Lord had said, all his words and all his laws. "And these you must obey," he finished.

The people answered with one voice: "We will do everything the Lord has said!"

Early the next morning Moses arose and built an altar at the foot of the mountain of God, with the twelve pillars for the twelve tribes of Israel, and sent the young men of the camp to bring oxen to place as burnt offerings on the altar. Together, all the children of Israel worshiped the Lord, and Moses once again told them the words of God. When the service was over he feasted with his elders on the mountainside, until the Lord called to him and said: "Come up to me on top of the mountain, and I will give you tablets of stone upon which I will write my law and the commandments with my own hand, so that you may teach them to the people."

Moses rose from the feast, bidding Joshua to join him. "Wait here for us, until we return again," he told the elders. "Aaron and Hur are with you; if any man has any matters to decide, let him go to them."

And Moses went up into the mountain, taking Joshua with him almost to the summit, and then he climbed onto the cloud-capped peak alone.

To the children of Israel, watching from below, the glowing cloud looked like a blaze of glorious, heavenly fire; and they knew that their leader Moses was within it communing with the Lord.

This time the Lord spoke to him about the building of a tabernacle, a tent sanctuary which the Israelites could take with them on their journey. In it, the Lord would meet with Moses, and the children of Israel would hold services in worship to their God. It was to have several rooms, and the innermost chamber would be the most sacred of all. For this room the people must make an ark, or chest, of acacia wood and gold, and the two stone tablets bearing God's commandments were to be placed in this ark and revered forever. To build and furnish this tabernacle the people must bring offerings, with willing hearts; and many such offerings would be required.

"Gold, silver, and brass shall they bring," said the Lord, "and fine linens in blue, purple, and scarlet; goat's hair, and ram skins dyed red, and acacia wood; oil for the light, spices and incense; onyx stones and other jewels. And the goat's hair shall be used as curtains in the tabernacle; and the acacia wood will support the covering of the tent which must be made of the dyed ram skins. . . ."

Moses listened intently to the detailed instructions given to him by the Lord. The hours and days passed into weeks while he remained within the cloud, but he was not aware of time.

"From the fine linens and jewels," said the Lord, "you shall make ornaments for the tabernacle and holy garments for the priests; and your brother Aaron the Levite and his sons shall be the first of the priests."

There was more, much more, and even while Aaron was being mentioned as a holy priest by the speakers in the cloud, he was performing priestly duties down below. But, although he was a good man, there was wickedness in what he did now.

For forty days and forty nights Moses spoke with God on the cloud-topped mountain. And the people began to be afraid that he would never come back. "We are lost!" they cried to Aaron. "What has happened to Moses, the man who brought us out of the land of Egypt? Make us gods to go before us, so that we shall not be deserted."

Aaron was deeply distressed, but he did not have the courage to refuse in the face of their rising restlessness. "Bring me all your golden ornaments and earrings," he said sadly.

They brought him what they had, all the earrings that they wore, and he took them for his work. He melted them down and fashioned the molten gold into the figure of a calf. It was a shape the people knew and secretly admired, for the Egyptians and other pagan peoples often worshiped such things as bulls and calves.

"This is our god!" the Israelites shouted joyfully. "These are the gods, O Israel, that brought you out of the land of Egypt!"

Aaron saw their great delight and, having already broken the commandment against making graven images, committed an even greater blasphemy. He built an altar before the golden idol so that a ceremony of worship might be held, and he made a proclamation.

"Tomorrow is the feast of the Lord!" he shouted, though the Lord's feast it certainly was not. "Bring offerings, and food, and let us feast!"

Early next morning the children of Israel, happy and excited as they had not been for many days of fear, brought offerings to the altar. They worshiped the false idol, ate and drank until they could fill themselves no more, and then rose up to play. Soon they were in a frenzy of singing and abandoned dancing.

The Lord God on the mountaintop knew at once what they were doing.

"Go!" he said to Moses. "Get down to your people that you led from Egypt, for they have already disobeyed me and made a molten calf to worship. 'These be your gods, O Israel,' they are saying to each other! They are a stiff-necked, stubborn people. Leave me now, for my anger has grown hot against them for their wickedness. Of you, I shall make a great nation; but those people, I shall destroy."

"Lord, do not destroy them," Moses pleaded. "Why be angry against the people you brought out of Egypt with your own mighty hand? Then will the Egyptians say, 'It was for an evil trick that their Lord led them out, so that he might kill them in the mountains and destroy them from the face of the earth.' I pray you, Lord, have mercy on your people and remember your vow to Abraham, to Isaac, and to Israel, that their race would be great upon this earth and inherit the land."

The Lord heard him, and repented of his wrath. Whatever he would do, he would not destroy them.

Moses hurried down the mountainside, taking with him the two precious tablets of stone on which the Lord had inscribed his commandments with his own hand. Joshua met Moses on the way, for he was waiting for him still.

"There is a noise of war in the camp!" Joshua said urgently.

"No, that is not the noise of war," Moses answered grimly. "That is the sound of revelry and singing."

When he came to the camp the sight that met his eyes was even worse than he had imagined. He saw the calf with Aaron standing by it; he saw the meat, the drink, the worshipers, and the wild, abandoned dancing, and he was hot with anger. There was scarcely a commandment that had not already been broken. Then they might as well be truly broken! In the white heat of his rage Moses raised the sacred tablets of stone high above his head and flung them down with all his strength against a rock at the foot of the mountain. They shattered noisily into tiny pieces; and with the shattering sound the children of Israel suddenly grew silent. Aaron turned pale and trembled. The whole assembly looked at Moses, and he stared back at them.

After many months of guidance through the desert, after coming to a holy place and hearing God, after receiving his commandments and his laws of conduct and of justice, they had brought themselves to this.

The precious tablets lay like dust upon the ground.

The Cloud
Moves on from Sinai

✛✛✛✛✛✛✛✛✛✛✛✛✛✛✛✛✛✛✛✛✛✛✛

The godless image of a calf stood upon its pedestal amongst the people, unseeing and unsightly. But many of the Israelites were still defiant of Moses and would rather keep their useless idol than follow their stern leader.

Moses turned with fury upon the golden calf that Aaron had made and flung it into the fire. When it had melted into a shapeless mass and cooled into an ugly lump, he ground it into powder and put the fine gold dust into the drinking water. It tasted bitter and poisonous, but Moses forced each man and woman to drink it.

Then he sought out Aaron, who stood aside, shame-faced and silent.

"What did the people do to you, that you have brought so great a sin upon them?" he demanded.

"Do not be angry with me," Aaron begged him

humbly. "You know the people, and the wickedness of their hearts. For they said to me, 'Make us gods to go before us, for we do not know what has become of Moses who led us out of Egypt.' I told them, then, to bring me gold. So they gave it to me, then I cast it into the fire, and there came out this calf."

Moses' anger still burned hotly. These rebellious people must be made to realize that they could not sin without being swiftly punished! And although he did not want them to be destroyed by the wrath of God, examples must be made among them or mutiny would wreck the expedition. He therefore stood at the gate of the camp and called out: "Who is on the Lord's side? Let him come to me!"

The idol worshipers hung back, muttering among themselves against God and their leader. But all of the tribe of Levi, those destined to be priests, gathered by his side.

Moses gave his orders. And there fell by the sword that day many men who were not on the side of the Lord.

On the following day Moses said to his people: "You have sinned a great sin, and the anger of God is mighty. But I will go up to the Lord now, and perhaps I may obtain forgiveness for your sin."

With heavy heart he climbed the mountain once again and returned to the Lord to beg forgiveness for his people.

"O Lord, these people have sinned terribly," he said. "They made for themselves gods out of gold. Yet I beg your mercy. And if you cannot forgive their sin, let me die, I pray you, to atone for them."

"No, you shall not die for them," said the Lord. "Whoever has sinned against me shall suffer for his own sins. Now return to your people, and tell them that I will plague them for their wickedness. And say also that you shall still lead them into the land flowing with milk and honey; but my angel shall go before them, and not I. I will not be with them, for they are such a stubborn and sinful people that I might destroy them on the way."

And the Lord did plague the people, because they had made the calf; but they were more troubled by the Lord's words than the plague. When they heard that God would no longer lead them himself they mourned with all their hearts and cried with sorrow.

Their penitence was so sincere and their sorrow so deep that the Lord felt pity for them. Moses saw them praying, and he saw the honesty with which they worshiped, and once again he spoke for them with his Lord.

Then God relented. "I will be with you on your way," he said, "so that it shall be known that you and your people have found grace in my sight. For this nation is my chosen people. Now cut two more tablets of stone, like the first, and I will write upon those tablets the words that were on the first tablets that you broke. Be ready with them in the morning, and come to me alone on the top of the mountain."

Moses cut the two new tablets of stone, and in the morning he went up the mountain with them as the Lord had commanded him.

The Lord descended in the cloud and stood with Moses as before. Again, it was many days before the leader of the Israelites left the presence of his God, but this time there was no murmur of rebellion from his people.

When Moses came down from Mount Sinai he carried with him a new set of written laws, for upon the second pair of stone tablets were written the words of the Lord's covenant, the ten commandments of the Lord. He did not know that his very being shone from talking to God; and when Aaron and all the children of Israel saw Moses and the strange light that glowed from his face they were afraid to come near him.

Moses called to them, for he had much to say to Aaron and all the rulers of the congregation; and he put a veil over his face to shield them from the light that frightened them so much. Afterward he gathered to

him all the children of Israel and told them what God
had taught him on the mountain: all about the laws they
were to follow, about their duties, their offerings, and
the building of the ark and tabernacle.

Then every man and woman with a willing heart
went to their tents and came back with offerings of
materials for the tabernacle. Lovingly, and with the
greatest skill, they built the holy tabernacle and all the
furnishings within. And when it was complete they
placed in it the ark containing the stone tablets on
which the Lord had written his commandments.

There in the wilderness they celebrated the first an-
niversary of the passover, and Aaron and his sons
began their priestly duties. On the day that the sanctuary of the Lord was made ready for worship—one
year after the children of Israel had made their camp at
the foot of Mount Sinai—the cloud of the Lord settled
upon the tabernacle. That meant that Moses would no
longer have to go up into the mountain to commune
with God; and also that they had an unmistakable sign
to follow as a guide. The cloud was with them always, a
smoky covering by day and a pillar of fire by night.

When the cloud lifted from the tabernacle and
moved on ahead, the children of Israel continued on
their journey. But when the cloud stopped and covered
the tabernacle, they pitched their tents and rested. And
so it was, throughout the remainder of their journey,
that at the commandment of the Lord they rested in
their tents, and at the commandment of the Lord they
journeyed on. As the cloud traveled, so did they.

On the twentieth day of the second month of the
second year of their wanderings, the children of Israel
followed the cloud of the tabernacle out of the Wilderness of Sinai toward the Wilderness of Paran. After
three days' journey the cloud searched out a resting
place for them, and there they stopped.

During all this time the Lord had sent them manna
for their daily bread. Every day the people gathered it:
they ground it to fine flour in their mills, and they beat
it in their mortars; they baked it in pans and made

bread or cakes of it; they boiled it, and they sliced it
and roasted it, and they ate it in as many ways as they
could think of, and it tasted like fresh oil and honey.
And always when the dew fell upon their camp toward
morning, the manna fell upon it.

Manna! Every meal was manna. The children of
Israel began to long for other food; they hungered for
the taste of meat and the fresh fruits they had known
before. Again they complained and wept as though
they were the most miserable and neglected of all people. "Who shall give us meat to eat?" they cried.
"Where is the other food we used to eat? We remember
the fish, which we did eat in Egypt freely; the cucum-
bers, and the melons, and the leeks, and the onions,
and the garlic. But now there is nothing at all before
our eyes except this never-ending manna!'

From every tent door came the sound of their weeping and their moaning. The Lord heard them, and was
angered by their complaints; Moses also was displeased. He went to the Lord with shame and sadness
in his heart.

"Why do you punish me, O Lord?" he begged. "Why
have I not found favor in your sight, that you should
lay the burden of these people upon me? They are not
my children, that I should carry them like a father
carrying babies to the land you promised them! Where
in this wilderness shall I find meat to give to all of
them? For they groan to me, and weep, crying for meat
to eat. I cannot bear the burden of these people all
alone; it is too heavy for me."

The Lord took pity on him, for he could see that
Moses' burden was heavy indeed and that he needed
help. "Gather seventy men of the elders of Israel, those
you know to be the leaders among them, and bring
them into the tabernacle," he commanded. "I will come
down and talk with you there, and my spirit shall be
upon the elders so that they shall share the burden of
the people with you and you will no longer have to
bear it alone. As for the people who are crying out for
food, call them together and say this: 'You shall eat

meat—not only for one day, nor two days, nor five days, nor ten days, nor even twenty days, but for a whole month, until it comes out of your nostrils and is loathsome to you!' So shall it be because they have despised the Lord with their weeping and complaints."

"But there are six hundred thousand people with me!" Moses objected. "And you say that you will give them meat to eat for a whole month! Shall the flocks and herds be killed for them? Or shall the fish of the sea be gathered together so that they might eat? How else will they have enough?"

"Is my power less than before?" said the Lord. "You shall see now whether my words come true or not."

Moses went out and told the people what the Lord had said, and chose seventy elders to take with him to the tabernacle. There, as the Lord had promised, a new spirit came upon them and brought with it new strength and wisdom so that they might help Moses in his difficult task of leading six hundred thousand wayward people.

Then a wind from the sea blew masses of quail toward the camp of the Israelites. Great flocks of them flew near the ground on either side of the camp. At once the people stopped everything else they were doing and rushed out to gather the meat they had longed for. They gathered the birds all that day, all that night, and all the following day, and by the time they had finished the man who had gathered least had about a hundred bushels. With great joy the children of Israel brought the food back to the camp and spread it about for everyone to eat. It was indeed enough food to last them all for at least a month.

But even while they were eating, the Lord, who was angered by their greed and their everlasting complaints, sent a plague upon them. Many became sick, and many died, and even before the meat was finished there were burials in that land. It was another lesson to those who still lived when the plague was over, if they could only learn.

And it was time they learned, because now that they were in the Wilderness of Paran they stood very close to the borders of the promised land. Only if they were worthy could they cross into the land of Canaan.

Land of
Milk and Honey

✠✠✠✠✠✠✠✠✠✠✠✠✠✠✠✠✠✠✠✠✠✠✠✠✠

The cloud over the tabernacle rose up and drifted through the wilderness to a place very close to the southern border of Canaan. Here at Kadesh, as the site was called, the children of Israel stopped to water their cattle and make plans for their final march. While they pitched their tents and settled into camp, Moses sought counsel from the Lord.

"Send out men to search the land of Canaan, which I am giving to the children of Israel," said the Lord. "Choose one man from every tribe, each one a ruler among his people."

So Moses by the commandment of the Lord chose twelve men, all of them headmen of their various tribes, and instructed them to spy out the land of Canaan to see what lay ahead. Joshua, of the tribe of Ephraim and already Moses' chief military leader, was to lead the scouting expedition; and Caleb, a valiant

185

young captain of the tribe of Judah, would act as his second-in-command.

"Go up into the mountains of the south," said Moses, "and see what the land is like. Find out what kind of people live there; whether they are weak or strong, or few or many. Make note of the cities that they live in, whether they are tents or strongholds. See if the land itself is good or bad, rich or poor; and whether it has wood or not. Go now, and be of good courage. Bring back some of the fruit of the land so that we all may see."

This was the time for the first ripe grapes, and therefore there should be no difficulty in bringing back some sample of the riches of Canaan. So the twelve spies went on their way. From the heights of Hebron, once so well-known to Abraham, they viewed the valleys below. There, they saw, were small, pleasant villages and great walled cities, and fields that were carpets of fresh young corn.

The spies went down from the mountains and went carefully through the land. The soil was rich and prosperous, and trees grew up the slopes toward the hilltops. Sheep grazed in green, well-watered pastures; people lived in well-fortified towns. And those people looked very strong and vigorous, especially those of the tribe of Anak.

Joshua led his scouts through the land for forty days, until they had seen hills, plains, valleys, and the coast, and they knew they had indeed come upon a fertile land. They also knew that it was already occupied by various tribes, each of which no doubt intended to keep occupying it.

They went on, and they came to a gently flowing brook with lush vineyards on either side. From a great vine they cut a branch bearing one huge cluster of grapes, and so marvelous was this cluster that two men had to carry it between them hung upon a staff. The place they called Eshcol, meaning "cluster," because of the grapes they had found. They found ripe pomegranates, too, and figs; and saw all manner of flocks and herds and fruits of the field. Many of the fruits and crops were the same as they had known in Egypt, and there were even some that they had never seen before.

After the forty days they returned to their camp at Kadesh in the Wilderness of Paran, taking with them the huge cluster of grapes, the pomegranates, the figs, and many a tale of the wonders they had seen. They reported at once to Moses and to Aaron, and all the children of Israel crowded around to listen.

"We went into the land to which you sent us," Joshua began. "It surely is flowing with milk and honey, and this is the fruit of it." He showed the people what his spies had brought back, and they delighted in the sight.

"But the people are strong who live in that land," said another of the spies, "and the cities are walled and very great. And moreover, we saw the children of Anak there. The Amalekites live in the south, and the Hittites and other strong tribes live in the mountains, and the Canaanites live by the sea. Altogether there are many powerful and warlike people in that land." Nine other spies nodded agreement as he spoke, and added their own words of alarm about the dangers of the land.

Their listeners murmured unhappily. Caleb silenced them and turned to Moses. "It is a good land, well worth having. Let us go up at once and take possession," he said boldly. "We are well able to overcome it."

But all the other spies who had been with him, except Joshua, shook their heads in gloom and said: "No, we cannot go against those people. They are much stronger than we. We shall have no chance at all."

And the spies gave an evil report to the children of Israel about the lovely land which they had searched. The more they talked, the less they said about its riches and the more they said about its dangers. What they had seen, they exaggerated; and what they had not seen, they imagined. "There are giants in that land!" they said. "All the people that we saw in it are men of a great stature, but especially the sons of Anak who are descended from the giants. Beside them, we were no more than grasshoppers; and to them, we were no more than grasshoppers that they could easily crush beneath their feet."

The children of Israel were terrified, and deeply disappointed. All this way through the wilderness, only to come to a land they dare not enter! There was weeping in the camp that night; and a murmuring against Moses and Aaron.

"Would God that we had died in the land of Egypt!" they cried out to their leaders. "Or that we had died in the wilderness! Why has the Lord brought us to this land? Are we to fall by the sword of these giants in Canaan, and have our wives and children taken as prisoners? Would it not be better for us to return to Egypt?"

The suggestion caught fire and ran through the camp. They said to one another, "Let us choose a captain for ourselves, and let us return to Egypt. Moses shall not lead us any longer, for see where he has brought us."

The sounds of their rebellion came to their leader's ears. Both Moses and Aaron fell on their faces in front of all the people, praying God that the children of Israel should overcome their cowardice. And to the people themselves Moses cried out: "Why can you not obey and trust the God who has helped you so many times before when you have thought that all was lost?"

Joshua and Caleb tore their clothes in great dismay. Out of all the twelve spies, they were the only two who tried to reason with the people; for they were brave men, and they had faith in God. "It is a good land, and a fertile one!" they said. "It truly flows with milk and honey. Why do you have doubts, when you know that if the Lord is pleased with us he will lead us there and give it to us? It is promised to us! Only you must not rebel against the Lord, nor be afraid of the people of the land. We can crush them easily, for they have no defense when the Lord is with us. Fear them not!"

But the Israelites were too afraid to listen to words of reason, and their fear showed itself in anger against

Caleb and Joshua. They reached for stones to fling at them, and would have stoned not only the two brave spies but Moses and Aaron as well if a strange and wonderful distraction had not suddenly occurred.

The glory of the Lord appeared in the form of a brightly glowing light from the tabernacle, in front of all the children of Israel. And the voice of the Lord came from the brightness.

"Moses! How long will these people provoke and disobey me? How long will it be before they believe in me, after all the signs that I have shown them? I will send a plague to wipe them out; I will disinherit them. Of you, and you alone, shall I make a great and mighty nation."

But Moses pleaded for them, as he had done countless times before. "Do not destroy them, Lord, I beg you; not after having brought them all this way and becoming famed as the Lord who leads by cloud and fire and talks to his people face to face. If you should kill them here, then the nations which have heard of your fame will say that you were not able to bring your people into the land you promised them, and that you therefore destroyed them in the wilderness. You are long-suffering, O Lord, and of great mercy. Pardon, I pray you, the wickedness of the people in accordance with the greatness of your mercy, as you have forgiven them since leaving Egypt even until now."

The Lord listened, and relented; but not altogether. "I will pardon them, as you ask," he said. "They shall not be destroyed, nor will I disinherit them. But because all these men, who have seen my glory and my miracles which I did in Egypt and in the wilderness, have not listened to my voice and have tempted me now ten times, they shall none of them see the land which I promised to their fathers. Tell them this: 'Not one of you who is twenty years or older, and has murmured against me, shall ever go into that land. Only Joshua and Caleb, who have been faithful to me, shall be allowed to live in Canaan. And the little ones, whom you feared would be made prisoners, shall grow up to inherit the land which you have despised. But as for the rest of you, you shall stay in the wilderness and wander there until you die. And your children shall wander in the wilderness for forty years, one year for each of the days in which you searched the land, until they are grown and you are gone.'"

The children of Israel were overcome with grief. The thought of wandering in the desert for a lifetime was more than they could bear, and they quickly changed their minds about the dangers of entering into Canaan. "Caleb and Joshua have said that we are well able to take that land," they told each other. "Let us go and do so. It was wrong of us not to trust the Lord."

It did not even occur to them that they had lost their chance, and that what they were planning now was fresh disobedience. Even when all the spies except Caleb and Joshua died by the plague as punishment for bringing back an evil report and causing the murmurings among the congregation, they would not realize that there was no escape from the wrath of God except through absolute obedience.

They rose up early in the morning and gathered on the mountain that overlooked their camp. "See, we are here," they said to Moses. "We will go now to the place which the Lord has promised us, for in our fear we sinned. Now we are not afraid."

"But you are sinning again!" said Moses. "Why do you go now against the commandment of the Lord? Do not go, for you will surely fall by the sword. The Lord will not be with you because you turned away from him, and the Amalekites and the Canaanites will strike you down."

But they would not listen to him, and they rushed upon a hilltop that was occupied by the people of Canaan. Without Moses, without the ark and tabernacle, without the cloud that guided them and without the Lord, they had no chance. The Amalekites and Canaanites fell upon them from the hill. The battle was quick and bloody. Many of the Israelites were killed outright, and all the rest were driven away with their enemy at their heels.

Defeated and despairing, they gathered in their camp and made ready to go once more into the wilderness.

"Now turn you," said the Lord. "Leave this land and get you into the wilderness near the Red Sea."

They turned sorrowfully away from the borders of Canaan and went back to their wanderings. The promised land was still their goal, but their route would be long and devious and the journey was to last them many years because they had not trusted God.

The miles and the years dragged slowly by. They moved on, made camp, moved on again. And the Israelites found many causes for complaint. Again they were thirsty, again they were hungry, again they rebelled, and again they fought with hostile tribes. And each time they were in need, the patient Moses called on God to help them. His own faith never wavered.

At long last, after what seemed like endless hardships and setbacks, the children of Israel once again came within sight of the land of Canaan. This time they approached it from the country of Moab, near the river Jordan and the valley of Jericho. The forty years were drawing to a close, and all the people who had murmured against God had died and had been buried in the wilderness. The new generation of Israelites were seasoned shepherd-farmers of the desert, skillful in battle against enemy tribes, hardened by their wanderings, and strong in their faith. Aaron had died, and Miriam was gone; of those who had made their camp at Kadesh and hoped to enter Canaan through the southern hills, only Moses, Caleb, and Joshua still lived.

And Moses was a very old man, and his days were coming to an end. He gathered the children of Israel together, the new generation, and once again taught them all the judgments and commandments of God. To each of the tribes he gave a special blessing, and to all he renewed God's promise that Canaan would be theirs. "You will cross the Jordan into Jericho," he said, "and although the Lord has told me that I will not be with you, Joshua shall lead you and you will put your trust in God. For the Lord our God is one Lord, and you shall love the Lord your God with all your heart and with all your soul and with all your might."

Then he spoke these words to all the people of Israel:

"I am a hundred and twenty years old this day. I can no longer lead you. But God will go with you and you shall possess the promised land. And Joshua shall be your leader; he will take you over Jordan." To Joshua he said, in the sight of all Israel: "Be strong and of good courage. For the Lord has given you the task of taking these people into the land which he promised their fathers, and you shall cause them to inherit it."

Then the Lord spoke to Moses, saying: "Go up to the top of Mount Nebo, which is in the land of Moab near the Canaanite city of Jericho. And behold the land of Canaan which I give to the children of Israel for a possession. You shall see the land before you, though you shall not enter it."

So Moses went up from the plains of Moab onto the mountain of Nebo, to the peak of Pisgah near the city of Jericho. And the Lord showed him all the promised land that he was giving to each of the tribes of Israel. Moses looked down and across the valleys; he gazed at the plain of Jericho, and raised his eyes to scan the farthest sea. He looked to the south and saw its beauty, and he looked at Zoar, city of the palm trees; and he saw all the green hills and fertile valleys that his people would soon be seeing for themselves.

"This is the land that I promised to the children of Abraham, of Isaac, and of Jacob," said the Lord. "I have caused you to see it with your own eyes, though you shall not go there. For the end of your days has come."

So Moses, the servant of the Lord, took one last, long look at the land of milk and honey, and died there in the land of Moab. He was buried in the valley; and to this day no man knows where his grave may be.

And the children of Israel wept for Moses in the plains of Moab for thirty days.

When the days of mourning were over they turned to Joshua for leadership, for the spirit of God was upon him. But never again in all Israel was there a prophet like Moses, whom the Lord knew face to face.

Joshua Fights the Battle of Jericho

✶✶✶✶✶✶✶✶✶✶✶✶✶✶✶✶✶✶✶✶✶✶✶✶

On one side of the river Jordan was the camp of the Israelites; on the other, the Canaanite city of Jericho. If the children of Israel were to enter Canaan by this route then they would have to capture that great walled city first. They knew this, and they felt confident of success. The people of Jericho, for their part, were growing increasingly alarmed by the presence of the armed camp across the river. They had heard about the wonders of the God of Israel and the many victories the Israelites had won against the wilderness tribes, and even behind the great walls of their fortified city they trembled with fear.

Now after the death of Moses the Lord said to Joshua: "Arise, go over the river Jordan with the children of Israel. All the land that your feet shall tread upon, from the wilderness to the great river Euphrates and to the edges of the great sea toward the west, shall

194

be yours to divide among your people for their inheritance. As I was with Moses, so will I be with you. I will not fail you or forsake you. Therefore be strong and of good courage, and obey me always. Then shall you succeed in whatever you do, for the Lord your God will be with you wherever you go."

Joshua called his officers to him and gave them the first command of his campaign against the Canaanites. "Go through the camp and tell the people to prepare food and gather their possessions, for within three days we will cross the Jordan and possess the land." And while the people were making their preparations, Joshua sent two men across the river to spy out the territory beyond. "Go view the land and the city of Jericho," he told them, "so that we may know the weaknesses of the place and what manner of men we shall have to fight."

The two spies stole quietly across the river and scouted the land around the city. Then, seeing that the gates of the city were still open for the daylight hours, they slipped stealthily into Jericho to mingle with the people and study the fortifications. When evening came they went into the house of a woman named Rahab to find lodgings for the night. So far as they knew, Rahab did not recognize them for what they were, nor had their movements been noticed by anyone else; but even while they talked to Rahab someone was hurrying to the king of Jericho to tell him that two scouts from the camp were in the city to spy out the land for the forces of Israel.

The king at once sent soldiers to Rahab's house to find the strangers.

"Bring out the men who came here tonight!" the soldiers told her roughly. "They are spies come here to search out our land so that they might conquer us."

But Rahab, from her house on the city wall, had seen the vast camp of the Israelites across the river and come to certain conclusions of her own. And she had also seen the king's men coming to her house.

"Why, there were two men here earlier," she said thoughtfully, "but I did not know where they had come from. They left here not long ago, at about the time of the shutting of the gate when it was getting dark. Where they went I do not know, but if you go after them quickly you will surely overtake them."

They took a swift look over her house in case she had been lying to them, for she was not known to be a very honest woman but they did not find the spies. Rahab had taken them up to the flat roof of her house and hidden them beneath the stalks of flax that she had been drying in the open air, and the searchers did not think to look there for the spying Israelites.

Rahab watched the searchers running out through the city gates and saw the gates being firmly shut behind them. Then she went up to the roof. "They have gone," she said, and removed the flax that covered the spies. "The gates are locked, but I will see that you leave the city safely."

The two men looked at her and wondered why she had not betrayed them.

As if in answer to the question that they did not ask, she said: "I know that the Lord has given you this land. All the people here have heard it, and they faint with terror because of you. For we know how the Lord dried up the water of the Red Sea for you, and how you have destroyed your enemies as you came this way. As soon as we had heard these things our hearts did melt, and there is not a man among us who has any courage left. We can see that the Lord your God is God in heaven above and here on the earth beneath; I know that we cannot win against you."

Joshua's spies were greatly encouraged by these words, for surely people of such faint heart would easily be defeated. Yet, with the city gates closed upon them and the people of Jericho alerted to their coming, they could see no way of getting back to camp with their heartening news.

But Rahab knew a way. Her house was built into the very walls of the city and it was possible for agile men to come and go without using the heavily guarded gate.

"I pray you," she went on, "swear to me by the Lord

that you will show kindness to me and to my father's house, since I have shown kindness to you. Promise me that you will spare my life when you take the city, and that you will save the lives of my father and my mother, and my brothers and my sisters."

They gave their promise readily. "If you save our lives," they said, "we will save yours. But you must not say a word about this to any other soul. And when the Lord has given us this land, we will deal kindly with you and return your kindness."

She led them, then, to a high window and hung a strong cord down the outside of the city wall upon which she lived. "Let yourselves down upon this rope and go into the mountains instead of toward the river, so that your pursuers will not find you," she told the Israelites. "Stay there for three days until they give up the search and return here to the city. After that, you may go upon your way toward the camp."

They thanked her and made sure that their escape rope was secure. "We will keep our oath," they promised again. "When you see our forces coming into this land, take a piece of scarlet line and tie it in this window so that we may see it from outside. As soon as we are gone you must send secretly for your father and your mother, your sisters and your brothers, and all your father's household. Once they are here you must make sure that they do not go out of the doors of your house into the street. If they do, it will be their own fault if they die. But as long as they remain in your house we will be responsible for them."

"So be it," she agreed, and sent them on their way. They let themselves down on the rope that dangled from her window, and vanished into the darkness outside the city wall. When they had gone she bound the scarlet line in the window and sent urgent messages to the members of her family.

The two spies hurried into the mountains and hid there for three days while their pursuers searched vainly for them in the vicinity of the river Jordan. Then they came down from their hiding place, crossed the river, and took their story back to Joshua.

"Truly the Lord has delivered the land into our hands," they reported. "The inhabitants are faint with fear because of us! They themselves believe that we will conquer them, for they know the Lord is with us."

This was welcome news indeed for Joshua.

Early the next morning he arose and struck camp, moving all the children of Israel to the very banks of the river Jordan. For the next three days he let the citizens of Jericho see his vast forces, and then he said to his people: "Sanctify yourselves, for tomorrow the Lord will do wonders among you."

And it happened the next day that the priests carrying the ark of the convenant went ahead of the people; and as they dipped their feet into the brim of the river the waters of the Jordan rolled back to leave a path between the waters. All the Israelites crossed over on dry land while the waters held back, and they made camp in Gilgal on the eastern border of Jericho.

Forty thousand fighting men prepared themselves for battle in full view of the frightened people behind the city walls. Again they camped for several days before making their final move. On the first day they celebrated the passover. On the next day they ate parched corn and unleavened cakes. And on the day after that, the manna that had fallen on them for six days out of every week during their more than forty years of wandering after leaving Egypt ceased forever to fall. At last the children of Israel were truly in the promised land. From that day on they ate of the fruits of Canaan and never again saw the desert food they had called manna.

Now the great walled city of Jericho was shut up tightly and its gates were sealed. No one stirred through the gates for fear of the Israelites. Joshua, from the camp at Gilgal, surveyed the walls and saw how solid they were. Behind the fortified stone barriers the people of Jericho were armed and ready to fight. It seemed that only the mightiest of weapons could prevail against them. And yet the children of Israel, armed though they were, had only the most simple of weapons to use against those sturdy walls.

Then the Lord spoke to Joshua, saying, "See, I have given into your hands the city of Jericho, and its king, and all its mighty men of valor. And you shall march around the city, all you men of war, with the ark among you. And before the ark shall go seven priests with seven trumpets of rams' horns, and before them shall go your armed men. . . ."

Joshua listened closely as the Lord described how the city was to be taken. It was unusual strategy for war, but Joshua had no doubt that it would succeed according to the words of the Lord.

Then Joshua called the priests and all the people together to give them their instructions. "And you must not shout," he told them, as God had commanded, "nor make any noise with your voices, not even a single word, until the day I order you to shout. Then cry out with a great and mighty shout! Now go, and march once around the city, and let those of you who are armed march in front of the ark of the Lord."

And it did happen, after Joshua had spoken to the people, that the seven priests bearing the seven trumpets of rams' horns marched ahead of the ark of the Lord and blew upon their trumpets. Half of the armed men went before them, and the other half formed the rear guard that followed behind the ark.

From behind the walls of Jericho the city dwellers watched a strange and unexpected sight. The forces of Israel were marching around their city, making no attempt to scale the walls or batter down the gates; the priests among the Israelites did nothing but blow on trumpets, and the rest of the procession made no sound at all except with their steadily marching feet. When the marchers had gone once around the city, they turned and went back to their camp in silence. It was extraordinary, and it was disturbing. Only Rahab, watching with her family from her house, was not afraid.

On the second day the Israelites, with their ark, their silent marching men, and the trumpet-blowing priests, again circled the great city just once and then returned to camp.

For six days they marched around the city, once each day, and departed silently.

On the seventh day the Israelites rose early, at the dawning of the day, for this time they would have a very much longer march. Trumpets blasting, armed men silent, they marched around the city not once but seven times. On the seventh round the priests gave a great long blast on their trumpets and Joshua turned to face his forces.

"Now!" he ordered. "Shout, for the Lord has given you the city. The whole city and everyone within it shall be accursed; every living thing shall die but Rahab and the people that are with her in her house, because she hid the messengers we sent. Shout, O Israel!"

So the people shouted together in a mighty shout while the priests blew hard upon their trumpets. The walls began to tremble, to shake, and then to totter; and suddenly they all came tumbling down to lie flat upon the earth. The children of Israel turned where they stood and swarmed straight into the city. They took it easily, falling upon the terrified inhabitants and destroying with their swords every living thing they found.

But the two young men who had spied out the land were keeping their promise to the woman who had hung a scarlet line in her window for all of them to see. "Go to Rahab's house," Joshua had said, "and bring her out in safety as you promised."

So the two spies went into her house for the second time and brought her out, with her father and her mother, and her sisters, and her brothers, and everything they had. After escorting them safely to the outskirts of the Israelite camp, the spies went back to the broken city of Jericho to help their fellow soldiers finish their task. Between the lot of them they retrieved the city's silver and gold, and vessels of iron and brass, for the tabernacle of the Lord; and then the Israelites burned the city to the ground. Only Rahab and her father's household were spared; because she had given aid to Joshua's messengers, she and her family lived with the people of Israel all the days of their lives, and no harm came to them.

So the Lord was with Joshua in his onslaught against the first stronghold in Canaan. And the fame of Joshua and his God spread throughout the land.

In the course of the next few years the Israelites fought many times against the kings and tribes of Canaan. In time Joshua took the whole land in accordance with God's promise to Moses, and divided it among the children of Israel according to their tribes.

The Israelites settled down in the promised land after many years of hardship and of battle. And the land rested at last from war.

Gideon's Three Hundred

✠✠✠✠✠✠✠✠✠✠✠✠✠✠✠✠✠✠✠✠✠

Joshua died peacefully at a good old age, his task well done. The children of Israel spread throughout the land of Canaan to live contentedly in their allotted portions. Many of them became prosperous, and many of them married into the heathen tribes that were their neighbors. No longer did they need a prophet like Moses or a warrior like Joshua to lead them, for it seemed that they were finished with war.

But in their prosperity and contentment they gradually forgot the goodness of the God who had brought them out of the land of Egypt, and turned away from him to bow down to the gods of the people who lived round about them. These were the false gods called Baal and Ashtoreth, and in worshiping them the children of Israel did evil in the sight of the Lord.

Then the anger of the Lord was hot against them, and for their sins he punished them by allowing their enemies to come down upon them and enslave them. Yet even then he would raise up judges, or deliverers, to help them in their time of need. For a while they would repent, but when the judge was dead they would go back to their evil ways. And then a new enemy would come upon them to oppress them.

Their enemies were many. Within the borders of their land there still lived many Canaanites; and there were also Philistines, people from a far-off land who now lived along the coast and tried again and again to extend their power inland and capture Israelite territory. Outside their borders were the warlike Ammonites and Midianites, as well as Moabites and Amalekites, and even the tremendous forces of the Babylonians. All these people were ready to fall upon them when they found the Israelites in a state of weakness. But the children of Israel would not learn that whenever they deserted their God he punished them by letting them fall prey to one of these great enemies. Wise judges came and went—Othniel, Ehud, Shamgar, Deborah—and used their courage and wisdom to raise their people from oppression; but when they were gone the Israelites went back to their idol worshiping.

And because the children of Israel again did evil in the sight of God, the Lord delivered them into the hands of the Midianites for seven years. Their trials began one season after they had sown and their valleys were thick with ripening corn. Like a sudden swarm of starving grasshoppers, the Midianites and their allies the Amalekites descended on the tribes of Israel to ravage their lands and strip their homes. Year after year, for seven years, they became increasingly bold. At first they attacked from the borders of their own land. Then they invaded Israel and camped on Israelite soil, bringing in their own herds and flocks to graze upon other people's land and swooping down upon the grainfields whenever the crops were ripe. And finally they spread themselves throughout the land with their cattle and their tents and camels, plundering savagely as they went. There came a time when there was no food left for Israel, nor sheep nor ox nor ass, and even the people's homes had been taken from them. Terrified and helpless, they fled into the hills to make new homes for themselves in the mountain caves and dens. From these strongholds they crept out timidly to tend their tiny patches of corn and pray that the Midianites would not discover them.

So it was in the land of Israel when the angel of the Lord came down in the seventh year. Gideon, the son of Joash and descendant of Manasseh, was threshing his small crop of wheat in a hidden wine press to keep it from the Midianites; and while he worked the angel appeared before him and sat down beneath an oak.

"The Lord is with you, O mighty man of valor," the angel greeted him.

Gideon looked up, startled. He was no mighty man, nor did he believe that the Lord was any longer with the Israelites.

"My lord," he answered, "if the Lord is with us, then why have all these things happened to us? And where are all the miracles of which our fathers told us? No, we are forsaken. The Lord has delivered us into the hands of the Midianites and he has not been with us for these many years."

"You shall save Israel," said the angel. "Go out with all your might and you will overthrow the Midianites, for it is the Lord himself who sends you."

"I, save Israel?" Gideon was doubtful, for he was not only a humble man but a simple farmer who knew scarcely anything of war. "My lord, how shall I save Israel? My family is poor in the tribe of Manasseh, and I am the least in my father's house."

"The Lord will be with you," promised the angel. "You shall strike down the Midianites as one man."

"Then if I have found favor in your sight," said Gideon, "show me a sign that I am indeed talking to the angel of the Lord. Stay here, I beg you, until I come back and bring a gift of food to set before you."

"I will wait," the angel said.

Gideon went into his home and came back with

meat, unleavened cakes, and a pot of broth. These he set before the stranger underneath the oak.

"Take the meat and the unleavened cakes," said the angel of God, "and lay them upon this rock, and pour out the broth."

Gideon did so.

The angel of the Lord reached out his staff, and with the end of it he lightly touched the offering of food. Miraculously, fire flamed from the rock and burned the food to ashes. Then the angel of the Lord vanished from Gideon's sight.

When Gideon saw that he had, beyond a doubt, been talking to the angel of the Lord, he cried out with fear. "Alas, O God! I am afraid, for I have seen an angel of the Lord face to face and I shall surely die!"

"Peace be to you," answered the Lord. "Do not be afraid, you shall not die."

Then Gideon built an altar in that place, and called it by a name which means "The Lord is Peace." With the building of this altar, the first one built in honor of the true God for many years, the spirit of the Lord began once again to reach out to the children of Israel.

That night God spoke to Gideon again. "Take one of your father's young bulls," he said, "and tear down the altar that your father built to Baal. Cut down the grove of trees around it; build a new altar to the Lord in place of the heathen altar, and offer the young bull as a burnt sacrifice with the wood that you cut down."

Later that same night Gideon gathered together ten men. Under cover of the darkness and with their help, he did as the Lord had told him. When they had utterly destroyed the altar of Baal and cut down the grove of trees, the men built a great fire from the fresh-cut wood and sacrificed the young bull upon the new, and holy, altar.

When the men of the city arose early the next morning and came to worship Baal, they saw what had happened and grew hot with rage. "Who has done this thing?" they asked furiously. And as they inquired among the people they found one man who said: "It was Gideon, the son of Joash."

In their anger they went to Joash and told him what his son had done. "Bring him out!" they demanded. "He has thrown down the altar of Baal, and for that he will die."

But Joash, who himself had built the heathen altar, was loyal to his son. "Does Baal need you to plead for him?" he asked. "Why should you help Baal? If he is a god, let him help himself. Let him punish Gideon."

But Baal was a god in their imagination only. Such a god could not harm the man who had broken down his altar. After that the people had respect for Gideon. And when the Midianites and Amalekites banded together to launch another murderous drive from their war tents in the valley of Jezreel, it was to Gideon that the people of Israel turned for leadership. The spirit of the Lord came upon Gideon, and he felt inspired. At once he sent messengers throughout the land to sound a call to arms among his own tribe and among others; and more than thirty thousand men gathered by his side.

As his people came together Gideon called upon God to give him a sign that his attack against the Midianites would indeed have the help and blessing of the Lord. "O Lord God," he said, "let me have some token that you will help me save Israel. I will put this fleece of wool upon the ground. If, by morning, the fleece is wet with dew and all the earth nearby is dry, then I shall know that you are with me and will give to us the victory."

And it was so. When morning came Gideon arose and saw that the earth was dry, but the fleece was so heavy with dew that Gideon was able to wring a bowlful of water from it.

Again he prayed to God, saying: "O Lord, do not be angry with me, but give me one more sign and I shall not speak again. This time, let the fleece alone be dry, and let all the ground around it be wet with the dew."

And again it was so. When morning came there was

dew on all the ground, but none upon the fleece. Then Gideon no longer had any doubts about his victory. He swiftly assembled his army and pitched camp beside the well of Harod, across the valley of Moreh from the army of the Midianites.

But then the Lord said to Gideon: "You have too many people with you for me to let you have the victory. The men of Israel will boast that they have won by their own might. They must know that it is the Lord who has saved them. Therefore go to the people and say: 'Whoever is afraid and fearful, let him leave this place at once.' "

Twenty-two thousand men left Gideon's camp, and ten thousand stayed. But the Lord told Gideon that there were still too many, for only the bravest and most alert of men would be needed in the coming battle. "Bring all the men to the river," said the Lord, "and I will test them for you there. When you see how they drink, divide them into two groups according to the manner of their drinking."

So Gideon took his ten thousand men down to the water's edge and watched them as they drank. Most of the men laid aside their weapons and bent down low to drink. But three hundred men held their weapons ready, and each one of these scooped up the water and lapped it from one hand so that he could still keep watch while drinking.

Gideon arranged each group into a company, with those who bent down low to drink in one company, and those who lapped the water in the other. The second group looked very small beside the first.

"With these three hundred men who lapped the water with their hands shall I save you from the Midianites," the Lord told Gideon. "Keep them, and send the rest away."

Gideon did so. With his small company of three hundred men on the mountainside, he looked down upon the vast forces of Midian in the valley. That night, instructed by the Lord, Gideon and his servant

Phurah stole quietly down to the enemy camp to find out what the people there were saying.

The enemy forces looked even more formidable at close range: Midianites, Amalekites, and all the soldiers of the eastern lands were stretched out across the valley like a massive swarm of grasshoppers, and their camels were as many as the sands beside the sea. Gideon and his man approached cautiously and stopped in the deep shadows behind the tents on the outskirts of the camp. And here they overheard a soldier talking.

"I had a dream," said a voice from the tent, "and in my dream a cake of barley bread came tumbling into our camp. It rolled against a tent and struck it hard, so that the tent fell over and lay flat upon the ground."

"Oh! That can only mean that Gideon and the forces of Israel will defeat us by the sword!" said another voice. "Truly, the Lord has delivered us into their hands."

Then Gideon knew why God had told him: "When you have heard them talking, your hands will be strengthened to meet the enemy in battle." He offered up a prayer of thanks to God and then returned with Phurah to his waiting army. "The Lord is with us!" he said, as one inspired. "He has delivered the armies of Midian into our hands!"

He divided his three hundred men into three companies, and swiftly outlined his strategy. When they all understood exactly what they were to do, he gave them each a trumpet, and a deep pitcher with a burning flare inside. Armed with these unusual weapons, Gideon's men crept toward the enemy camp. No sound came from their stealthily moving feet, and no light showed from beneath the blazing torches hidden within the pitchers. The Midianite watchmen at their posts noticed nothing strange about the gentle rustlings of the night.

In silence the three companies took their places around the camp of the sleeping Midianites and waited for Gideon to give the signal.

Suddenly the shrill blast of a war trumpet pierced the stillness. It was Gideon's call to action: all at once, three hundred other trumpets blew their shattering sounds, and three hundred empty pitchers smashed against the rocks of the valley with one great echoing crash. Flaming torches, now held high in each man's left hand, flared around the outside of the camp. Trumpets blared again in a mighty chorus of sound. "The sword of the Lord and of Gideon!" the three hundred cried out in one tremendous voice.

The Midianites, shaken abruptly from sleep, rose from their tents and saw flashes of bright flame in all directions. Noise—triumphant shouts and trumpet blasts—came at them from every side. In their terrible confusion they were convinced that they were hopelessly outnumbered by those bellowing, blaring forces, and their one thought was to escape. They picked up their swords and ran in panic through the camp.

But in the darkness of the camp, made worse by the dazzling flares encircling it, they could not see where they were going nor could they tell friend from foe. The Lord turned each man's sword against each other, and Midianite killed Midianite as they stumbled blindly toward the outermost ring of tents. But neither was there safety for them there; wherever any man came through the chaos of screaming, frightened soldiers and falling tents, he met a warrior with drawn sword and flaming torch.

The rush to get away became a stampede, and the stampede became a total rout. Gideon's three hundred fell upon the men of Midian and pursued them to the borders of their land. Other men of Israel followed Gideon now, joining in to chase their oppressors out of the land of Canaan altogether; and they killed both kings and princes of the enemy on the far side of the Jordan.

Thus were the forces of Midian driven out by the children of Israel. A grateful people begged Gideon to be their king, but he did not want the trappings of royalty or believe that a king was right for Israel. Instead, he promised to rule them as their judge and use all his strength and wisdom to lead them in the way of the Lord.

And the country lived in peace for forty years, all the rest of the days of Gideon.

But peace did not last long after Gideon's death, for even while he still lived another powerful enemy was quietly building up its forces.

Samson and Delilah

✝✝✝✝✝✝✝✝✝✝✝✝✝✝✝✝✝✝✝✝✝✝✝

Years and rulers passed away. The Philistines along the coast grew mightier and mightier. But the children of Israel too easily forgot the lessons of their past, and turned away from the Lord to worship their neighbor's heathen gods. And because they were again doing evil in the sight of the Lord, they again fell into the power of their enemies.

For forty years the warlike Philistines, who themselves worshiped a strange, fishlike idol they called Dagon, oppressed the people of Israel. And among the loosely scattered tribes there was no leader close enough to God to find the strength to free the Israelites from their new enemy.

Yet there was a certain man named Manoah, of the tribe of Dan, who still loved and served the Lord. His wife had borne no children, and it seemed she never would. But one day an angel of the Lord appeared to

Manoah's wife and told her that she would have a son.
"Take care that you drink no wine or strong drink," the
angel said to her, "nor eat food that is not clean. For
you shall bear a son who will be a Nazarite, a man
who belongs to God, and he shall begin to deliver
Israel out of the hands of the Philistines. And he shall
not cut his hair for as long as he lives, for if his hair is
cut he breaks his vow with God and the Lord will no
longer be with him."

It happened as the angel said. The woman bore a
son, and called him Samson. The child grew into a
youth of extraordinary strength, and the long hair that
was a symbol of his covenant with God fell about his
shoulders. By the time he had reached manhood he was
the strongest man in all the land, blessed by God and
destined for great things. Yet though he felt the spirit of
the Lord moving in him at times, he was not always
wise. His hatred for the enemy Philistines did not prevent him from admiring their women. This, in time,
caused great trouble for him; and yet it also was the
cause of eventual disaster for the Philistines.

His feats of strength were many and marvelous. One
day, while he was on his way to meet a Philistine
woman whom he wished to marry against his parents'
wishes, a young mountain lion leaped down from its
lair and roared menacingly in Samson's path. The spirit
of the Lord came upon him, and Samson seized the
lion with his bare hands and tore it apart as easily as if
the wild and clawing creature had been a timid young
goat.

After that he went along his way to make the Philistine woman his bride. But the Philistines did not like
this Israelite, and even at the wedding feast they persuaded the woman to help them deceive Samson with a
trick. In his terrible rage at being deceived, Samson
used his great strength to kill thirty of their countrymen. And one awful incident led to another.

Again the Philistines cheated the young man with the
flowing hair, and again Samson swore vengeance.

This time he went out and caught three hundred wild

foxes and tied their tails together two by two. Then, between each pair of foxes, he tied a piece of dry wood to the knotted tails and set the wood on fire. When the firebrands were blazing hotly with great tongues of flame, he set the foxes loose to run through the tall ripe corn in the Philistines' fields.

In their agony and terror the foxes ran wildly from one field to another, and the blazing firebrands burned up the sheaves of harvested grain, the growing corn, the olive groves, and the vineyards of the Philistines.

Now the Philistines, in their turn, took their own terrible revenge. They went to the home of Samson's Philistine wife and burned it to the ground. Both the woman and her father died by fire.

Then Samson's anger blazed again. He leaped upon the Philistines with all his strength and slaughtered them in great numbers. "I will have vengeance!" he roared. "I will not cease until I am avenged of you!" When the dead lay thick in front of him he turned away and made a new home for himself in the land of the tribe of Judah.

The Philistines were not finished with him yet. An army of them went into the land of Judah and pitched their war tents in Lehi, hoping to find Samson and have done with him.

The men of Judah had been trying to keep peace with these savage Philistines, and when they saw the army their alarm was great. "Why have you come here?" they asked. "Why do you bring your forces here against us?"

"We have come to find Samson," they replied. "To capture him and bind him as a captive so that we can do to him as he has done to us."

The men of Judah knew where Samson could be found. They had no wish to betray him, but neither did they want the anger of the Philistines to be turned against themselves. So they went to Samson's home among the rocks and called him out.

"Do you not know that the Philistines are rulers over

us?" they said to him. "Would you have us suffer for what you have done to them?"

"I did nothing more to them than they have done to me," said Samson.

"Yet we will have to bind you as a captive and take you to them," the men of Judah told him, "or their anger will descend on us."

"Take me, then, and bind me," Samson said. "Only swear to me that you will not kill me yourselves while I am bound."

They gave their promise and bound him tightly with two new cords, then took him from his sheltering rock down to the waiting Philistines. When his enemies saw him coming, bound and apparently helpless, they shouted with triumph and bloodlust.

But Samson was far from helpless. Power surged through his mighty body, and strength poured into his limbs. He flexed his muscles and strained against his bonds; they burst from his arms and fell off in broken strands as if they had been flax burnt through by fire. When his hands were free he searched upon the ground and picked up the sun-dried jawbone of a long-dead ass, and with it he lashed out at the men who had come to take him. Again and again he struck his furious blows with the sharp side of the bone, until a thousand Philistines lay dead upon the earth around him.

"With the jawbone of an ass have I killed a thousand men!" his great voice bellowed out victoriously. And when he had done with killing he threw the bone away.

After that he was recognized as a powerful judge among the people of Israel.

But then, instead of staying away from the people who hated him, Samson went to Gaza. This was a great stronghold of the Philistines, and a dangerous place for any Israelite to visit, and dangerous especially for Samson.

Word flew around the city that he was there. "Samson is in Gaza!" so the people said. And the Philistines rejoiced at this unexpected chance to trap him. When evening came they arranged themselves around the great stone walls of the city and secured the heavy gates. All night they lay quietly in wait for him, planning to ambush him when he came out in the morning. But again Samson was too much for them. He did not wait for morning, but approached the gates at midnight. His huge arms reached for the barred gates and tore them from the walls—posts, crossbar and all—and carried them away upon his shoulders to drop them on a hilltop looking down on Hebron.

Some time afterward he came to love a woman in the valley of Sorek, a Philistine whose name was Delilah.

It was not long before his enemies discovered that Samson was bewitched with love for Delilah and that he was often to be found with her in her home. The lords of the Philistines went to her and proposed a bargain.

"Entice him," they said. "Use your wiles upon him to find out where his great strength lies and how we may defeat him. If you discover his secret we will each give you eleven hundred pieces of silver."

It was a large sum of money, an alluring offer. Delilah agreed.

The next time Samson came she began at once to coax his secret out of him. "Tell me," she said seductively, "what it is that makes you so wonderfully strong, and what manner of cords can possibly tame your marvelous strength."

Samson was not quite so easily enticed as she had hoped.

"If I were bound with seven green willow switches that have not been dried," he answered, "I should be as weak as any other man."

Delilah passed her report on to the rulers of the Philistines. They came to her house with the seven green willow switches and lay in wait while Delilah soothed Samson into sleep. Then she bound Samson with the supple green stems and called out: "Samson! Awake! The Philistines are upon you!"

Samson woke up and stretched. The willow bindings

broke as easily as a strand of rope is broken when it touches fire.

"You have mocked me," said Delilah sadly. "Why do you tell me lies, when you know I would not harm you? Now tell me truly: With what may your great strength be bound?"

"Only with new ropes that have never been used before," said Samson. "Then I shall be as weak as any other man."

Delilah therefore took new ropes and bound him while he slept. "Awake, Samson!" she called out. "The Philistines are upon you!" Samson got up lazily, and the ropes around him snapped like threads.

"You have mocked me again!" Delilah cried reproachfully. "You have told me lies. Now tell me truly how you may be bound!"

"If you weave my hair into the web of cloth you are weaving on your loom," he said, "then I shall be as weak as any other man."

Later, Samson slept again and Delilah quickly went to work at her weaving loom. She parted Samson's long, thick hair into seven strands and wove each one into the fabric on her weaving frame, then fastened the fabric securely with the sturdy pin of the loom to make doubly sure of subduing Samson.

"The Philistines are upon you, Samson!"

But the Philistines, still hiding, had no chance to fall upon him, for Samson was as strong as ever. He rose up without effort and walked away, dragging with him the weaving frame, the pin, and the web of cloth in which his long hair was entangled. Delilah was left with a broken loom and a growing fear that she would never see the silver promised her by the Philistine rulers.

Yet Samson kept coming back to her, and Delilah kept on trying to lure his secret out of him. "You have mocked me now three times," she rebuked him sorrowfully, "and still you have not told me where your great strength lies. How can you say, 'I love you,' when your heart is not truly with me?"

And she pressed him daily, pleading and coaxing

until Samson became harassed beyond endurance. Tired of her constant badgering, he at last gave up the secret that had been locked so long in his heart.

"There has never been a razor on my head," he said, "for I am a Nazarite, given to the Lord from birth. If I should let my hair be shaved, then my strength would go from me and I would truly be as weak as any other man."

Delilah saw that he was telling the truth at last. As soon as Samson's back was turned she sent for the Philistine lords. "Come up this one last time," she said urgently. "He has told me the secret of his heart."

The Philistine leaders went to her with the money in their hands. Delilah hid them and greeted Samson with smiles and words of love. When the big man was asleep she called out softly for a Philistine to come quickly with a razor. "Shave off the seven locks of his head," she ordered.

The man raised the razor deftly, slashed it through the thick tangle of hair. One after the other, the seven locks came off and dropped like dead leaves to the floor.

Delilah shook Samson roughly. "The Philistines are upon you, Samson!" she cried harshly, and struck him with her hand. He awoke out of his sleep, thinking that this time would be the same as other times. "I will shake myself," he said, "and go out as before." He did not know that his long hair was cut short, that his vow to the Lord had been broken for him, and that his heavensent strength had left him.

When the Philistines sprang from their hiding places he swung out to strike them down. To Samson's great alarm he suddenly felt as weak as any ordinary man and his blows were useless. His gloating enemies captured him with ease and cruelly thrust out his eyes to make certain that he never again could do them any harm. They took him back to Gaza, where they bound him with brass chains and thrust him into prison.

Day after day he labored in the prison house, turning

a heavy millstone and grinding corn to make bread for his enemies.

Meanwhile the rulers of the Philistines were gathering together from all corners of their land to prepare a great sacrificial offering to Dagon, their fishlike god, and to rejoice in their triumph over Samson. "Our god has delivered our enemy into our hands!" they said joyfully. "Samson, the destroyer of our country, who killed so many of us, will never again do any harm!" When the long preparations were complete and all the prayers had been offered up to Dagon, the Philistines thronged in even greater numbers than before into the huge stone temple of their false god, to feast and drink and celebrate their deliverance from the strong man whom they had managed to imprison several weeks before.

At the height of the merrymaking someone, one of the Philistine lords, shouted out drunkenly: "Call for Samson, so that we may have sport with him!" Others picked up the cry, and soon they called for Samson to be brought out of the prison house so that they might make fun of him. A young lad led him to the temple, in his rags and chains, and he was made to stand between the pillars of the temple where all could see and throw their taunts at him. There were three thousand men and women who stood there laughing at him for his helplessness, among them all the lords and rulers of the Philistines, and they gloated at the sight of a giant made blind and powerless by their cunning.

They did not notice how long his hair had grown during his time in prison.

As he stood between the pillars and heard their mocking shouts, Samson said to the lad who held him by the hand: "Let me feel the pillars that support this house, so that I may lean upon them."

He leaned upon them, as if weak and tired, and the people jeered.

"O Lord God," he prayed, "remember me, I pray you! Strengthen me only this once, O God, so that I may be avenged of the Philistines for my two eyes."

He took hold of the two middle pillars that supported the temple, and braced himself. "Let me die with the Philistines!" he cried.

Then Samson tightened his grip upon the pillars and bowed forward with all his might. The pillars crashed to the floor in a terrible rumble of sound; the temple shattered down and crumbled into ruins on top of all the people in it—all the merrymakers, all the priests of Dagon, and all the rulers of the Philistines.

Thus, in his death, Samson destroyed more Philistines than he had killed in all his life. And the power of the Philistines was broken with the temple. It was to be many years before they regained sufficient strength to again threaten the peace and freedom of the children of Israel.

The Story of Ruth

✚✚✚✚✚✚✚✚✚✚✚✚✚✚✚✚✚✚✚✚✚✚✚

Now it happened, in the days when the judges ruled, that there was a famine in the land. And a certain man of Bethlehem in the tribe lands of Judah took his wife and two sons into the country of Moab where the grass was green and food was plentiful.

The name of the man was Elimelech, and the name of his wife, Naomi. The two sons were named Mahlon and Chilion.

It was not a very long journey, for Moab lay directly across the Salt Sea from the land of Judah. Nor was the land itself unknown to the people of Israel, for it was from a mountain peak in Moab that Moses had seen the promised land for the first and only time. Yet it was a strange land, and it was no small venture for a family of Israelites to leave their home and friends to start a new life among strangers.

The Moabites were Gentiles and worshiped strange

gods. At times there was bitter warfare between them and the people of Israel. But this was a time of peace, and the family of Elimelech settled quietly in the country of Moab. They brought their own faith with them, and prospered in the land. Their new neighbors welcomed them with kindness; and the land was fertile so that there was always bread to eat.

Yet life was not always easy, and the woman Naomi suffered many tragedies. Elimelech, her husband, died, and she was left with her two sons to care for her. In the course of time her sons took wives from among the women of Moab; the name of Chilion's wife was Orpah, and the name of Mahlon's wife was Ruth.

For about ten years all was well. Ruth and Orpah became devoted to their mother-in-law, and she to them, and though they were Moabite women they gave up the gods of their people to worship the God of Israel. Then Mahlon and Chilion both died, leaving Naomi without either husband or sons. She wanted to return to her own country, for she was lonely among the Moabites without her family around her. Also, she had heard that the Lord had ended the famine in Judah and given his people bread, so that it was no longer necessary for her to stay away from home. So she left the place where she was living and started on her way back to the land of Judah. Her two loving daughters-in-law left with her, for with their own husbands gone it seemed to them at first that they had no one left but Naomi. They did not want to lose her, too, and they did not want her to be alone and sad.

But Naomi, for her part, had no wish for Ruth and Orpah to be lonely in the land of Judah as she herself was, now, in the country of Moab. When the three women had gone some little distance together she stopped, and they stopped with her.

"Go, now," she said. "Go back, each of you, to your mother's house. May the Lord deal kindly with you, as you have been kind to my sons and to me. And may he grant that each of you marry again, so that you may find rest and happiness, each in the house of her husband."

Then she kissed them, and the young women wept.

"We cannot leave you," they sobbed. "Let us go with you and live among your people."

But Naomi answered: "No, turn back, my daughters. Why should you go with me? Turn again, my daughters; go your way. I am old, too old to have another husband. And even if I should marry again and have more sons, would you wait for them until they were grown? Would you do that, instead of marrying other husbands here? No, you must stay, for I am grieved for your sakes and wish you to remain in your own land and be happy with your people."

Ruth and Orpah wept again, and Orpah said a sad farewell. She kissed her mother-in-law as the tears trickled down her cheeks. Slowly and sadly she turned away. But Ruth clung to Naomi and held her close.

"Look, your sister-in-law has gone back to her people and her gods," Naomi said gently. "You must go after her and do what she does."

"Do not make me leave you," pleaded Ruth. "Do not ask me to turn away from following you. For wherever you go, there will I go, too; and wherever you stay, there will I stay with you. Your people shall be my people, and your God shall be my God. Where you die, there will I die, and there will I be buried. May the anger of the Lord be upon me if anything but death parts you from me."

Naomi said no more. She could see that Ruth was steadfast in her purpose and would not be turned away. In silence she walked on. Ruth followed her. And in her heart Naomi was glad that Ruth was with her.

So the two women traveled together to the town of Bethlehem, arriving there at the beginning of the barley harvest when the fields were rich with grain and the people of Israel were rejoicing because the Lord had sent them plentiful crops. "Is this Naomi?" they cried out in welcome when they saw the women. Yet in spite of all their greetings it was a sad return for Naomi, who had left her home ten years before with a husband and two fine sons only to come back poor, empty-handed, and alone but for the Moabite girl Ruth.

Their first concern was to find food. In Moab they owned land, but here in Bethlehem they had nothing of their own and no means of earning silver even to buy bread. Now it was the custom among the people of Israel that every farmer, when he and his laborers reaped the grain and gathered it into bundles, would permit the poor and hungry to follow behind the reapers and gather all the loose stalks that had fallen by the way. And it so happened that one of the richest farmers in Bethlehem was a man named Boaz, who was not only a mighty man of wealth but a kinsman of Elimelech, Naomi's husband. Naomi did not know how rich he had become, nor did she give the matter any thought. But Boaz, too, was reaping at this time.

Ruth looked around the strange new land, saw the great harvest of barley being reaped on all sides of the town, and took note of the custom that permitted the poor to glean the fields for whatever the reapers might have left.

"Let me go now to the fields," she said to Naomi, "and gather grain from whoever allows me to glean."

And Naomi answered, "Go, my daughter."

So Ruth went into the fields and gathered the fallen stalks of grain left by the reapers. And it was her good fortune to chance upon a part of the great field belonging to the wealthy Boaz.

As the day passed Boaz came out of the city to watch his reapers at harvest. He walked slowly through the tall grain, looking about him at the workers and the growing piles of sheaves. Suddenly he saw a young woman who was a stranger to him. He saw, too, that she was fair of face and working diligently. "Who is she?" he asked his overseer. "She is the Moabite maiden who came back with Naomi out of the country of Moab," the overseer answered, for he knew her story. "She asked leave to glean and gather behind the reapers among the sheaves. I gave permission, and she has worked hard since morning with scarcely any rest."

Boaz looked at her with even greater interest. So this was the young woman who had come back with Naomi! He, too, had heard the tale of her departure from Moab and her devotion to his kinswoman. He watched her for a while, and then made his way between the sheaves to where she worked.

"Hear me, my daughter," Boaz said to her, and she raised her head to look at him. "Do not go to any other field to glean. Stay here with my maidens and follow after them. My young men will not disturb you; I will see to that. And when you are thirsty, go to the drinking vessels and drink the cool water which the men have drawn. Gather whatever you wish until the harvest is over."

Ruth bowed low to Boaz in her gratitude. "I thank you, my lord," she said. "But tell me why I have found favor in your sight, so that you take notice of me? For I am a stranger, and did not expect such kindness."

"I have heard all that you have done for your mother-in-law Naomi since the death of your husband," Boaz answered. "I know how you left your father and your mother and the land of your birth to come here to live among strangers, so that you could be with Naomi and care for her. May the Lord God of Israel, under whose wings you have come for protection, reward you in full for the good you have done!"

She thanked him for his kindness; yet there was more to come.

"Go and glean," he said, "but at mealtime come back here to eat bread with the reapers."

And so she did; she sat beside the reapers and they passed her parched corn until she had had enough. Then she arose, taking with her what she had not been able to eat, and went back into the field to glean. When she was out of earshot Boaz gave more orders to his men. "Let her glean all she needs," he commanded, "even among the sheaves you have already gathered. Also, as you reap, let some handfuls fall on purpose and leave them there for her. Do not reproach her no matter what she takes; it is my wish that she should have all that she can carry."

So she gleaned in the field until evening, gathering many more stalks than she had been able to find in the morning. When she beat out what she had gleaned she found she had about a bushel of barley, an unusual amount for one day's work. She took her barley and went into the city, and there she gave it to her mother-in-law with the food she had saved from her meal with Boaz and the reapers. Naomi was amazed.

"Where did you glean today?" she asked. "And how did you gather so much? Blessed be the man who took notice of you!"

"It was a man named Boaz with whom I gleaned today," Ruth answered.

"Boaz!" said Naomi, greatly pleased that Ruth should have been noticed by this man of all men. "May the Lord bless him for his kindness! The man is near of kin to us, one of our closest kinsmen. It is good that you are gleaning in his fields."

"He also said to me that I should stay with his reapers and his maidens in the fields until the end of harvest," Ruth told her.

"That is good, my daughter," said Naomi. "Then you will not need to look for any other field to glean in, and Boaz surely will protect you."

So Naomi was glad; and Ruth stayed with the maidens of Boaz, gleaning in his fields until the end of barley harvest and of wheat harvest. During all that time she lived with her mother-in-law and gave her comfort.

Naomi in her turn was concerned more for Ruth than for herself. Ruth was young and fair to look at, and it was right that she should marry again and find happiness in a home of her own. To live as Ruth was living now was not what Naomi wanted for her loyal daughter-in-law.

Therefore she said to Ruth at the end of harvest: "My daughter, shall I not seek rest for you, that you may have a home and be provided for? And Boaz, with whose maidens you have been working—is he not our kinsman? And you know that he is winnowing barley tonight upon the threshing floor. Bathe and anoint yourself with fine perfumes and put on your loveliest robes, and then go down there to him. Let him first eat and drink with his men, and afterward approach him. He will tell you what to do."

"All you tell me to do, I will do," said Ruth.

That night, when Boaz had done with eating and drinking and his heart was merry, he lay down on the threshing floor with his head on a soft heap of grain. At midnight he awoke suddenly and knew that someone was with him. "Who is it?" he called out, startled.

"It is Ruth, your handmaid," she answered. "I have come to you for help, for you are a near kinsman of mine through Elimelech."

"The Lord bless you, my daughter," Boaz said. "You have shown kindness again, for you have not followed the young men, either rich or poor, but have come to me. And now, my daughter, do not be afraid. I will do whatever you ask, and provide whatever you need. The people of this city know that you are a good and virtuous woman, and all will be well with you. Now it is true that I am your near kinsman, for I was related to your husband who died. But there is a man who is more closely related than I. Tomorrow we will find him out if he will do his part as the closest kinsman. If he does, then let him do it. But if he is not able to, then I shall do it in his place."

He did not say that he had come to love Ruth and had secret hopes that the closer kinsman would not be able to perform his family duty in caring for the daughter-in-law of the late Elimelech; and Ruth did not say that she had come to love Boaz and had no real interest in any closer kin.

Both she and Boaz would abide by the custom that the closest relative of a man who had died had first right to buy his property and marry the widow. He was also expected to take responsibility for the dead man's mother, if she was not still married herself. What Boaz must do before declaring his love for Ruth was to find out if the nearest male relative would claim his rights and duties.

The next day Boaz went to the city gate where the elders of the city were usually to be found and where, sooner or later, his kinsman would be sure to pass. Boaz sat down and waited.

Meanwhile Ruth had gone back to Naomi with six measures of barley as a gift from Boaz. "Do not go empty-handed to your mother-in-law," Boaz had said, and Ruth gave Naomi his present of food while she told the older woman every word that Boaz had said to her.

Naomi listened and nodded. "That is good," she said. "Now sit down and wait until you know how this matter will end. For the man will not rest until he has finished the thing this day."

Ruth waited with Naomi and Boaz waited at the gate until the kinsman of whom he had spoken came by.

"Ho!" Boaz called. "Turn aside, sit down here with me." The kinsman turned aside and sat down. Then Boaz sent for ten men of the elders to sit down with him and his kinsman to witness the discussion, and he spoke thus to the kinsman: "Naomi, who has returned from the country of Moab, has land to sell which was our relative Elimelech's. I ask you now, in the presence of these elders, if you wish to redeem it in accordance with your right. If you wish, then do so. If not, then I shall do so."

"I will redeem it," said the kinsman, glad of such an opportunity.

"But you know," Boaz reminded him, "that on the day you buy the land, you must take Ruth the Moabite woman, Mahlon's widow, to be your wife, so that she may have children and her family will not end with her. And you shall also care for Naomi, the woman's mother-in-law."

"That I cannot do," the man declared, "or I shall lose my own inheritance. For I have a family already. Take my right as your own; I cannot use it myself."

Boaz had heard all that he needed. In front of his kinsman and the ten elders, he announced what he would do: "You are witnesses this day that I am buying from Naomi all that was Elimelech's, all that was Chilion's, and all that was Mahlon's. Moreover, I am taking Ruth, the Moabite woman who was Mahlon's wife, to be my wife so that the family of Elimelech continues on this earth. Naomi, also, shall I care for until the end of her days. You are witnesses?"

"We are witnesses," the elders said. "May your house prosper!"

Then Boaz went back to Ruth where she awaited him, and took her for his wife. In happiness, they married; and soon the Lord gave Ruth a child.

The women of the city rejoiced with their friend Naomi. "Blessed be the Lord who has not left you without a kinsman!" they said joyfully. "May his family name be famous throughout Israel. And he shall be to you a restorer of your life and a comfort in your old age. You are blessed indeed, for the daughter-in-law who loves you and is better to you than seven sons, has borne a son to the family of Elimelech!"

Naomi laid the child on her bosom and was comforted. She nursed him lovingly through his babyhood, and the women said: "It is as if Naomi had a son herself." And it was so, for she loved him as her own.

Ruth and Boaz named their boy Obed, and in great happiness they watched him becoming a sturdy lad who walked in the ways of the Lord.

Obed grew to manhood and had a son named Jesse. Jesse, when he became a man, married and had several sons. One of them was David, the singing shepherd boy, who was to be a mighty king of Israel. And from David's family came the Savior of mankind, a baby born in Bethlehem.

Thus did Ruth, the kindly Moabite woman who believed in the God of Israel, give life to an Israelite family that led down through the years to Mary, Joseph, and the gentle Jesus.

Samuel the Kingmaker

****

There was a man named Elkanah who lived in the little hill town of Ramah on the slopes of Mount Ephraim, not far from Shiloh where stood the temple of the Lord and the holy ark. Every year he and his wife Hannah went to the temple with their offerings to worship God.

Hannah was a good woman whose husband loved her deeply. But she was sore at heart because she had no children. Year after year she prayed to the Lord to send her a son. As time passed and she remained without a child, she became more and more sad until she was overcome with grief and could not even eat for weeping.

Then she wept with bitterness in the temple of the Lord, and she made a solemn vow. "O Lord," she prayed silently, with the tears streaming down her cheeks. "Look on my sorrow, and remember me! Only give me a son and I will give him back to you to serve you all the days of his life."

The old priest of the temple, Eli, saw her tears and the silent movement of her lips. So strange and troubled did she look that he at first thought she had been drinking wine. Therefore he spoke sternly to her, and she answered humbly.

"No, my Lord," she whispered through her tears. "I have not been drinking wine. I have poured out my soul to the Lord, for I am a woman of sorrowful spirit. Out of the depths of my grief have I spoken to him."

Old Eli saw his error. "Go in peace," he said to her, "and may the God of Israel grant you what you ask."

Peace stole into Hannah's heart. She rose and went away. When she returned with Elkanah to their house at Ramah she wept no more, nor did she push aside her food untasted; and her face was no longer stained with tears nor marked by sadness.

Soon afterward the Lord remembered her. Hannah bore a son and called him Samuel, saying, "I have asked him of the Lord, and thus his name is Samuel." And in his babyhood the child was a great comfort and pleasure to his mother.

When Samuel was old enough to be of service to the priests in the temple, Hannah took many offerings to the house of the Lord in Shiloh. And she also took the child. When she had given up her gifts of wine and meat and flour, she gave the boy into the care of the old priest, Eli.

"O my lord," she said to Eli, "I am the woman who stood by you in the temple, praying to the Lord. For this child did I pray, and the Lord has given me what I asked of him. Therefore, as I vowed, I do lend him to my God, and as long as Samuel lives he shall belong to the Lord."

Then she prayed, and worshiped there in the temple with her husband and her son, and returned home with Elkanah. The boy Samuel stayed with Eli, and the old man taught him how to serve the Lord. And Samuel was happy in the temple.

Every year Hannah would make a new coat for her son and take it to him when she and Elkanah went to Shiloh to offer up their yearly sacrifice. Eli gave them good reports about their son and blessed them, for he was glad to have a boy like Samuel with him to grow up in the service of the Lord. Nor was Hannah left without a son in her own home, for as the years passed the Lord gave her three more boys and two lovely daughters.

Now Eli had two sons of his own who were also priests. But they did not love the Lord and did many evil things, so that the people of Israel despised them. Eli spoke many times to his wicked sons, begging them to change their ways, but they would not listen to their father's voice. God warned Eli that their punishment would be terrible and that the honor of serving as high priest in the holy temple would be taken away from them and placed in more worthy hands. But still the sons of Eli went their way and sinned against the Lord.

Meanwhile the child Samuel grew, and found favor in the eyes of men and the Lord. Eli, watching him and guiding him, was more than ever glad to see the goodness of the boy, for the word of the Lord was seldom heard in those days and the Israelites needed someone of strong faith to come among them as their judge and leader.

One night, when all was quiet in the temple and Eli had lain down to sleep, a voice called Samuel's name.

"Here I am!" said Samuel, and he ran to Eli. "You called me; I am here."

"I did not call," said Eli. "Lie down, boy, and sleep."

Samuel went to his bed and lay down, but he did not sleep.

The voice called again. "Samuel!" Samuel arose and ran to Eli.

"Here I am, for you called me," he said.

"I did not call, my son," said Eli. "Lie down again."

Samuel went back to bed. The voice called him again. "Samuel!" The boy arose and went to Eli.

"Here I am," he said, "for you did call me."

Then Eli realized that the Lord had called the child. "It was not I," he said. "Go, lie down. If you hear the voice again, say, 'Speak, Lord, for your servant hears.'"

So Samuel went and lay down once again. This time he lay wide awake and waiting, with great awe in his heart.

Once more the Lord spoke in the night. "Samuel, Samuel!"

And Samuel answered, "Speak, Lord, for your servant hears."

Then the Lord said to Samuel: "Behold, on an appointed day I will do in Israel a thing that will cause the ears of everyone that hears of it to tingle. On that day I will do to Eli all the things of which I warned him concerning his household and his sons. For I have told him that I will judge his house forever for the evil which he knows his sons have done, and from which he did not stop them. Therefore I have sworn to the house of Eli that the evil of his house shall not be cleansed by sacrifice or offerings, but shall be punished. And when I begin, it will be the end for them."

Samuel lay awake until morning, thinking about the strange voice in the night and its ominous message. At daylight he arose and opened the doors of the temple as he always did. But he did not seek out Eli, for his heart was heavy and he did not want to tell Eli what he had heard.

Eli waited for him, and still he did not come. At last the old man called for him. "Samuel, my son!"

Samuel went to him. "Here I am," he answered.

"What is it that the Lord told you last night?" the old priest asked him gently. "I pray you, do not try to hide from me anything he said."

Samuel sadly told him everything the Lord had said, hiding not a word

Eli lowered his head in sorrow. "The Lord has spoken," he said. "So be it. Let him do whatever seems good to him."

But the time had not yet come, and the house of Eli was safe as Samuel grew to manhood. And the Lord was with him as he grew, so that Samuel spoke true words of prophecy and wisdom. All the land of Israel, from Dan even to Beersheba, came to know that Samuel was to be a prophet of the Lord.

Yet even though the Israelites trusted Samuel as a wise man who spoke the true words of the Lord, many of them disobeyed God and began again to worship heathen idols. And because they sinned, the Lord turned their powerful, land-hungry neighbors against them.

In the years after the death of Samson, the Philistines of the coastal plains had gradually built up strength until they were in control of the five great cities of Ekron, Ashdod, Ashkelon, Gaza, and Gath, and with this great power and wealth at their disposal they were prepared to attack the loosely scattered tribes of Israel. And this they did: with all their great might they descended upon the leaderless children of Israel and laid waste their land. Four thousand men of the Israelite forces were killed in one terrible battle, and God's country was again in the hands of Israel's archenemies.

Afterward, when the remaining Israelites were gathered together in their camp, the elders of Israel said: "Why has the Lord let us be defeated by the Philistines? Let us fetch the ark of the Lord out of Shiloh and carry it into battle with us. Then surely we will win."

They would not understand that they had been defeated again because they had been sinful and had turned away from God. And instead of praying to their Lord before going into battle, they took the ark of the Lord with them against the army of the Philistines. In their blindness they were sure that the enemy would be terrified by the presence of the Lord among them. But they were wrong; for, in truth, the Lord was not with his people, for they were not with him.

And the Philistines did not allow themselves to be afraid. "Be strong!" the Philistine leaders told their men. "See, God is in their camp, and it will go hard with us if we do not battle mightily. Acquit yourselves like soldiers, O ye Philistines! Do not become slaves to the Hebrews because their ark is with them. Be men, and fight!"

Trumpets sounded and the battle began. Eli's two sons themselves carried the ark of the Lord before them, convinced that by merely carrying it they would win the day.

But the Philistines fought like men inspired; and they won. Thirty thousand Israelites fell dead. Eli's two sons were killed, the ark was captured, and the few Israelite soldiers who were left alive ran screaming to their tents. A soldier from the tribe of Benjamin escaped from the dreadful slaughter and ran to Shiloh with the news. Eli waited near the temple for word of his sons and the missing ark.

"Israel has fled before the Philistines," the man cried out. "Your two sons are dead, and many others as well, and the ark of God is taken!"

When Eli heard these awful words he fell back and died, an old man with a broken heart. He had judged Israel for forty years, and he had not done well.

Then Samuel became chief priest and judge of Israel in old Eli's place. Strange things began to happen to the Philistines. Wherever they took the captured ark, the people of the town became tormented by all manner of plagues. Horrible diseases spread from town to village and across the plains; boils and sores attacked both young and old; their fishlike idol, Dagon, toppled from his place. At last, in desperation, the tortured Philistines returned the ark to the people of Israel.

It was then that Samuel showed his strength.

"Gather together, all you children of Israel!" he cried. "Return to the Lord with all your hearts and put away the strange gods of the heathens. Serve the Lord only, and he will deliver you out of the hands of the Philistines!"

Then the children of Israel put aside their heathen gods and served their Lord. And on a day when Samuel offered up a burnt offering to the God of Israel in the presence of a multitude of his people, the armies of the Philistines drew near to do battle with the Israelites. A cloud rolled over the sun. And, that day, the Lord thundered with a great thunder against the Philistines; and the enemy from the coastlands fled in terror and complete defeat.

There was peace for a time. Samuel grew to middle years and to old age, and he judged Israel for the rest of his days. He was a wise man, and he was good, but like Eli he had sons who made false judgments and took bribes. And his people grew greatly concerned as Samuel aged.

The elders of Israel gathered together and came to Samuel with troubled hearts. "Behold," they said, "you are old and you will not always be with us. What of the future? Your sons do not walk in the ways of the Lord as you do, and we do not want them to judge us when you are gone. Therefore make us a king to judge us, like all other nations."

But this was displeasing to Samuel, for he did not think that a king would be right for his people. He prayed to the Lord for guidance.

"Give the people what they want," the Lord told him. "It is not you they are rejecting; they are rejecting me, so that I should not reign over them. Since the day I brought them out of Egypt they have been forsaking me for false gods. Therefore listen to them and do as they say, but warn them what manner of man shall reign over them as king."

Samuel went back to them. "So you will have a king!" he said. "Know, then, that he will take your sons and make them work for him as drivers of his chariots, and as horsemen, and as runners before his chariots. And he will make them servants in his armies, and servants in his fields, and servants to make his instruments of war. He will take your daughters to be cooks and bakers in his palace. He will take your fields,

your vineyards, your olive groves, the best of everything you have, and give it all to his own officers and
favorites. He will take your sheep, your asses, your
finest young men, your maidservants, your menservants
to be his own and put them to his work. And you will
cry out because of the king that you have chosen, and
the Lord will not hear you on that day!"

But the people refused to take heed of the warning
voice of Samuel.

"We will have a king!" they demanded. "Let us have
a king so that we may be like other nations, with a king
to judge us, to go out before us and lead us into
battle."

Samuel argued no more. "Go back to your homes,"
he told them, for he knew he would have to find the
king they had demanded.

Now there was a man named Kish, of the tribe of
Benjamin, who had a son named Saul. And Saul one
day went out looking for his father's asses that had
strayed. In his search he came to the house of the wise
man Samuel, and Samuel told him where he would find
the wandering asses.

Samuel looked at tall young Saul, a strong and stalwart man of fine and handsome face. And the voice of
the Lord told Samuel in his ear: "Behold, this is the
man! Anoint him, for he shall be king and reign over
the people of Israel!"

The old prophet took a vial of oil and poured it on
Saul's head. And he gathered the people together, and
all the people shouted: "God save the king!"

And so the proud young Saul, a noble warrior who
stood head and shoulders taller than his fellow men,
became the first king of the children of Israel at their
demand.

It was not long before he proved himself. With great
courage he led his forces into war against Israel's
sworn enemies, the Ammonites and Philistines and
Amalekites, and as he skillfully won battle after battle
he also won the support of all the people of his land.
As time went by, his young son Jonathan joined him on

the battlefields to fight with equal bravery, and all Israel rejoiced because of their prowess in war. They were glad, then, that they had found a king so bold and strong, with so fine a son to be his heir.

King Saul went from one great success to another, and another. He pleased his people greatly. But he did not please the Lord.

Again and again he broke the Lord's commandments; again and again he caused grief to Samuel for his headstrong ways. Black moods came upon him and he turned away from God. He began to quarrel with the man who had made him king of Israel.

And at last Samuel had to tell him what the Lord had told him to say: "You, Saul, have disobeyed and rejected the word of the Lord. And therefore the Lord has rejected you from being king. Neither shall your son be king, for you are stubborn and sinful. The time will soon come when you shall no longer reign."

"I have sinned!" Saul cried out remorsefully. "Turn again with me, I beg you, so that I may be honored in the eyes of Israel and worship the Lord your God!" And bold, proud Saul clutched desperately at Samuel's cloak as the old prophet turned away. The cloak tore in his hands.

"It is too late," said Samuel sadly. "As you have torn my cloak today, so shall the Lord tear the kingdom of Israel away from you and give it to another man, a better man than you. To repent is not enough; for a man who sins and lies and then repents cannot be the strength of Israel."

Samuel went away, and he came no more to see Saul all the days of his life. But he mourned in his heart for the brave young man who had proved to be so great a fighter and so bad a king.

David the Shepherd Boy

****

I repent that I made Saul king of Israel!" said the Lord. "So rebellious and stubborn a man is not fit to rule my people."

Samuel knew this well, yet he had learned to love the tormented, sinful Saul almost as though the son of Kish had been his own son. Therefore he wept for Saul in the bitterness of his grief, and found no comfort anywhere.

Then said the Lord to Samuel: "How long will you mourn for Saul, seeing I have rejected him from reigning over Israel? Fill your horn with oil and go from here to Jesse in the town of Bethlehem, for I have provided me a king among his sons and you shall anoint him against the time when Saul shall cease to rule."

"How can I go?" said Samuel. "If Saul hears of it, he will kill me."

"Take a heifer with you as an offering," said the Lord, "and when you come to Bethlehem, say, 'I have come to make a sacrifice unto the Lord.' And call Jesse to the feast. When he is there with all his sons I will show you what you must do, and whom you shall anoint as king. Saul will not know of this, you need not fear."

Samuel did as the Lord had said. He prepared the offering, filled the anointing horn with oil, and journeyed to the town of Bethlehem where lived Ruth's grandson Jesse and his eight strapping sons. The elders of the town trembled at his coming, for the visit of their high priest and prophet was usually a sign of God's displeasure and a warning of punishment to come. "Do you come in peace?" they asked fearfully.

"Yes, I come peaceably," said Samuel. "I have come here to make a sacrifice to the Lord. Therefore prepare yourselves, and come with me to the sacrifice." Then he called for Jesse and his sons to join him at the feast.

Now Jesse was a farmer and his sons were shepherds, and when Samuel sent word that he wished them to be with him at the sacrifice they came hurrying to him across the fields and pastures. Seven of them, all tall and fine-looking young men, came with their father Jesse; but one stayed with the sheep out in the grazing lands.

He was young, no more than a boy and not yet as tall and well-muscled as his brothers, but already he was known for his courage. More often than not it was peaceful among the sweet grasslands and cool, refreshing streams, but sometimes his lambs would fall down a rocky hillside or climb too high to leap to safety; and then the lad would risk his life to climb after them and bring them back into the flock. Once a lion had leaped upon his flock and dragged away a frightened lamb; the boy had gone after the lion and killed it singlehanded. And once a bear had attacked the sheep, only to be driven off and killed by the shepherd boy with his simple, herdsman's weapons. He was brave among brave men, for the shepherds of his time needed strength and courage, and he was well known for his fighting skill.

There was something else about the boy that made him different from his fellow shepherds. He played the harp like a dreamer with music in his heart and fingertips, and in his mind he made up songs of praise to the Lord. As he watched his flocks, always keeping his staff and sling beside him in case of attack from any wild beast, he would draw his fingers across the strings of his harp and sing about the wonders of the Lord and all the sweet beauty of the hills and fields about him. And because he was a shepherd he sang as a shepherd would sing and thought as a shepherd would think:

"The Lord is my shepherd; I shall not want.
He maketh me to lie down in green pastures,
He leadeth me beside the still waters, He restoreth
    my soul;
He leadeth me in the paths of righteousness for his
    name's sake.
Yea, though I walk through the valley of the shadow
    of death,
I will fear no evil, for thou art with me;
Thy rod and thy staff, they comfort me.
Thou preparest a table before me in the presence of
    mine enemies;
Thou anointest my head with oil! My cup runneth
    over.
Surely goodness and mercy shall follow me all the
    days of my life,
And I will dwell in the house of the Lord for ever."

And on this day, while the lad was singing songs of glory in the fields, his father and his seven brothers were presenting themselves to the prophet Samuel and looking forward to the feast.

Samuel looked them over one after the other, seeking for the one who was to be the Lord's anointed. First,

Eliab, Jesse's oldest son, came before him. Samuel gazed at his great, towering body and his handsome face, and approved of what he saw. "This, surely, is the Lord's anointed," he said to himself.

But the Lord said to Samuel, "Do not judge him by his face or by his height, because I have refused him. This is not the chosen one. The Lord does not see as a man sees; for man looks at the outward appearance, and the Lord looks into the heart."

Then Jesse called his second son Abinadab and made him pass before Samuel. He, too, was big and bold-looking; but the Lord made no sign to Samuel.

Samuel shook his head. "Neither has the Lord chosen this one," he said.

Then Jesse called his son Shammah. Again, Samuel shook his head. "Neither is this the chosen man," he said.

Jesse called another; and went on bringing his sons before Samuel until all seven had been scrutinized and turned away.

"The Lord has not chosen any of these," Samuel said to Jesse. "Are all your children here? Have you no other son?"

"I have one more," said Jesse doubtfully, "only David, the youngest. He is out in the fields, caring for the sheep."

"Send for him," said Samuel. "Bring him here, for we will not sit down and feast until he is among us."

So Jesse sent a messenger out into the green pastures to call young David from his flocks.

Samuel waited patiently. The Lord had said he would find a king among the sons of Jesse, and a king he knew he would find.

When he saw the boy leaping down the hillside and running swiftly toward him where he waited at the place of sacrifice, Samuel felt in his heart that his search was ended. David was young and vigorous and good to look at, and his fine, almost beautiful face was tanned and ruddy from his life outdoors.

They boy stopped in front of Samuel and gave him

courteous greeting. In his clear eyes and his bright, open countenance, Samuel could see the goodness of young David's heart.

"Arise," said the Lord to Samuel. "Anoint him, for this is he who shall be king."

Then Samuel took the horn of oil and anointed David's head in the presence of his brothers. The spirit of the Lord came upon David from that day forward, and the lad knew that some day he would rule all Israel under the guidance of the Lord his God.

But that time was not yet come. Saul was still ruler in the eyes of the people, and David was still a youth with much to learn.

Samuel left Bethlehem and returned to his home with a lighter heart now that Saul's successor had been chosen; and David went back with his flocks into the green hills that he loved. And again he sang:

"Thou anointest my head with oil! My cup runneth over.
Surely goodness and mercy shall follow me all the days of my life.
And I will dwell in the house of the Lord for ever!"

And David was happier than he had been in all his life.

But the spirit of the Lord departed from Saul, and an evil spirit from the Lord came upon him instead and troubled him deeply. He knew nothing of the anointing of David as future king; nothing of the shepherd boy of the tribe of Judah who would rule and whose sons would rule in place of Saul's own heirs; but he did know that the Lord had turned away from him for his pride and disobedience. Moods of black despair descended on him, and there was no one in his household who could help him.

He suffered long and terribly. Then, at last, his attendants thought of something that might ease his troubled mind. They went to the king, for they loved him and wished him to be well, and said: "We see that an evil spirit from God is troubling you. Command us, our lord, to seek out a man who is a skillful player on the harp. Surely it will come to pass that, when the evil spirit is upon you, he will play soft music on his harp and you will then be well."

Saul thought about it. Soothing music on a harp? It might be pleasant. Nothing else had helped his misery; perhaps music would.

"Do it, then," he said. "Find a man who can play well, and bring him to me."

"Jesse of Bethlehem has such a son," one of the servants said. "I have seen him myself, and although he is not yet a grown man he is valiant and courageous, as well as being a musician of great skill. Also he is wise, a young man both discreet and tactful. He is good to look upon, a comely person, and the Lord is with him."

"Then he shall play for me," declared the king, and at once sent messengers to Jesse with an urgent command. "Send me your son, David, who is with the sheep," the messengers repeated when they arrived in Bethlehem, and Jesse was proud that the king had sent for his son.

He called David from the pastures and told him to prepare for his journey while he himself made ready a gift for Saul. "Now take yourself and these presents to King Saul," he said to David, "and do whatever he asks of you."

David left Bethlehem with bread and meat and wine and traveled to the town of Gibeah. There he presented himself to Saul and gave the king his father's gifts. Saul looked upon him; and he liked the lad. To Saul's tired eyes the boy was good to look at and pleasant in his manner, and the music that he played upon his singing harp was soothing to Saul's uneasy soul.

The days passed and Saul came to love the boy as one of his own, for David was indeed wise and his music did much to ease the king's dark spirits. Saul therefore sent a message to Jesse, saying: "Let David, I pray you, stay with me, for he has found favor in my sight." Jesse was glad that David could be a comfort to the king, and he willingly agreed to Saul's request.

From that day on, David was always welcome in Saul's court. Saul was so pleased with him that he made the boy his armor bearer, which was a great honor for the shepherd boy who was destined to be king.

And whenever the evil spirit was upon Saul so that his heart was heavy with despair, David took up his harp and played his melodies upon it. Even though he knew that there would come a day when he would take the place of the man at whose feet he sat, he served Saul faithfully and with love. Saul was his king, and his king needed him. Saul's heart was eased as David made his harp sing between his skillful fingers, and the black despair fell away as the lad raised his clear young voice in songs that told of his faith in the Lord his God.

"I will lift up mine eyes unto the hills, from whence cometh my help.

My help cometh from the Lord, which made heaven and earth.

He will not suffer thy foot to be moved; he that keepeth thee will not slumber.

Behold, he that keepeth Israel shall neither slumber nor sleep.

The Lord is thy keeper; the Lord is thy shade upon thy right hand.

The sun shall not smite thee by day, nor the moon by night.

The Lord shall preserve thee from all evil; he shall preserve thy soul.

The Lord shall preserve thy going out and thy coming in from this time forth, and even for evermore."

And Saul's dark spirit departed from him, so that he was refreshed in his mind and strong in his body. The time came when he felt he no longer needed David and his soft and soothing music to be with him all his days, and he sent the boy back to Bethlehem to mind his father's sheep. He knew that David would come back whenever he was needed.

David sang in the fields as before, but with a new knowledge of what it was to be king and a new understanding of how privileged he was to be chosen by the God of Israel. His own faith grew strong and sure as he tended his flocks and waited for the day when he would be called to duty by the Lord.

"Make a joyful noise unto the Lord, all ye lands!" he sang.
"Serve the Lord with gladness;
Come before his presence with singing.
Know ye that the Lord he is God;
It is he that hath made us, and not we ourselves;
We are his people, and the sheep of his pasture.
Enter into his gates with thanksgiving,
And into his courts with praise;
Be thankful unto him, and bless his name.
For the Lord is good; his mercy is everlasting;
And his truth endureth to all generations!"

David and Goliath

✛✛✛✛✛✛✛✛✛✛✛✛✛✛✛✛✛✛✛✛✛✛✛

All during the days of Saul there was bitter war against the Philistines. Now once again the invaders from the coastal plains threatened to lay waste the land and destroy the cities. In great numbers, and with all their mighty weapons of war, they marched boldly into the land of Judah and pitched their war tents on a mountainside at Shochoh.

Saul and his warrior son Jonathan hastily gathered together the men of Israel and pitched camp on a mountainside directly across from the forces of the enemy. Between the two encampments lay the valley of Elah, and it was in this valley that the battle was expected to take place. Saul therefore drew up his forces into battle array and prepared to meet the foe.

But instead of an army, one man came out from the camp of the Philistines and cried out a scornful challenge to the men of Israel.

"Why are you arrayed for battle?" he boomed across the valley. "I am only one man, and one man only do I call to combat!"

Only one man; but he was a giant, and the men of Israel were afraid.

Goliath was the Philistine's name, and he was more than nine feet tall. Neither Saul nor Jonathan, in all their years of battle, had ever seen a man so huge and fearsome. He wore a great brass helmet on his head and he was sheathed in a heavy coat of mail the likes of which no man of Israel had ever seen before. Enormous plates of brass covered his shoulders and his legs, and there was scarcely any part of his great body that was not encased in armor. He carried a spear twice as big and weighty as any ordinary man could even hold; and a man walked in front of him bearing a mighty shield.

King Saul stared down the mountainside at the giant and repented that he had turned away from God and lost the prayers of Samuel, for now he was in desperate need.

There was no man in the ranks of Israel who could match the Philistine.

Twice each day, in the morning and the evening, the giant Goliath came down into the valley and roared his challenge to the armies of Saul, daring any man among them to leave the shelter of the trenches and come out to fight him man to man.

"Choose a man," he shouted, "and let him fight with me. Am I not a Philistine, and you the servants of Saul? There is no need for battle. Let one man come down to me!"

But there was no man in the camp of Saul who dared to fight him, not even Saul himself. The men of Israel watched the giant and listened to the thunder of his voice, and their courage melted.

Day after day Goliath stalked the valley and roared his message to the Israelites. "I defy the armies of Israel this day! Give me a man, that we may fight together. If he kills me, then we will be your servants.

But if I kill him, you will submit to us and be our slaves."

Saul trembled with dismay. He knew he had no chance against this giant Philistine.

Now David, at this time, was at home in Bethlehem minding his father's sheep. Three of his older brothers were in Saul's army, and one day his father Jesse sent him to the camp with supplies of food for his brothers and their captain. David left his sheep in the care of a keeper and went along his way with the corn and loaves and cheeses.

For forty days the giant Goliath threatened the men of Israel, and each time he came out to challenge them the Israelites were more ashamed. And yet they still could find no man to go out and meet the challenge, for none of them were giants.

David reached the camp and greeted his brothers. As he spoke to them a great voice boomed across the valley. "Choose a man! I defy you, men of Israel!" Now David heard the challenge, but he heard no answer. Instead, he saw the men of Israel turn pale with fear and run back to their tents.

"Did you see the giant?" they asked David.

"Does no one dare to fight him?" he asked in turn. "Who is this Philistine, that he should defy the armies of the living God?"

"Goliath of Gath," they answered, their voices hushed with awe. "For forty days he has defied Israel, and we have no one to meet his challenge. The king has said that if any man will go out and kill the Philistine and save us from our shame he will be rewarded with great riches and high rank, and the king's own daughter will be given to him as his wife."

Young David wondered at their words. It was not that he was interested in riches; but he could not understand why any man of Israel should be afraid of any Philistine, giant though he might be. He was not impressed by Goliath's size or armor, and he said so.

David's brother Eliab heard him talking to the men, and was angry and embarrassed. "Why did you come here?" he asked roughly. "And who is looking after the sheep while you are gone? I suppose you have come here just to see the battle!"

"I see no battle," David said, "only a man who puts us all to shame. If no one else will go, then I myself will fight this enemy of God's people."

Eliab grunted scornfully and turned away. To him, David was only a younger brother speaking proud words that meant nothing. But there were others among the soldiers who took him more seriously, and soon David's words reached the ears of Saul. Saul sent for him at once.

Looking at him the king saw a handsome, clear-complexioned youth, not yet fully grown; a boy of whom he had thought highly enough to make him his own armor bearer, and whose music had often soothed his troubled soul. But he had never thought of this poetic shepherd boy as a warrior. He eyed David doubtfully.

David spoke up. "Let no man's heart fail because of Goliath," he said earnestly. "I, your servant, will go out and fight this Philistine."

Saul smiled. "You, fight the giant?" he said gently. "You are but a youth, and he is a man of war with many years of battle behind him. How can you go out against him?"

"It is true that I have not fought men," said David. "But I have kept my father's sheep. And when the lion and the bear have come to take lambs out of my flock, I have gone out after them. And with my hands, I have killed the beasts and saved the lambs. This giant is the same to me as one of those wild beasts. The Lord delivered me out of the paw of the lion and out of the paw of the bear, and he will deliver me now out of the hand of this Philistine."

Saul gazed back at him. It seemed impossible, and yet the boy might have a chance. There was something about him that inspired confidence. He nodded slowly. "Go, then," he said, " and the Lord be with you."

But first he gave his own armor to the shepherd boy:

a great brass helmet, a coat of mail, and a heavy sword to wear about the waist. David staggered under the weight. He was not used to the uniform of war, and he found it clumsy. "I cannot even walk with this," he said to Saul, and took off the armor. "I can only fight in my own way, with the things that I am used to."

So he took up his wooden staff, and chose five smooth stones from the nearby brook and put them in his shepherd's bag, and he carried his leather sling ready in his hand.

He walked down the mountain slope to meet the Philistine. The giant strode toward him; and they looked at each other across the valley of Elah.

Goliath, like Saul, saw a slim young lad, but he did not see the courage in the boy's heart nor the sling in his hand. All he saw was a boy with a shepherd's stick, and when he spoke it was with contempt for Israel's puny little challenger.

"Am I a dog, that you come at me with staves?" he roared, and cursed David by all the heathen gods. "Come, then! and I will give your flesh to the fowl of the air and the beasts of the field!"

There was still some distance between them. The slight boy walked calmly toward the giant of a man and called his answer to the Philistine:

"You come at me with a sword and a spear and a shield, but I come to you in the name of the Lord of Hosts, the God of the armies of Israel, whom you have defied! This day will the Lord deliver you into my hand. Not I, but you the Philistines, will be given to the birds of the air and the wild beasts of the earth, so that all the earth will know that there is a God in Israel. All here shall know that the Lord does not save by sword and spear, for the battle is the Lord's, and he will give you into our hands!"

The giant roared with rage and lumbered forward to meet this impudent boy. Behind him, the great army of the Philistines watched and waited, sure that their champion would crush this slender, almost unarmed lad. Behind David, the men of Israel stood arrayed for battle; and Jonathan looked on and prayed.

David stepped forward and reached a hand into his shepherd's bag. Quickly, he placed a smooth stone in the sling. Then he raised the sling above his head, took aim, whirled it swiftly in the air, and threw with all his strength and skill.

The stone flew out of the sling, swift and straight as an arrow to its target, and struck the giant hard between the eyes. Goliath swayed and fell like a great tree toppled by an axe.

The champion of the Philistines, the giant Goliath, had been dropped with a sling and a stone!

On one side of the valley, the Philistines gasped with disbelief and horror. On the other, the men of Israel saw the man who had terrorized them for forty days struck down by a pebble from a boy's slingshot; and they thought they had surely seen a miracle.

David ran toward the gigantic fallen body to make sure the duel was over. He pulled the giant's great sword from its sheath, brought it down with all his force, and cut off the Philistine's head.

And when the Philistines saw their champion would never rise again, they turned and ran away in terror. The men of Judah and Israel plunged after them with great shouts of joy and triumph, and pursued them deep into their own land, even to Goliath's town of Gath.

After the forty days of shame and fear, it was a glorious victory for the forces of Saul. David's name became known and praised throughout the land of Israel. When the conquering forces returned from the slaughter of the Philistines, women danced in the streets and sang their songs of praise to Israel's two greatest fighting men.

"Saul has slain his thousands," they sang joyfully, and Saul was pleased. "And David his ten thousands," they sang on.

But this did not please Saul.

The Enmity of Saul

☀☀☀☀☀☀☀☀☀☀☀☀☀☀☀☀☀☀☀☀☀

Now Israel had a new hero, and all the land rejoiced. Even Saul, stabbed by jealousy and tormented with black moods, still loved the lad David and admired his courage. After the battle with Goliath he took David home with him to his court and would not let him go back to his father's house.

Saul's son Jonathan had seen young David conquering the giant and he, too, had great esteem for a warrior so bold and youthful and yet so humble of spirit. And it happened, as he came to know David in the palace of Saul, that Jonathan came to love his new friend David as a brother.

"Let us make a covenant," he said to David. "May the Lord be between you and me forever, that we may be true friends as long as we shall live."

David took his hand and clasped it warmly. "You

have my oath on it," he said. "We shall be friends forever in the sight of God."

And the friendship between the prince and shepherd boy was known throughout the land.

Saul himself was pleased with David and entrusted to him many important duties. David went wherever the king of Israel sent him, and behaved himself so wisely that Saul gave him command over all his men of war. David was soon accepted as a leader by all the people of the land and by all the nobles and attendants who served Saul. Everybody loved him; everybody praised him. As a warrior he was winning victory after victory, and as a man he was winning countless friends.

It was good for Saul that his bold captain should be so victorious in war, and at first he was glad that David was successful. But as time went by his jealousy grew within him and turned slowly into deep dislike. There came a day when he had seen enough of victory celebrations and heard too much of the women who played upon their taborets and sang their never-changing song:

"Saul has slain his thousands,
And David his ten thousands!"

On that day Saul's rage boiled over. "So they think he is greater than I, who am king!" he said angrily. "To him they credit *ten* thousands, and to me, only thousands! If he is ten times better than Saul, what more can he have but my kingdom itself?"

From that day forward Saul eyed David with growing hatred and suspicion. So jealous and outraged was he that, on the very next morning, the evil spirit from the Lord came on him once again and he acted like a madman before all the people of his house. David came to him with his harp and tried to soothe the troubled king.

But Saul could not bear the sight of him. David's very presence drove the king to greater frenzy. "I will kill this David. I will pin him to the wall!" he screamed, reaching for his javelin. With all his maddened might he flung the sharp-tipped spear across the room at David. But the lad was swift; he dodged and ran. Twice it happened; twice David moved away in time and saved himself from the flying javelin.

Then Saul became afraid. It was clear to him that the Lord had gone from him and was with David. And he began to plot other ways of disposing of Israel's young hero. He removed David from his post as commander over all the army and made him a captain of a thousand only, and then he sent the youth away from the palace as a gesture of his great displeasure.

"Now," thought Saul, "the people will despise him. And perhaps he will be killed in battle!"

But David was not killed, nor did the people of his land despise him. He accepted his demotion humbly and behaved with wisdom, for the Lord was with him all the time.

Saul was even more afraid. Within his troubled heart he knew that this wise and brave young man would somehow take his place, and he longed to kill David outright. Yet he knew, too, that Judah, David's tribe, and all of Israel as well, loved David too much to forgive his murderer. Therefore the king thought long and hard until his cunning mind produced another plan. Some time before, when he had been hard-pressed by the Philistines, he had promised his elder daughter Merab to whomever killed Goliath. Thus far he had not fulfilled his promise. Now he said to David: "Be valiant for me, and fight the Lord's battles, and you shall have my daughter Merab as your wife." And to himself he was thinking: "Let not my hand be against him; let him be killed by the Philistines."

David went out against the enemy once more and battled valiantly. But the Philistines did not kill him. And when the time came that Saul's daughter should have been given to David for his wife, Saul gave Merab to another man. Yet David did not concern himself over this insult, for he was a humble man and felt himself unworthy of being son-in-law to the king. Saul was very much displeased that David showed no anger.

Now it happened that Michal, Saul's younger daughter, was in love with David. And, according to the king's advisers, David looked with favor on Michal. This was pleasing to the king: here, he told himself, was a better opportunity to get rid of David. "I will offer her to him," he thought to himself, "and use her as a snare! This time I will make sure that he falls by the hand of the Philistines."

He called David to him and forced himself to speak pleasantly, although hatred was eating at his heart. "You shall have my other daughter Michal," he said, in his most friendly manner. "You will yet be my son-in-law!"

David still thought he was not worthy of any daughter of the king. Then Saul commanded his servants to talk in secret with him and persuade him that the king wanted nothing more than that David should marry Michal. "Speak to him thus," said Saul. "Say: 'The king delights in you, all his servants love you, and it is good that you should be his son-in-law. As for the dowry, it does not matter that you are poor, for the king desires no dowry. All he wants is that you kill one hundred Philistines.' "

Saul sat back and waited, satisfied with his cleverness. Now David would certainly be killed!

But David was not killed. With a group of chosen men he went into battle and killed, not one hundred, but two hundred Philistines. Saul's heart sank and his spirit despaired for now he had to give Michal to David as his wife.

His hatred blazed into an even brighter flame as he saw his daughter with this man he feared. She was happy, she loved David, and this was more than Saul could bear. He was convinced now that David was being guided by the Lord and had been chosen as the future king. Within himself, in his great fear, he swore everlasting enmity. To persecute David without mercy became his one desire.

The Philistines attacked again. Once more David

went out to meet them, and he fought more bravely and wisely than any of Saul's favorites. His fame continued to spread throughout the land of Israel, and Saul's rage knew no bounds. His dark mood descended on him even more heavily than before, and David, loving his king still, brought his harp into the presence of Saul and tried to ease his troubled spirit. When Saul saw David and heard the soft music that no longer soothed him, he picked up his javelin and again flung it furiously at the man he loathed. David nimbly stepped aside. The sharp weapon bit into the wall and hung there quivering while Saul raged and David slipped away into the night.

In his blind anger Saul sent men to lie in wait at David's house to kill him as he came out in the morning. But Michal heard of this and warned her husband. "You must go tonight, or in the morning you will die!" she told him urgently. So she let him down by rope through a window, and put pillows under his bed-clothes to make it look as though he was still there, sleeping. When Saul discovered this deception he was even further outraged, yet angry as he was, he could not harm his daughter.

Now David sought out Samuel and remained in hiding with him for some time. Eventually he came back, hoping to make peace with Saul, and went at once to his friend Jonathan.

"What have I done?" he begged. "What is my sin before your father, that he seeks my life?"

"I do not know of any sin," said Jonathan. "My father would surely tell me if he had a reason to want your life. But God forbid that you should die! Tell me what you want me to do and I will do it, for you know that I wish to do all in my power to help you."

It was agreed between them, then, that Jonathan should find out what Saul's feelings were and report his findings to David by means of a secret signal. The two young men again swore everlasting friendship, and Jonathan left his friend in hiding while he approached his father to sound him out about his intentions toward

David. He was hoping, too, that he could reason with his father and convince him that the shepherd-warrior meant him no harm.

But it was useless. Saul's anger blazed and turned against his son. "You son of a perverse, rebellious woman!" he screamed at Jonathan. "Do I not know that you have chosen the son of Jesse as your friend, to your own downfall? And do you not know that as long as he lives you will not be king? Now bring him here to me, for he shall surely die!"

"But why should he die?" asked Jonathan. "What has he done?"

In answer, Saul's face darkened and he flung his javelin at his own son Jonathan with a cry of fury. Jonathan stepped aside and the javelin missed; but he knew then that his father was determined to kill David and would let nothing stop him. In an anger almost as fierce as his father's he left Saul's house to tell his friend there was no hope of mercy from King Saul.

David came toward him from his hiding place.

"He has not repented," Jonathan told David sadly. "Go in peace, for we two shall be friends forever. The hand of Saul my father shall not find you, and you shall indeed be king of Israel, as he fears. Yet let nothing come between us, and may we always have our covenant before the Lord."

They clasped hands once again. Jonathan went slowly back to the house of Saul, saddened by the terrible enmity between his best friend and his father, and David went into the wilderness to seek refuge in the wild hills near the Salt Sea.

It was a time of wandering and persecution for him, for Saul would not relent. David was a hunted man. With no weapon but the great sword of Goliath, with barely any food, and with only a handful of loyal fighting men, he found refuge in the cave of Adullam, deep in the wilderness.

His place of hiding was not altogether secret. All his brothers and all the members of his father's house came to know about the cave of Adullam, and joined him there. All the men who were discontented under Saul, and all who were distressed by reason of debt or other hardship, gathered together and joined David in the hills. Yet not one of them, nor any of the people who knew where David and his band of outlaws had their camp, breathed a word to Saul. And Saul ranged desperately back and forth across the countryside with great companies of armed men, searching relentlessly for the man he hated.

Several times he came very close to David. More than once he inflicted dreadful punishments on people for not telling him where he could find his quarry. "You have all conspired against me!" he would scream. "Why does no one tell me where this man hides and lies in wait for me? Are you all in league with him?"

People died for David but David did not die. Hunted though he was, he moved safely through the wilderness from one stronghold to another while Saul sought him every day, yet could not find him, for the Lord was David's strength and safety. Saul's wild pursuit of an innocent man and his ruthless slaughter of David's friends caused the people of Israel to turn increasingly against him and begin to hope for his downfall. It was not only that they loved David, but also that they needed a king who would keep them strong against their enemies instead of stalking their greatest friend.

There came a day when Saul, in his never-ending search, did come dangerously close to where David and his men lay quietly in hiding. He knew that David was somewhere near him in the wilderness of Engedi, but he did not know exactly where. Weary from a battle with the Philistines and his endless pursuit of the son of Jesse, Saul went into a great cave to lie down and rest. While he slept, a silent figure came toward him from the dark recesses of the cave and stood looking down upon him. It was David; and Saul was in his power. He raised his sword and he brought it down swiftly and with one quick slash cut away a piece of King Saul's robe. But that was all he did, for he could not bring himself to take Saul's life. When Saul awoke and saw how he had been spared, he wept with remorse for his own wickedness and went away with shame and sorrow in his heart. For some time he gave up his murderous quest and left David in peace.

Then again the madness came upon him and he went out after David with a great company of men. And again David, who now knew the wilderness as if he had been born to it, saw Saul's forces from afar and kept his own men hidden while the king's men pitched their camp. In the dark of night David and his companion Abishai crept silently among the tents to the middle of the camp where Saul rested, his people pitched around him. Saul lay sleeping in a trench, his spear stuck in the ground beside him and a cruse of water near his head. No one stirred; no one saw the two men staring down at Saul.

"God has delivered him into our hands this day!" Abishai whispered triumphantly. "Let us kill him now, with one thrust of his spear."

David shook his head. "No, we must not kill the Lord's anointed. Leave him to the Lord; his day will come to die." And instead of plunging the convenient spear through the sleeping Saul, David pulled it quietly from the ground and carried it off. Abishai, disappointed but obedient, picked up the cruse of water that stood beside Saul's head. Then, as quietly as they had come, the two men left the camp taking with them the trophies of their visit.

Saul awoke next morning to the sound of David's voice calling to him from the hills and begging Saul to give up hunting him like a partridge in the mountains. The king looked about him and saw at once that his spear and water cruse were missing; and when he discovered that he had again been spared, his conscience burned within him once more.

He called back to David: "I have sinned! Return to me, David my son. I will do you no more harm, for my life was precious to you this day. Blessed may you be in the eyes of the Lord, for you shall do great things!"

There was truce between them, then, though David did not go back with Saul to his palace. They went their separate ways in peace, but David knew in his heart that Saul would change his mind again, so he went to a far place called Ziklag to escape the king. Saul did indeed change his mind and did seek David, but when he heard that his rival had gone so far away, he gave up pursuing him and devoted his declining strength to fighting off renewed attacks by the forces of the Philistines.

By now the Philistines knew that Israel had been weakened by the poor leadership of the moody Saul. They knew, too, that Saul's own subjects and the men of his army had lost faith in him. Therefore they massed all their armies on the soil of Israel, determined to crush the Hebrews during this time of opportunity. Saul saw their enormous forces and trembled with fear. David was not with him, old Samuel was dead, and Saul's own fighting spirit had been sapped by his bouts of hatred and madness.

Yet he rallied together his sons and his soldiers to meet the vastly stronger Philistine armies on the slopes of Mount Gilboa.

It was disaster from the start. Hundreds and thousands of Philistine arrows carried swift death into the Israelite ranks. Hundreds and thousands of Israelite warriors broke and ran down the mountainside or fell dead before the overwhelming onslaught. Brave Jonathan, fighting at his father's side, died with an arrow in his heart. Then his two brothers dropped to the bloodstained earth and died. At last great Saul, wounded almost to death by the enemy archers, fell upon his own sword and ended his tumultuous life. Now hordes of triumphant Philistines poured unchecked into the land of Israel. It was a terrible defeat.

When David heard the dreadful news he mourned for Saul as though the tortured king had been his lifelong friend instead of his sworn enemy. He and all the men with him wept and fasted until evening of that day, mourning for Saul and Jonathan and all the people of Israel.

In his sorrow David lamented with this song:

"The beauty of Israel is slain upon thy high places;
How art the mighty fallen!
Tell it not in Gath,
Publish it not in the streets of Ashkelon,
Lest the daughters of the Philistines rejoice,
Lest the daughters of the heathen triumph.
Ye mountains of Gilboa, let there be no dew,
Neither let there be rain, upon you, nor fields of
      offerings,
For there the shield of the mighty is vilely cast
      away,
The shield of Saul, as though he had not been
      anointed with oil.
Saul and Jonathan were lovely and pleasant in
      their lives,
And in their death they were not divided;
They were swifter than eagles,
They were stronger than lions;
Ye daughters of Israel, weep over Saul!
How are the mighty fallen in the midst of the battle!
O Jonathan, thou wast slain in thine high places;
I am distressed for thee, my brother Jonathan.
How are the mighty fallen,
And the weapons of war perished!"

Thus did David mourn for his lost king and for his good friend Jonathan, while the land of Israel lay kingless and in ruins.

The Triumph
and Tragedy of David

✛✛✛✛✛✛✛✛✛✛✛✛✛✛✛✛✛✛✛✛✛

David could not mourn long for Saul and Jonathan, for his land was sorely troubled and in great need of him. When he had done with weeping and lamenting he inquired of the Lord what he should do.

"Go back to Judah," said the Lord. "Go to Hebron, and dwell there."

So David journeyed back to his own land, taking with him his several wives, all the men who had been with him during his years of exile, and all the people of their households. The men of Judah came to welcome him; and there in Hebron they anointed David king over the house of Judah.

But to be king of Judah was not to be king of all Israel, and those who were left of the house of Saul were by no means ready to give up their claim. Abner, once captain of Saul's army, chose to suppport Saul's one surviving son as king, and succeeded in making him ruler over eleven tribes of Israel. Saul's son reigned for two years, but the house of Judah remained faithful to David.

Now there was long war between the house of Saul and the house of David. Abner fought hard for Saul; and David's nephew Joab gathered forces to destroy the armies of Abner. David gradually grew stronger and stronger while the house of Saul became weaker and weaker. When at last both Abner and the son of Saul were dead, all the leaders of the tribes of Israel came to David at Hebron. "Behold," they said, "we are your brothers. In time past when Saul was king, it was you who led the armies of Israel and brought us victory. The Lord then said to you: 'You shall feed my people Israel, and you shall be a captain over Israel.' Therefore make a league with us before the Lord, that you will rule us from this day on."

David vowed before the Lord to rule with all his might and wisdom, and the elders of Israel anointed him that day as king over all twelve tribes of Israel. Thus was Israel once again a united nation.

As king of all the land, David needed a great city for his stronghold. The fortified hill town of Jerusalem seemed ideal to him. It was occupied by the Jebusites, people of the land that had once been known as Canaan, and they boasted that their town was so strong that the blind and lame could hold it against any foe. But they were wrong; David drove them out and took their city easily, and from that time on Jerusalem was known as the city of David.

The city grew in size and wealth, and David himself grew powerful and great. He took more wives and concubines, and he had many sons. His fame spread rapidly to many lands, and their kings sent gifts to him. Hiram, king of the Phoenician city of Tyre, sent gift-laden messengers to David, as well as cedar trees, and carpenters, and masons; and they built David a royal palace. David thanked the Lord for his good fortune, for he saw that the Lord had indeed established him as king of Israel and that the Lord had exalted his kingdom so that the children of Israel might be great upon the earth.

But the Philistines were still strong in many of the cities of Israel, and when they heard that David had been anointed king of Israel they determined to destroy him. They marched their mighty armies toward Jerusalem and spread across the valley of Rephaim south of the city. David looked down at their vast forces and enquired of the Lord how he should meet this new threat.

"Shall I march against the Philistines?" he asked. "Will you be with me, and bring me victory?"

"You shall not go out to meet them face to face," said the Lord. "Instead, you must go around behind them so that they do not see you, and array your forces beneath the mulberry trees. And let it be that when you hear the wind blow through the tops of the mulberry trees, you will go into battle and attack them from the rear; for the sound among the trees will be a sign that the Lord is moving before you to destroy the Philistines."

David did as the Lord commanded him. When he heard the wind sighing through the treetops he launched a swift surprise attack that drove the Philistines out of the land of Israel and broke their power for many years to come.

Now Israel truly was a nation worthy of respect, and Jerusalem was a capital fit not only for a king but for the house of God. David, in his gratitude and triumph, decided to bring the ark of the Lord to the royal city. Therefore he built a small tabernacle to house it until such time as he could build the magnificent temple that he had begun to plan, and he gathered together all the chosen men of Israel to join in a triumphal procession to carry the ark to its new resting place. On that day he laid aside his kingly robes for the simple garments of a priest, and as the great procession wound toward the hills of Jerusalem he danced joyfully before the Lord with all his might. Trumpets, harps, cornets, and cymbals sent their exultant noises to the skies. All the house

of Israel shouted out their gladness and sang songs of
praise to the Lord their God; and the priests of David
set the ark down reverently in the simple tabernacle.

"O come, let us sing unto the Lord!" the joyous
    voices sang.
"Let us make a joyful noise to the rock of our sal-
    vation.
Let us come before his presence with thanksgiving.
And make a joyful noise unto him with psalms!"

With renewed faith in God, and the ark in their
midst, the people of Israel prospered mightily under
David's rule. The scattered tribes were now one people,
and in their new strength they successfully drove off
invading hordes of Ammonites and Syrians and
Moabites, until it was no longer necessary for David
himself to lead them into battle. Joab, captain of the
Israelite armies, was well equipped to handle the border
skirmishes that still took place. David ruled long and
wisely, and in his time Israel was great.

Yet David was not wise in everything he did. One
evening he rose from his bed and walked upon the flat
roof of his palace, and from the roof he saw a very
beautiful woman whom suddenly he loved. He inquired
after her and learned that her name was Bathsheba and
that she was the wife of one Uriah, a soldier in his own
army. Now David did a very sinful thing. He commanded Joab to send Uriah into the forefront of the
battle so that he would be struck down and killed. And
Joab did assign Uriah to the most dangerous part of
the battlefield where fighting was at its hottest peak.
Uriah fought valiantly, for he was a dedicated soldier,
until he fell beneath an enemy sword and died there
on the battlefield in the service of his king.

When word came to him of Uriah's death, David
married the widow of the man whose death he had so
cruelly arranged, and soon Bathsheba had a child.

But the Lord knew what David had done. In punishment to David he let Bathsheba's first child sicken and

die. David was grieved, but since his remorse for the terrible thing he had done was greater than his grief, the Lord gave him and Bathsheba another son, whom they named Solomon.

David had many other sons by other wives, and among them he had one great favorite whom he dearly loved. His name was Absalom. In all Israel there was none so praised for his manly beauty as this princely youth: from the sole of his foot to the crown of his head he was perfect in every outward way. His own pride and joy was in the long flowing hair that he cut only once a year, when it was heavy on him and became a burden.

David did not realize, however, that Absalom had dreams of being king, and that he was already making plans to win the people to his side, preparing chariots and horses and fifty men to run before him so that Israel would take note of him and see his splendor.

Thus displaying himself to be admired, Absalom made it a practice to rise early in the morning and go to the gates of the city so that any man coming with a cause to lay before the king would see him first. Then the handsome prince would call out in a friendly manner and say, "Where do you come from, and what troubles you?"

The man would answer, and explain why he had come to the city of David seeking judgment to settle a claim.

"Your claims are good and right," Absalom would say. "What a pity it is that there is no one appointed by the king to hear and help you! If only I were judge in the land, then every man with suit or cause could come to me, and I would do him justice!"

His kind words and friendly manner had great effect on those who came to see the king. Not only did he always find their causes to be right and just and express a warm desire to help; he also treated them with courtesy, so that when they wished to bow to him he would restrain them gently and instead take each man by the hand and graciously bestow a kiss. In this way did he treat all those he met on their way to David; and with his courtesy and kindness he won the hearts of the people of Israel.

One day Absalom went to David and said: "Let me go, I pray you, to Hebron to fulfill a vow which I made unto the Lord, for I did swear that I would serve the Lord in Hebron."

"Go in peace," King David said, not knowing or suspecting that Absalom was using his vow as an excuse to leave Jerusalem and pursue his own plans for the kingship. Indeed, David knew nothing of what his son was doing.

Absalom took two hundred men with him from Jerusalem, innocent men who did not understand that he was making use of them. Upon his arrival in Hebron, Absalom sent spies throughout all the tribes of Israel, saying: "As soon as you hear the sound of the trumpet, then you shall cry out, 'Absalom is king in Hebron!'" For here in Hebron, too, Absalom had many friends, and he intended to gather his followers at this place and quickly build an army. Thus the conspiracy grew strong. The people turned increasingly toward the handsome, well-loved Absalom, and supporters flocked to his side in Hebron. Soon they would be ready to attack the city of Jerusalem and force David from his throne.

Then, just before Absalom's preparations were complete, a messenger hurried to David, saying, "The hearts of the men of Israel are with Absalom your son." And the man told him what was happening at Hebron. David's distress was great. His favorite son, his Absalom! To war against him was unthinkable; to let him succeed in what he was doing would be sheer disaster. Scarcely knowing what to do, David decided that there was no way to save the city of Jerusalem from ruin but to leave it with all haste. "Arise!" he told the faithful followers who were still with him. "Let us flee, for we shall not else escape from Absalom. Quickly, get ready to depart, or he will overtake us here and destroy the city."

So the king left the city with his household and his men, leaving only the priests to guard the ark of the Lord, and a handful of women to keep the royal house in order. If the Lord was with him, David thought, he would return to the city of Jerusalem. And if not, it was better that the ark should remain in the tabernacle.

David and all the people with him crossed over the brook Kidron and gathered together in the wilderness. Then David climbed slowly up the Mount of Olives, weeping bitterly for the favored son who had turned against him and for the people who had conspired with Absalom for his downfall. Meanwhile Absalom, with his forces, entered into the city of Jerusalem only to find that it was almost empty. With his counselors he made cunning plans to seek out David and attack him.

Now David, saddened though he was, was still a king and still a fighting man; and although he did not want to harm his son he knew that he must stop this revolt or his country would suffer badly. Therefore when he had composed himself he led his forces by night over the river Jordan to the town of Mahanaim, where the people treated him with kindness and offered full support. There at Mahanaim he prepared for battle, dividing his army into three divisions with an experienced captain over each. One division came under the leadership of Joab, one under Abishai, and one under a man named Ittai who had volunteered his services to David after seeing the king's need. And David said to his people as they gathered in their strength: "I will go forth with you and lead you."

But the people answered: "No, you shall not go into battle. If we flee, it will not matter. Nor will it matter if half of us should die. But you are worth ten thousand of us, so you shall not either flee or die. Therefore stay here in the city and help us from this place."

"I will do whatever seems best to you," said David humbly, and he stationed himself beside the city gates. All the people came out by their hundreds and their thousands to hear his words and do battle for him. As Joab and Abishai passed by with their divisions he commanded them: "Deal gently for my sake with the young man Absalom." And all the people heard him when he gave these orders to his captains.

So the forces of David went out into the field against those who followed Absalom, and David waited at the gates of Mahanaim for news. The battle took place on the wooded slopes of Mount Ephraim and in the valley below, a vast stretch of forest land that was a tangle of great oaks and heavy undergrowth, and Absalom in his great confidence went forth ahead of his untried band of men.

The two forces clashed head-on, and one was far superior to the other. David's three divisions of loyal and experienced fighting men quickly got the upper hand over the poorly led and ill-advised army of his son Absalom. The battle spread through the vast woods and over the face of the country; thousands of men fell by the sword and thousands more ran panic-stricken through the confusion of trees and vines to lose themselves in the great forest. There was a great and terrible slaughter that day of twenty thousand men; and the people of Israel, the followers of Absalom, fell in great numbers before the loyal followers of David.

Absalom, in his vanity, had not thought to cut his richly flowing hair before going into battle. Here and there he galloped on his mule, rallying his forces and demanding victory. And as his men scattered in retreat he rode behind them, searching desperately for a way out of the dark woods. On all sides he saw the soldiers of his father David, and he whipped his mule to greater speed so that he might ride between them. His long hair blew high as he rode; and his frightened mule darted beneath the trees and ran under the low-hanging, clutching boughs of a great oak. And suddenly Absalom was swinging between heaven and earth, the lovely long hair of which he was so proud caught on the branches of the tree. The mule galloped desperately away from under him and left him hanging there.

One of David's soldiers saw him dangling in mid-air. Remembering his king's words he did not harm the prince but hurried to his captain Joab. "Behold!" he said. "I saw Absalom hanging from an oak by his long hair!"

"You saw him helpless and you did not strike him to the ground?" Joab said roughly. "I would have rewarded you with ten shekels of silver if you had killed the traitor Absalom!"

"I would not put forth my hand against the king's son for a thousand shekels of silver," said the man, "for we all heard the king charging you and Abishai and Ittai not to touch the young man Absalom. You yourself would have been the first to blame me if I had."

"I cannot waste time with such as you!" said Joab, for he had no such scruples. With three darts in his hand he strode off to the oak from which Absalom hung, still alive and struggling painfully to free himself. And Joab thrust the three darts into the heart of David's son. Then he blew his trumpet, and his men returned from pursuing the fleeing forces of Absalom. They took his limp body from the tree and cast it into a deep pit in the forest; and then they filled in the crude grave and built a great mound of stones above it. Now all was over for the followers of Absalom. There was nothing left for them to fight for; nothing left for them to do but run and hide.

David still waited at the city gates of Mahanaim for word of the battle. A watchman on the roof above him lifted up his eyes and saw a man in the distance, running toward the city. The watchman called out and told the king. "If he is alone," said David, "he must be bringing news." And he waited anxiously.

Then the watchman saw another man running. "Behold, another man running alone!" he called out. "But the one in front looks like Ahimaaz, the son of Zadok the priest."

"If it is Ahimaaz he is a good man," said the king. "Therefore he must be coming with good tidings."

Ahimaaz called out as he drew near: "All is well! The victory is ours!" And he fell down to the earth upon his face before the king, saying, "Blessed be the Lord God, who has delivered into your hands the men who rebelled against my lord the king."

The king had but one question. "Is the young man Absalom safe?"

Ahimaaz knew the answer; but he loved his king and could not bring himself to tell David what had happened. So he turned his head away from the kings gaze, and he lied. "When Joab sent me on my way," he said, "there was great noise and tumult. But I knew not what it was."

The second runner came to a stop in front of David.

"Stand aside," the king told Ahimaaz, and turned his attention to the second messenger. Ahimaaz waited with a sinking heart as the man Cushi gave his message.

"News, my lord the king!" Cushi began. "For the Lord has given you vengeance this day against all those who rose against you."

Again the king had but one question. "Is the young man Absalom safe?"

Cushi hesitated, choosing his words carefully. Finally he said: "May the enemies of my lord the king, and all that rise against you to do you harm, be as that young man is now." Then David knew that Absalom was dead. And instead of rejoicing in his victory, he mourned bitterly for his lost son.

The rebellion had been broken and David needed only to return to Jerusalem and reunite his people, for now they needed him more than ever before. But for days he covered his face and wept, and cried out: "O my son, Absalom, my son, my son Absalom! Would God I had died instead of you, O Absalom, my son, my son!"

And the great victory of that day was turned into mourning for all the people, for they heard how David grieved and cried out in his anguish: "O Absalom, my son, my son!"

The Wisdom of Solomon

++++++++++++++++++++++

Now King David was old and his days were drawing to a close. In spite of occasional rebellion he had succeeded in welding his kingdom together so that it was strong and worthy of respect. His life had been full; apart from his sorrow over Absalom he had but one regret, and that was the Lord's refusal to allow him to build a temple for the ark. David's hands, the Lord had told him, were too bloodstained by war. Some day his son would build the holy house instead.

He had many sons, but his wife Bathsheba had made him swear that Solomon would be king. Therefore when David felt the day of his death to be drawing near he saw to it that Solomon was anointed king, and he told all Israel what the Lord their God demanded of a king.

Said David: "The God who is the Rock of Israel spoke to me and said, 'He that rules over men must be just, ruling in the fear of God. And he shall be as the light of the morning, when the sun rises, a morning without clouds; he shall be as pure as the tender grass that springs out of the earth in the clear sunshine after rain.' Let Solomon be such a king, for then the Lord will be a tower of salvation and will be merciful to his anointed."

Then David called Solomon to him and spoke to him for one last time.

"I go the way of all the earth," he said. "Be strong, therefore, and show yourself a man. Keep the commandments of the Lord your God and walk according to his ways. Obey his statutes, and his judgments, and his testimonies, as it is written in the law of Moses, so that you may prosper in everything you do. Then will the Lord fulfill the promise which he made to me, saying, 'If your children take heed of their ways and walk before me in truth with all their heart and with all their soul, then shall there always be a man among them on the throne of Israel.' Moreover, you know who has been faithful to me and who has not. Do therefore according to your wisdom; show kindness to those who have shown kindness to me, and do what you will to those who have done evil."

So David slept with his fathers, and was buried in the city of David. He had reigned over Israel for forty years: seven years in Hebron, and thirty-three years in the city of Jerusalem.

Now Solomon sat upon the throne of David his father, and under him a mighty kingdom was established. In accordance with his father's wishes he dealt out swift, stern punishment to those who had wronged David in his lifetime, and also to those who had threatened his own throne at the beginning of his reign. But he dealt kindly with those who were loyal to the house of David. To forestall war between Israel and the neighboring countries he made alliances with foreign kings, the first and most powerful of whom was Pharaoh, king of Egypt. Solomon married Pharaoh's daughter, making her the first of his many alien wives, and he brought her to live in the city of David. Then he devoted himself to securing his city and his kingdom. With the vast wealth inherited from David, he began to strengthen the great wall around Jerusalem, to build storehouses for storing grain against leaner times, and to build both a fine palace for himself and a temple for the Lord.

But until the house of the Lord was completed the people of Israel worshiped and made their sacrifices on the tops of hills. King Solomon loved the Lord and walked in the ways of David his father; and he, too, sacrificed and burnt incense in high places to the God of Israel. Often he would go to Gibeon to make his sacrifices there, for Gibeon was a great high place, and there he offered a thousand offerings upon the altar of the Lord.

In Gibeon the Lord appeared to Solomon in a dream by night; and God said to Solomon: "Ask of me what you will, that I may give it to you."

Solomon was humble of heart, and he knew that he needed much wisdom and heavenly guidance to rule his kingdom well.

"You showed great mercy to my father David because he walked before you in truth and righteousness," he said. "And in your kindness you gave to him a son to sit upon his throne, as it is this day. Now, O Lord my God, I your servant am king instead of David. But I am like a little child and know not how to rule. I am in the midst of your chosen people, a great people who cannot be counted for they are so many, and it is for me to lead them. Give to me therefore an understanding heart to judge your people, so that I may know the difference between good and bad. For without God's wisdom, who would be able to judge so great a people as yours?"

It pleased the Lord that Solomon had asked this thing. He said to Solomon: "Because you have asked this, and not for long life or riches for yourself, nor for the lives of your enemies, but for understanding to make wise judgments, I will give you what you ask. I give you this day a wise and understanding heart, so that there shall never have been a man like you before you nor shall there ever be in time to come. And I also give to you that which you have not asked: both riches and honor, so that there will not be anyone among the kings like you in all your days. And if you will walk in my ways and keep my laws and commandments, as your father David did, I will also lengthen your days."

Then Solomon awoke and knew he had been dreaming. Yet he was sure that the Lord had indeed spoken to him in his dream. He therefore went back to his city of Jerusalem to make offerings before the ark of the Lord; and he called all his servants and attendants to a great feast of thanksgiving.

It was apparent before long that the prayer of his dream had been answered, for there came to him one day two women, who stood before the king with a case for him to judge. With them they had brought a tiny baby.

"O my lord," the first woman said, "this woman and I live in the same house. And a child was born to me while she was in the house. It happened then that on the third day after I had my child, this woman also bore a son. Only we two were in the house; there was no one with us but the babies. And this woman's child died in the night, and she arose quietly at midnight and took my boy from beside me while I slept. Then she laid him on her bosom and put her dead child in my arms. When I rose from my bed in the morning to nurse my child, I saw that the child I held against me was no longer living. When I looked at him in the light of dawn I found that it was not my son that I was holding in my arms."

"It is not so," the woman said. "The living is my son, the dead is yours."

"No, the dead is your son!" the first woman said again. "The living child is mine."

Thus they spoke in anger to each other before King Solomon.

The king listened closely, and then he said: "The one

says, 'This is my son that lives, and yours is the dead.' And the other says, 'No, but your son is dead, and my son is the living.' Therefore let us see which of you is telling the truth."

He turned to his guards. "Bring me a sword," he ordered. They brought it to him. "Now," said Solomon, "divide the living child in two, and give half to one woman and half to the other."

"O my lord, no!" cried the woman whose son it truly was, for her heart yearned for her son and she wanted him to live. "Give her the living child and do not kill it!"

The other woman said only, "Let it be neither mine nor yours. Let it be divided."

But Solomon had no intention of doing so cruel a thing. He had been testing both women, and one of them had failed.

"Give the child to the woman who does not want the child divided," he ordered his men. "By no means harm it; she is his mother, for she would rather give him up than allow him to be hurt."

All Israel heard of the judgment which the king had made, and their respect for Solomon was great. They saw that the wisdom of God was indeed in him so that he made judgments that were fair and wise.

Solomon ruled well over Israel, and he had peace on all sides round about him. The people of his kingdom lived in safety, every man under his vine and under his fig tree from Dan even to Beersheba for all the days of the son of David. God gave him much wisdom and understanding and largeness of heart, as much as the sand that is on the seashore. His wisdom excelled that of all the sages of the east and all the people of Egypt; he was wiser than all men, and his fame spread to all the nations round about the land of Israel.

It seemed that there was nothing that Solomon did not know; nothing that he could not explain for everyone to understand. He spoke learnedly of trees and herbs, of beasts and birds, of creeping things, and of the fishes of the sea; and there were some who said that he could even speak the language of the beasts and talk to them in their own tongues. Like his father David, he made songs about things of beauty under the Lord's sky, and he spoke three thousand proverbs to guide his people in the ways of righteousness.

And these are some of the three thousand sayings:

> Hatred stirreth up strifes,
> But love covereth all transgressions.

> A righteous man regardeth the life of his beasts,
> But the tender mercies of the wicked are cruel.

> The way of the foolish is right in his own eyes:
> But he that is wise hearkeneth unto counsel.

> A soft answer turneth away wrath:
> But a grievous word stirreth up anger.

> Pride goeth before destruction,
> And a haughty spirit before a fall.

> He that is slow to anger is better than the mighty;
> And he that ruleth his spirit than he that taketh a
>   city.

> A merry heart is good medicine:
> But a broken spirit drieth up the bones.

> Even a child maketh himself known by his doings,
> Whether his work be pure, and whether it be
>   right.

> A good name is rather to be chosen than great
>   riches,
> And loving favor rather than silver and gold.

And people of all lands came to hear the wisdom of Solomon, even the kings of the earth who had heard of his great knowledge.

Hiram, king of Tyre in the land of the Phoenicians,

sent goodwill messages to Solomon, for Hiram had been David's friend.

Solomon received his greetings gladly and sent back his own messengers, saying: "You know how my father David could not build a house unto the Lord his God because of the wars which were about him on every side. But now the Lord has given me peace so that there is neither enemy nor evil happening to prevent this work, and I intend to build a temple to the Lord my God. Therefore, I beg you, command your servants to cut me cedar trees out of Lebanon. My servants shall work with yours, and I will pay your men for help, for you know that there is none among us with the skill of your people."

When Hiram heard these words from the messengers of Israel he rejoiced greatly, and said: "Blessed be your Lord this day, who has given David a wise son over this great people."

So he sent to Solomon all the cedar trees and timbers of fir that the king of Israel wanted for the temple, and skilled workmen to help with the building of it. Solomon, in exchange, sent great quantities of wheat and oil for Hiram's household; and the two kings made a pact together that they would always live in peace.

It was in the four hundred and eightieth year after the children of Israel escaped from the bondage of Egypt, and in the fourth year of Solomon's reign, that he began to build the house of the Lord. And he commanded first that his servants bring great stones, cut stones and costly ones, to lay the foundation of the temple. In accordance with his wishes the stone was made ready before it was brought into the city of Jerusalem so that there would be no sound of ax nor hammer nor any tool of iron in the Lord's house while it was being built.

Now, though David had not been permitted to build the Lord's house himself, God had told him that his son would build it in his time. Therefore David had prepared many rich things and materials for the temple, and he had told his son Solomon: "Behold, I have prepared for the house of the Lord a hundred thousand talents of gold and a hundred thousand talents of silver; and brass and iron so abundant that it cannot be weighed; timber also and stone I have prepared, and you may add to it. Here also is pure gold for the candlesticks and bowls and basins; as well as onyx, and other precious stones of many colors, and marble in abundance." Then David had given to Solomon the pattern for the main building, the porch, and all the rooms, and for the inner holy chamber where the ark of the covenant would rest.

Therefore Solomon sent also for the riches stored by David, and proceeded to build the Lord's house according to the pattern laid out by his father. The outside walls were gigantic blocks of stone. The walls, floors, and ceilings of the temple were solid boards of cedar; and when the floors had been laid Solomon covered them with planks of fir. And the cedar of the house within was carved with knobs and open flowers: no stone showed inside, for all was cedar and much of it was carved into lovely, intricate shapes. Then Solomon covered the whole house, and the whole altar in the holy of holies, with the purest gold. And he carved all the walls of the house with figures of cherubim and palm trees and flowers in bloom, and covered them all with gold.

Solomon spent seven years in building the house of the Lord, and when it was done there was nothing like it for magnificence in all the earth. He brought in all the things that David had gathered and dedicated to the Lord: the gold and silver, the vessels and the candlesticks, the precious stones; and he put them among the treasures in the Lord's house. So ended his work.

Then he called together all the elders of Israel and the heads of the tribes so that they might bring the ark of the Lord into the beautiful new temple and give thanks unto the Lord for his many blessings. With their hearts full of praise and gratitude to God, the priests brought the ark of the covenant of the Lord to its new resting place. There was nothing in it but the two tablets of stone which Moses had put into it at Sinai, but it was the most glorious and holy thing in Solomon's temple.

And when the ark had been put in place, the glory of God filled the house of the Lord with so bright a light that the priests could not look upon it.

Solomon stood before the altar of the Lord in the presence of all the people of Israel and stretched his hands toward the heavens. "Blessed be the Lord God of Israel!" he said prayerfully. "I have built you a house to live in, a settled place for you to abide in forever, and a place where the ark of the covenant may rest eternally. Blessed be the Lord who has given rest unto his people Israel, as he promised. O God of Israel, hear your servant and your people when they pray toward this place, and may they trust and honor the Lord all the days that they live in the land!" Then Solomon blessed all the congregation of Israel, and held a great feast of thanksgiving for all his people.

When all the feasting was over and the people had departed to their homes, the Lord again appeared to Solomon in a dream by night as he had done at Gibeon.

"I have hallowed this house that you have made," said the God of Israel, "and I shall be with it as long as your heart is with me. If you walk in my ways as your father David walked, being upright and keeping always my commandments and my laws, I will bless you and your children forever with the throne of Israel. But if you or your children turn away from following me and go to worship other gods, then I will leave this house that you have built; I will cut Israel out of the land which I have given them, and much sorrow shall fall upon the people."

Solomon would have done well to heed these words of the Lord, for in them was not only a blessing but a warning.

The Division of the Kingdom

✛✛✛✛✛✛✛✛✛✛✛✛✛✛✛✛✛✛✛✛✛✛

After completing the house of the Lord, King Solomon devoted himself to further strengthening his kingdom and building up his capital ciity of Jerusalem. He had spent seven years in building the temple, but he was thirteen years in building his own palace.

It was a magnificent structure of cedar and great stones, with a throne of ivory overlaid with gold. Six high, wide steps led to the throne. On either side stood the gigantic figure of a lion; and twelve more lions stood upon the steps, six on either side. There was nothing like his glorious throne in all the kingdoms of the world. The drinking vessels of the royal house were of the purest gold, for silver was not rich enough for such a noble king. Solomon sent to sea a great navy that sailed to many far places and brought back to him much gold and silver, ivory and spices, apes and peacocks, and all the wonders of the world beyond the

borders of the land of Israel. Soon he exceeded all the
kings of the earth not only in wisdom but in wealth as
well, as the Lord had promised.

Now there was a queen of the land of Sheba, a great
and wealthy country on the other side of the Arabian
sands across from Israel, who herself had much wealth
and wisdom. When she heard of the fame of Solomon,
the wisdom given to him by the Lord, and the wonders
of his growing nation, she determined to visit him and
test him with hard questions. It was not easy for this
great queen to believe that Solomon could be so much
greater than she, and she wished to know if he were as
wise as she had heard it said.

So she traveled many miles across the desert from
her own country with a vast train of camels and attendants; and on the camels' backs were stores of spices,
gold, and precious stones, rich gifts for a king who was
already more than rich. When she came to Solomon she
talked with him of everything that was in her heart,
asking him many questions that she thought he could
not answer.

Solomon answered everything she asked, for in the
Lord's wisdom there was nothing that he did not know
and nothing that he could not tell her. She was amazed
by his vast knowledge, for it had seemed impossible
that any man could be blessed with so much learning
and with such an understanding heart. Each question
that she put to him was more difficult than the last,
dealing with great mysteries of nature, science, and
religion, yet Solomon's wisdom was without end and
he knew far more than she could ask.

With eyes wide open in wonderment she surveyed
the glorious temple he had built to honor the Lord, and
never had she seen such magnificence in all her days.
She gazed admiringly at the great cedar pillars and
overlays of gold in the house of the Lord, and at
Solomon's own throne of ivory and gold with the lions
on either side. She took note of his splendid chariots
and many stalls of spirited horses, and she saw the
great array of food upon the royal table. Queen though

she was, she was impressed by the fine manners of his multitude of ministers and servants and the richness of their clothing, by the golden goblets brought in by his cupbearers and by their costly robes; and the many beautiful buildings he had built for his huge family struck her almost speechless for their number and their elegance. Having heard so much of his wisdom and seen the wonder and glory of Jerusalem, the Queen of Sheba no longer doubted that Solomon was all that people had said of him. Everything she saw and heard convinced her of the extraordinary might and learning of this king who ruled his nation under God's command.

"It was a true report that I heard in my own land about your great deeds and your wisdom," she told Solomon at last. "But I did not believe the words I heard until I came here and saw with my own eyes. Now I know that the half was not told me of the wisdom and glory of King Solomon. Happy are your men, and happy these your servants, who are with you all the time to hear your words of wisdom. Blessed be the Lord your God, who delights in you, for setting you upon the throne of Israel! It is because the Lord loves Israel that he has made such a man as you king over these people, to make judgments and do justice."

Then she gave the king a hundred and twenty talents of gold, and very great stores of spices and of precious stones. In return King Solomon gave the Queen of Sheba all she desired and whatever she asked, and many more wonderful things as well. And so she turned and went back to her own country with her servants, and with even more riches than she had brought to Solomon.

The king's wealth continued to increase. He built towns throughout his land: cities to store his treasures and his crops, cities to house his chariots, his horses and his horsemen. He had forty thousand stalls of horses for his tremendous fleet of chariots, and twelve thousand horsemen to ride them and to drive them. Tax money poured in from the Canaanites still living in the land, and gold flowed in from the foreign cities with which the king conducted trade. His merchants brought not only coin but horses, linen yarn, spices, and silverware from the far-off lands, and his treasure coffers were filled to overflowing. Yet he easily found ways to use the money, for he was always building and acquiring sustenance for his huge household.

Thousands of Israelites were put to work as builders of his cities, and as soldiers in the armies that never went to war because of his agreements with the neighboring lands. Twelve officers were sent over all Israel to see that the king and his household were well provided with food, each officer making provision from his appointed district for one month out of the year. And Solomon's provision for one day alone was three hundred bushels of fine flour, and six hundred bushels of meal; ten fat oxen, and twenty other oxen from the pastures; one hundred sheep, as well as deer and buck and fatted fowl; and barley and straw for all his camels and his horses.

Solomon reigned over all the kingdoms from the river Euphrates to the land of the Philistines, and to the border of Egypt. All of them brought presents to him and served him all the days of his life. All the kings of the earth that sought his presence to hear his wisdom brought presents to him, too: vessels of silver and vessels of gold; fine wearing apparel and sweetsmelling spices; horses and mules, harnesses and armor, cedar trees and fir, and all manner of riches to make Israel the wealthiest nation in the world and Jerusalem its most magnificent city. The people of Judah, Solomon's own tribe, and the rest of Israel multiplied and became many. They worked long and hard but they profited by the wealth of the land. They were at peace, Solomon administered their national affairs with the firm hand that they needed; and they ate well, drank well, and made merry.

But King Solomon loved many women who were strangers to the land of Israel, and in making his political alliances he had married the daughters of a great many foreign kings. Beside the daughter of Pharaoh, he had married women of the Moabites, Ammonites, Edomites, Sidonians, and Hittites, heathen peoples whose women were expressly forbidden to the children of Israel. Of them the Lord had said: "You shall not take wives among them, nor shall your women take husbands, for surely they will turn your hearts toward their own gods." But Solomon did take them as his wives.

He had seven hundred wives, all princesses, and three hundred concubines. And, as the Lord had warned, they did turn away his heart. As he grew old he tried to please his wives by allowing them to worship in their own heathen ways, and with the passing of time they turned his heart toward their gods. Now Solomon, less wise than in his youth, built an altar to the evil Ashtoreth, goddess of the people of Sidon in Phoenicia, and worshiped at that heathen shrine himself. Then he built a high place for Chemosh, god of the Moabites, on a hill before Jerusalem; and then another for Molech, vile false god of the Ammonites. Thus he did evil in the sight of the Lord, building all these altars not only for his foreign wives but for himself. He still made offerings to the God of Israel three times every year; but far more often did he burn incense and make sacrifices to the strange gods of his many wives.

The Lord was angry with him because his heart had strayed away from the God of Israel. He said to Solomon: "Because you have not kept my laws and covenants I will take your kingdom from you and give it to your servant. For David your father's sake I will not do it while you live, but I will take the kingdom from the hand of your son. One part of it only will I give your son for David's sake, and for my chosen city of Jerusalem. The rest shall be divided from your house, from the house of David."

Now, though Israel was mighty and full of riches under Solomon's rule, there were many people who had become dissatisfied with the evil of his later days and with his extravagance. His own palace was even more magnificent than the temple of the Lord; his household consumed great quantities of food which the people had to provide; taxes were high, because of Solomon's costly buildings and the sacrificial edifices he erected for his wives. The treasury was being strained to danger point, and many people were forced to spend far too much time in building and repairing structures that were nothing more than luxuries. And so, when the Lord made adversaries to rise up against King Solomon, some were enemies from beyond the borders of Israel but one was a young Israelite named Jeroboam who had become displeased with Solomon's rule. The son of Solomon's most trusted servant, Jeroboam was an industrious worker and a mighty man of valor. Solomon had taken note of his fine qualities, and had placed him in a position of some power. And now the Lord caused this young leader to lift his hand against King Solomon and gather followers round about him who were also discontented.

One day when Jeroboam went out of Jerusalem the prophet Ahijah met him on his way; for it was in Solomon's time that the great prophets began to speak for the Lord. When the two men were alone in the field the prophet caught at the new cloak he was wearing and tore it into twelve ragged pieces.

"Take ten pieces," he said to Jeroboam, "for the Lord God of Israel has said that he will tear the kingdom out of the hand of Solomon and give ten tribes to you. Thus said the Lord: 'Because Solomon and his house have forsaken the way of the Lord to worship heathen idols, I will give Israel to Jeroboam. Yet I will not take the whole kingdom away from the house of Judah but will give one tribe to the son of Solomon, for my servant David's sake. And Solomon shall be prince all the days of his life, but after him his kingdom shall fall. Only one tribe will stay with his son, so that David my servant may always have a light before me in Jerusalem, the city in which I have chosen to put my name.' But you, Jeroboam," the prophet Ahijah continued, "shall reign over the ten tribes of Israel, and if you walk in the ways of the Lord, he will be with you. But walk with care; the Lord has said that the house of David shall be thus afflicted, but not forever. There will yet come a great and powerful king from the line of Jesse, David, and the sinning Solomon."

Jeroboam went on his way and pondered the prophet's words. And when Solomon heard about the prophecy he tried to kill the rebellious young leader, but Jeroboam fled into Egypt until it was time for him to act.

Solomon reigned for forty years and then died, a great but sinful king who had wasted his wisdom as he had wasted the treasures of his kingdom. He was buried in the city of David; and Rehoboam his son reigned in his stead.

By this time all the people of Israel had become thoroughly dissatisfied with their lot under Solomon, and they hoped for less harsh treatment from their new king, Rehoboam. Jeroboam came back from Egypt on hearing of king Solomon's death, and went with the congregation of Israel to petition the new king.

"Your father made our burden grievously heavy," the people said to Rehoboam. "Our work was hard and our taxes were exceedingly high, so that we had little for ourselves. Now therefore lighten the heavy load he put upon us, and we will serve you well."

Rehoboam did not answer them at once. He had grown up in ease and wealth and luxury, and he knew nothing of what it meant to be a king. "Leave me for three days," he said. "Then come again to me, and I will answer you." When they had gone he consulted with the old men who had served his father Solomon, and asked: "How do you advise that I may answer the people?"

"If you want to serve your people well," they said, "then speak good words to them and answer their request. What they asked was right and fair. Be their servant, and they will be your servants forever."

But Rehoboam was not pleased with the advice of the old men; he had no desire to be the servant of his subjects. He went to consult with the idle young men who had grown up with him. "How shall I answer the people who have asked me to lighten the yoke my father laid upon them?" he asked these wealthy, indolent young princes.

"Answer them like a true king, harshly and with price!" they told him arrogantly. "Tell them that their load has not been heavy enough, and that you will make it worse."

Therefore, at the end of the three days the king went back to his people and spoke roughly to them, ignoring the counsel of the wise old men and following the foolish advice of his spoiled young friends.

"If my father made your yoke heavy," he said to the people of Israel, "I will make it heavier! My father punished you with whips: I will chastise you with the lash of scorpions!"

There was silence for a moment, then a rising murmur of horror and rebellion. Jeroboam arose in the forefront of his outraged countrymen.

"What share do we have then in the house of Israel and of David?" he cried out, and the people echoed him with angry shouts. "Go to your tents, O Israel! Depart from Rehoboam, son of Solomon and king of Judah, for he shall not be our king! And you, the people of David and Judah, see to your own house, for we will have no more to do with you!"

So, hot with rebellion, the ten tribes of Israel turned their backs on Rehoboam and followed Jeroboam. Only the people of Judah and the tribe of Benjamin stayed with Rehoboam, unworthy successor to the house of David. The land of Israel was torn apart like the prophet's cloak, so that the ten tribes of Israel were ruled by Jeroboam in the north and the two tribes of Judah were misruled by Rehoboam in the south. There were two Hebrew nations now; and the division of the kingdom was the beginning of the end of the Israel envisioned by Moses, captured by Joshua, and united by David and Solomon.

The land and people of Judah still had Jerusalem as their capital, so that all those in the southern lands who loved God could still worship at the holy place. But under Rehoboam's rule they did evil in the sight of the Lord, building heathen idols and altars on every high hill and under every green tree. Bad times came upon them, and the king of Egypt attacked Jerusalem while the strength of Judah was at its lowest ebb. There was nothing to stop the Egyptian invaders; they stripped both the king's house and the house of the Lord of all their treasures, even taking away the shields of gold which Solomon had made. And these lovely, priceless things never were replaced with anything of equal value, for Rehoboam did not have the resources of his father Solomon.

The northern kingdom of Israel established its capital at Shechem, and Jeroboam resolved to lead his people well. But he was afraid that his people would go up and make their sacrifices in the sacred city of Jerusalem, the city chosen by the Lord, and then be persuaded to turn against their leader in rebellion to rejoin Rehoboam and the house of Judah. Therefore he gave his people something to keep them satisfied in Israel: At the two strategic points of Bethel and Dan he placed two calves of gold for his people to worship, saying, "It is too much for you to go up to Jerusalem to worship and offer sacrifice. Here, O people of Israel, are the gods that brought you out of the land of Egypt!" And both Jeroboam and his people worshiped these false gods.

Thus, in the eyes of the Lord, there was little to choose between Judah and Israel, the two parts of what was once the promised land. United under a strong and godly ruler, the twelve tribes might have remained a mighty nation. Divided, each kingdom was weak, and both halves were in danger not only from their outside enemies but from each other. Civil war raged between Israel and Judah for all the days of Jeroboam and Rehoboam.

Years passed; the kings of both Hebrew countries died and were succeeded by their sons, and they in turn gave way to other kings. Among them, there were good kings and there were bad; there were weak and there were strong; there were those who worshiped the true God, and those who burned incense to strange idols. Brief periods of peace were shattered by the noise of battle. War followed war, defeat followed defeat. In spite of an occasional lull in the shedding of blood and the worshiping of graven images, both north and south sank ever deeper into sin and treachery and degradation.

Elijah and the Prophets of Baal

****

Of the two countries, Israel's disadvantage was the greater. Though it was twice the size of Judah to the south and had three times as many inhabitants, its geographical location placed it virtually in the midst of enemies and exposed it to their marauding expeditions. Judah, on the other hand, was a compact land, protected to a degree by Israel to the north and by such natural barriers as the Salt Sea and the desert of Arabia. Also, once the riches of its temple had been plundered, its empty treasure coffers and barren land were not as tempting to an invader as the storehouses and rich pastures of Israel. And although the people of Judah periodically turned to the worship of foreign idols, they still had a true national capital and religious center in their city of Jerusalem. Israel, however, had no permanent capital at all, either political or religious, to bind her people together. Each succeeding king chose his own favorite city for his capital; and each king, no matter what his early intentions, drifted into idol worship.

Ahab, the son of Omri, chose Samaria for his capital and reigned over Israel for twenty-two years. Those were bad years for all Israel, for Ahab did more evil in the sight of the Lord than any king before him. As if it were nothing to him to follow in the wicked ways of Jeroboam, who had built golden calves for his people to worship, Ahab took to wife the heathen woman Jezebel. She was the daughter of Ethbaal, king of the Phoenician city of Sidon, and in all the history of Israel there never had been nor ever would be a woman so vicious and sinful. Jezebel was an ardent worshiper of the idol Baal; and from her own land she brought hundreds of heathen priests so that the religion of Baal might be forced upon her husband's people.

Ahab made no attempt to turn her toward the God of Israel. He turned, instead, toward her false religion with a burning enthusiasm. He built a temple to Baal in the very heart of the city of Samaria. In the temple he placed an elaborate altar; and at the altar he worshiped the false god of the wicked Jezebel. But one altar to one false god, it seemed, was not enough: Ahab made a grove of trees where other false gods could be worshiped, and he did more to provoke the Lord to anger than all the kings of Israel who had gone before him. More altars sprang up throughout the land, so that the four hundred and fifty priests or prophets of Baal and the four hundred other prophets of the grove were kept well occupied with their evil work.

True believers, those among the men of Israel who had remained faithful to the one God, cried out against the excesses of Ahab and the terrible wickedness of Jezebel. But Ahab did not hear and Jezebel did not care. She meant to force her religion upon the people of Israel if she had to kill the lot of them. And many of them did die. She began a dreadful reign of terror in which all the old altars to the God of Israel were thrown down by her priests and soldiers, and faithful

Israelites fell by the hundreds in a ruthless slaughter. God's priests and prophets ran into the caves and wildernesses of the land to hide from the wave of killing, and people who were not priests quaked before the onslaught and turned in fear to worship Baal. And so it was that the name of God of Israel was no longer heard in Ahab's court nor even in the land.

And then one day a strange figure with ragged robe and tangled beard and burning eyes appeared before King Ahab and gave him dire warning. The man was Elijah from the land of Gilead, the one true prophet with the courage to meet with Ahab face to face. His only garment was his shabby cloak of camel skin; his only food was what the Lord in his mercy provided in the wilderness; and he lived under no shelter but the trees of Gilead. And he was the first of the great prophets with the power to perform wonders with the help of God.

He stood before the weak and sinful Ahab and fixed the king with his burning stare. He spoke but once, and said: "As the Lord God of Israel lives, the Lord before whom I stand, there shall not be dew nor rain these years until I say there shall be!"

Then he was gone. To the astonishment of Ahab's court, it was as if the strange old man had vanished.

The word of the Lord came to Elijah, saying: "Get away from this place and turn eastward; hide yourself by the brook Cherith which flows into the Jordan. You shall drink of the brook while it yet flows, and I have commanded the ravens to feed you."

So Elijah went and lived beside the brook Cherith as the Lord had commanded him. It was soon clear to all that his prophecy had become an established fact.

Neither dew nor rain fell upon the land; drought and famine fell together upon Israel like a terrible plague. Ahab sought in desperation for Elijah to put an end to it, but Elijah was nowhere to be found. The Lord had safely hidden him and was caring for his prophet.

Elijah lived upon the bank of the brook Cherith and drank its waters. The ravens brought him bread and meat in the morning, and bread and meat in the evening, so that he always had enough. For months he lived there in solitude, and he drank what he needed until the brook dried up.

Then the word of the Lord came to him again. "Arise," said the Lord, "and go to Zarephath, which belongs to Sidon. I have commanded a widow woman there to care for you and give you food."

So Elijah left the dried-up brook and traveled through the drought-stricken countryside to Zarephath in the land of the Phoenicians. When he came to the gate of the city he saw a woman gathering stray sticks for a fire, and he knew that she was the woman to whom the Lord had sent him. He could also see that she was poor and that she was in deepest despair.

He called to her and she turned to him. "Bring me, I beg of you," he said, "a little water in a vessel, so that I may drink." She nodded. As she was on her way to fetch it for him he called out again: "Bring me, I pray you, a little morsel of bread, for I am weak with hunger."

She looked at him. "I cannot," she said sorrowfully. "As God lives, I swear I have not the smallest cake in the house but only a handful of meal in a barrel and a little oil in a jar. I am gathering sticks now to make a fire, so that I may go in and prepare what is left for me and my son. It is very little; we will eat one last time and then we will die."

"Do not fear," Elijah said. "Go and do as you said, but first make me a little cake from what you have and bring it to me. Afterward bake cakes for yourself and your son, for there will be enough. The Lord God of Israel has said that the barrel of meal shall not become empty nor shall the cruse of oil run dry until the day that the Lord sends rain upon the earth."

The widow went into her house and followed Elijah's instructions. And she found that when she had baked a small cake for the prophet there was still meal and oil enough to feed herself and her son. Every day thereafter, for many weeks and months, there was enough in the widow's house for three people to eat. The barrel of meal did not become empty, nor did the cruse of oil run dry. And there was no longer any question of the small household dying for want of food.

But as time passed it happened that the woman's son fell sick. So very ill was he that the breath went out of him and it seemed that he was dead. The woman's heart was broken, and in her grief she turned upon Elijah.

"What have I to do with you, O man of God!" she cried. "Have you come to me to remind me of my sins and punish me by killing my son?"

"Give me your son," said Elijah gently. And he took the lifeless boy from her arms and carried him up to the loft where he was staying. Then he laid the child down on the bed and called upon the Lord.

"O Lord my God! Have you brought evil upon the widow who has been kind to me, by letting her son die? I pray you, let this child's soul come into him again; let him be restored to life." Then he stretched himself out upon the child three times, and three times prayed. The warmth of his body warmed the body of the child and the breath of his mouth entered the mouth of the child.

And the Lord heard the voice of Elijah. The soul of the boy came back into the young body, the breathing became deep and regular, and the child revived. Elijah picked the boy up in his arms and took him down to his weeping mother. "See!" he said. "Your son is alive."

The woman ceased her sobbing and grasped her child with loving joy and wonderment. "Now I know you are a man of God!" she said, reverent with gratitude. "By this miracle I know that the word of the Lord comes from your mouth and what you speak is the truth."

For three years there was meal in the barrel, oil in the cruse, and drought throughout the land. Neither dew nor rain fell upon Israel, and King Ahab was hard put to feed his household and keep his horses alive. His messengers went far and wide in search of the missing Elijah, hunting at the same time for far-off brooks that perhaps might have a trickle of water left and seeking pastures that might yet be green. They found nothing. But the misery and hunger in his land did not persuade the king to turn away from Baal and back to God. As for Jezebel, she persecuted the followers of the one true God even more relentlessly.

The word of the Lord came to Elijah in the third year of the drought, saying: "Go, show yourself to Ahab, and I will send rain upon the earth." So Elijah went to show himself to Ahab while the famine was still sore in the land. There was every chance that Ahab, in his anger, would try to kill the prophet who had brought the drought upon him, but Elijah was strong in the knowledge that God had sent him.

King Ahab scowled at the ragged figure of the elusive prophet.

"Are you the man who troubles Israel?" he demanded.

Elijah shook his head and answered calmly, "It is not I but you who have troubled Israel, you and your father's house. For you have forsaken the commandments of the Lord and worshiped Baal, and thus you have made the trouble."

Ahab was astounded and mightily displeased. Yet he remembered that Elijah had spoken the truth three years before and he knew that his land was desperately in need of rain, so now he listened to the prophet in silence and laid no hand upon him.

Elijah went on speaking, and he proposed a test: "Send out and gather together all the people of Israel at Mount Carmel. Gather also the four hundred and fifty prophets of Baal, and the four hundred prophets of the gods of groves, those who eat at Jezebel's table. Then we will see which god is the mightier."

So Ahab sent messages to the children of Israel. Great crowds of people and false prophets gathered together at Mount Carmel.

Elijah stood before them at an ancient altar that now

lay in ruins, as did all the altars of the God of Israel in his time.

"How long will you hesitate between two faiths?" he began. "If the Lord is God, follow him and do not waver; but if Baal is God, then follow him."

The people answered not a word.

"You must decide," Elijah said. "See, I alone remain a prophet of the Lord, but Baal's prophets are four hundred and fifty men. Let them therefore give us two bullocks. Let them choose one for themselves, and cut it into pieces and lay it upon wood, but put no fire under it. Then let the heathen call on the names of their gods, and I will call on the name of the Lord. Whichever God answers, let him be the one God."

"It is well spoken!" said the people. But the prophets of Baal had nothing to say. They did not look foward to the test, but they could not refuse before the gaze of all the people. And there was Ahab, too, looking on and praying to his false god for rain to end the drought and famine. The challenge had to be met.

The bullocks were quickly provided for this strange contest between gods. "Choose yours first," Elijah told the heathen priests, "for you are many and I am only one. And call on the name of your god to put fire beneath your sacrifice!"

The prophets of Baal took their bullock and cut it into pieces

And they started praying to their god to send them fire.

From morning until noon they prayed with rising desperation for something that they knew within their hearts could never be.

"O Baal! Hear us!" they cried. But there was no answer from their idol: neither a voice crying out to aid them, nor a flash of fire to burn the pile of waiting firewood. Their frenzy rose and their voices became louder and more wild, and they leaped upon the altar which they had made to Baal.

All their leaping and their shouting had no effect on Baal.

"Cry more loudly!" Elijah mocked. "He is a god; and perhaps he is already talking so that he cannot hear, or he has other business, or he is on a journey; or perhaps he is asleep and must be wakened."

They cried more loudly and cut themselves with knives according to their strange custom so that blood flowed out and stained their priestly robes. But no mysterious fire came to light the woodpile underneath their bull.

Midday passed, and afternoon; and evening came. But still there was no answer to their frantic pleas: no sign, no voice, no indication that their cries were heard.

"Enough!" Elijah said at last. "Your god does nothing for you." He turned to the waiting people of Israel. "Come near to me and see what I do now." They came close to him and watched his every move. First he rebuilt the ancient altar of the Lord, the fallen stones which had been disused for many years. He chose twelve large stones, one for each of the tribes of Israel, and made them into an altar in the name of the Lord. Next he dug a trench around it, deep and wide; and then he cut his bullock into pieces and laid his sacrifice on the wood upon the altar.

The crowd watched him expectantly. But Elijah was not ready yet.

"Fill four barrels of water," he ordered, "and pour it over the dry wood and the sacrifice until it is so wet that it is impossible for fire to burn it." Four barrels of water in a drought was a difficult request, but they obeyed in silence. "Again!" he said. They poured a second time. "Do it a third time," said Elijah. They poured again. The water overflowed the altar and ran about it so that it filled the trench up to the brim.

"Now," he said.

It was the time of the evening sacrifice; Elijah came near to the water-soaked altar and lifted up his hands in supplication. And he prayed: "Lord God of Abraham, of Isaac, and of Israel, let it be known this day that you are God in Israel and that I am your servant, and that I have done all these things at your command.

Hear me, O Lord, hear me! Hear me, that this people may know that you are the Lord God, and that you have turned their hearts back to yourself again."

He looked up into the heavens, and the eyes of thousands followed his calm gaze. With a shocking suddenness, bolts of fire flashed down from the skies and fell upon the altar and the sacrifice. The water became a hiss of steam; the bullock, the wet wood, the drenched stones and the very dust itself went up in sizzling smoke and tongues of fire and the smell of the burning sacrifice rose toward the sky. The fire of the Lord ate down through the stones, licked up the water in the trench and left a ring of burnt-out soil. Finally it died out, leaving no trace of bullock, water, stones, or altar for the astonished multitude to gaze upon.

When the people of Israel saw this spectacular sign from heaven they fell upon their faces in awe. "The Lord, he is God," they cried. "The Lord, he is the only God!"

"Take the prophets of Baal!" said Elijah. "Let none of them escape." For he knew that this was his great chance to break the power of Baal in the land of Israel, and he meant to use it. So the people fell upon the sinful heathen prophets who had led them astray, and killed them all beside the brook of Kishon. When they had done their work that day there were no longer any priests to serve the evil Jezebel or minister at the altars of false gods.

Ahab looked on and said nothing, for there was nothing he could say. Even to him it was obvious that Baal and his priests had been completely routed and discredited by the God of Israel.

Then Elijah turned to Ahab on this dry and cloudless day. "Go now, and feast," he said, "for there is a sound of abundant rains."

Ahab heard no sound of rain, but he went to eat and drink as Elijah had said. Elijah himself went up to the top of Mount Carmel and cast himself down upon the earth to pray. One servant only waited near him while Elijah spoke to God.

"Go higher," said Elijah to his servant. "Look toward the sea and tell me what you see."

The servant climbed a high rock and looked into the distance.

"There is nothing," he reported to Elijah.

"Go again," said Elijah. "Go seven times, and tell me what you see."

Seven times the servant climbed to the lookout point and peered across the sea while the prophet prayed. The seventh time he came back and said: "Behold! A little cloud, no bigger than a man's hand, is rising from the sea."

This was the sign Elijah had been waiting for.

"Go to Ahab," he told his servant. "Tell him to prepare his chariot and hasten from here so that the cloud shall not overtake him."

The king looked at the tiny cloud, and doubted. But he prepared his chariot. The little cloud grew rapidly and came in swiftly from across the sea, and Ahab rode swiftly to the safety of his city while the heavens became black with heavy clouds and boisterous with wind. Great drops came pelting down. By the time King Ahab reached his palace gates the rain was falling down in torrents upon the thirsty land and running into small dry brooks that soon became wide life-giving rivers.

Now all the children of Israel knew that God had done what Baal and his sinful priests could never do. The Lord God had sent fire down from heaven, and he had sent the welcome rain. The years of drought and famine were over.

Elijah and Elisha

✠✠✠✠✠✠✠✠✠✠✠✠✠✠✠✠✠✠✠

Jezebel was so far from being glad of the torrential rains that she flew into a violent rage. When Ahab told her what the prophet Elijah had done, and how he had ordered her own prophets slain by the sword, she snarled with fury and sent a messenger to seek out Elijah with an ominous yet foolish message: "Let the gods destroy me if I do not take your life as you have taken theirs, by tomorrow at this time!"

It was foolish because it gave Elijah a chance to run for his life, and he did so with all speed. Fed and guided by the angel of the Lord, he remained hidden in the wilderness for forty days and forty nights. While he hid from Jezebel's cruel hand he became increasingly despondent over the state of Israel. Nothing, it seemed, had changed. Even though Baal's prophets were dead, there were always more where they came from; and Ahab and Jezebel still ruled. While they lived the peo-

ple of Israel would continue to be persecuted and
would never find the courage to break away from
Baal.

God let Elijah rest in a cave on Mount Horeb, which
was also called Sinai, but at last he spoke. First there
was a great and powerful wind across the mountains,
which blew against the rocks and smashed them into
crumbling pieces, but the Lord did not speak in the
loud voice of the wind. After the wind an earthquake
came and shook the earth beneath Elijah's feet; but the
Lord was not in the thunder of the quake. After the
earthquake there was a fire that swept through the trees
and left a blackened trail; but the Lord was not in the
crackling and the roaring of the flames. After the fire
there was a still, small voice calling to Elijah to come
out from the cave. When Elijah heard it he covered his
face with his rough cloak, for even he was afraid to
look upon the glory of the Lord. He went out to stand
near the entrance of the cave to hear the word of God.

"Elijah! What are you doing here? Why do you
hide?"

"I have loved the Lord God of Israel and done all
things faithfully," Elijah answered sadly, "but I am
downcast and discouraged. The children of Israel have
forsaken your covenants, thrown down your altars, and
killed your prophets by the sword. I, and I alone, am
left, and now they seek my life."

"You are not alone," said the voice of God. "I have
seven thousand people left in Israel who have never
bowed before the false god Baal. Therefore take heart,
and go from here. Syria will war with Israel; Ahab
shall not forever be king but shall lose his house to one
Jehu. And you must seek out Elisha, son of Shaphat,
and anoint him to be prophet in your place when you
are gone. For there are still good men in Israel."

Elijah took heart and left his cave in Mount Horeb.
He found Elisha, son of Shaphat, plowing with twelve
yoke of oxen in a field. Elijah went up to him and
threw his mantle over the young man's shoulders, a sign
both men knew to mean that Elisha was to continue the

old man's work as God's prophet when the right time came. Elisha begged leave to say farewell to his mother and his father; and he killed the oxen to give a feast to the people he was leaving. Then he arose and went after Elijah, and served him faithfully for all the days of the old man's life.

Ahab, in the meantime, had mended his ways to some slight degree. God therefore gave him victory in a battle with attacking Syrians, northern neighbors of the people of Israel who had been building up their strength throughout the years of the divided Hebrew kingdom. Under Ahab's leadership the land of Israel was temporarily spared from the doom that hovered over it. But Jezebel had not improved by any means, and once again she plotted with her husband to do a wicked and greedy thing. It was a small thing, by her standards, but it was thoroughly evil.

It so happened that a man named Naboth owned a vineyard that king Ahab coveted. The place was close to Ahab's palace, and the king told Naboth, "I should like to have it as a garden of herbs, for it is a pleasant place and near to my house." He offered money; he offered a better vineyard; but Naboth respectfully declined to give up the inheritance of his forefathers.

Ahab stalked back to his palace in a childish rage. He lay down on his bed, turned his face to the wall, and refused to eat. When Jezebel inquired what ailed him, he told her about Naboth's refusal to part with his family's vineyard.

"Ah, well, if that is all," said Jezebel, "it is easily remedied. Are you not the king? Arise! Be merry! You shall have the vineyard of Naboth."

And Ahab did acquire the coveted vineyard. The wicked Jezebel bribed two men, almost as evil as herself, to accuse Naboth of blasphemy against God and the king. And, exactly as she had planned, the elders and nobles of the city took the innocent Naboth out of the city and stoned him cruelly to death.

"Arise now," said Jezebel to Ahab. "Take possession of the vineyard of Naboth which he refused to give you, even for money. For Naboth is no longer alive, and a dead man cannot possess a vineyard." So Ahab took possession of it and strolled about it proudly, planning his new herb garden.

Elijah found him there.

"Have you found me, O my enemy?" cried Ahab, alarmed by the anger that burned in Elijah's deep-set honest eyes.

"I have found you," said Elijah grimly. "And I tell you now that I will bring evil down upon you and your house. Your sons shall die, and another shall be king; and for Jezebel also shall there be a fitting and most horrible end." And he proceeded to tell Ahab exactly what frightful things would happen.

And they did. Some time later Ahab was mortally wounded in battle with the Syrians, and he bled to death. The two sons who followed him to the throne died, each in his turn, by violence. The next king, Jehu, was indeed not of Ahab's house, for he gained the throne through bloody rebellion. And Jehu killed all Ahab's sons, all the great men of Ahab's court, all his kinsmen, and all the priests of Baal. When Jehu had done with slaughter there was not a man left of Ahab's family or followers.

But these things took place years after Elijah's prophecy, and the old prophet had other tasks in the intervening time. And he did not live to see all his words come true. There came a time when he was very old and had only one task left: to turn his work over to his young successor. The faithful Elisha went with him everywhere he went, learning from the old man and following in the ways of the Lord.

It was while Elijah and Elisha were together in Gilgal that the Lord made known his wish to take Elijah into heaven by a whirlwind. The two men set out together for Bethel and Jericho, where there were young priests studying to serve the Lord, and when they were along the way Elijah said: "Stay here, Elisha, for the Lord has sent me to Bethel."

But Elisha answered, "As the Lord lives, and as

your soul lives, I will not leave you." So they went
together to Bethel. And the followers of the prophets
who were at Bethel came out to Elisha and said: "Do
you know that the Lord will take your master from you
this day?"

"I do know," said Elisha. "Hold your peace."

And Elijah said to him, "Elisha, wait here, I beg
you, for the Lord has sent me on to Jericho."

"As the Lord lives and as your soul lives," answered
Elisha. "I will not leave you."

So they came together to Jericho, and here also the
young prophets spoke to Elisha saying, "Do you know
that the Lord will take your master from you this
day?" As before, Elisha answered, "Yes, I know it.
Hold your peace."

Then Elijah said again to him: "Stay here, I pray
you, for the Lord has sent me to the Jordan." Elisha
answered again, "As the Lord lives, and as your soul
lives, I will not leave you." For he knew very well that
the old man's last day upon the earth had come, and he
did not wish to be away from his beloved master at the
end.

So the two prophets traveled on together until they
reached the banks of the Jordan.

Fifty men of the followers of the prophets went after
them and stood a short distance away to watch. Elijah
and Elisha stood together upon the bank of the swiftly
flowing river.

The old prophet took off his cloak, folded it together, and struck the waters; they divided to leave a path
of dry ground upon which a man could walk. The two
men crossed the Jordan by this miraculous ford, and
the waters closed behind them.

When they reached the other side Elijah turned to
his companion and said: "Ask, Elisha, what I shall do
for you before I am taken from you."

"I pray you," said Elisha, "to let a double portion of
your spirit come upon me."

"You have asked a hard thing," said Elijah, "for that
is given by God. Nevertheless, if you are able to see me

when I am taken from you, you shall have your wish. But if you cannot see me, it shall not be as you ask."

They walked slowly away together on the far side of the Jordan, still talking. And suddenly a chariot and horses blazing with strange fire swept across the sky and came down low between the two prophets. A great whirlwind swirled around and picked up old Elijah, lifting him toward the heavens on the fiery chariot.

Elisha saw it. "My father, my father!" he cried out. "It is the chariot of Israel, and its horsemen!" Then there was nothing more to see but Elijah's mantle fluttering to the ground. Elijah himself was gone, never to be seen again. Elisha tore his clothes in grief. When he had mourned and prayed he picked up the old prophet's mantle.

The young men watching from the other side of the Jordan saw him strike the waters of the river with the mantle, and they heard him cry out: "Where is the Lord God of Elijah?" And they saw that the Lord God was with Elisha, who had seen Elijah when he was taken from him by whirlwind and fiery chariot, for when Elisha struck the waters they parted for him even as they had parted for Elijah. The new prophet of Israel crossed over on dry ground.

"The spirit of Elijah has come to rest upon Elisha!" said the followers of the prophets, and they bowed low upon the ground before him.

It soon was clear to all the people of the land that Elisha was a worthy successor to his departed master. He, too, was capable of filling empty jars of oil, of raising children from the dead, of feeding many with small supplies of bread. And on one great occasion he even healed an enemy of the people of Israel. It happened during a brief truce in the intermittent warfare between Israel and the people of Syria, the invaders from the north who frequently crossed the frontier to raid Israelite towns and carry off their inhabitants into slavery.

Naaman, captain of the great army of the king of Syria, was honored as a great man by his master and his fellow citizens. To him the Lord had given much success in battle; and it was due to him that Syria was free. Naaman was a mighty man, and a man of valor, but he was a leper.

Under his bold leadership the Syrians had brought many captives from the land of Israel. One of them was a little maid, who became maidservant to Naaman's wife. Both her master and her mistress were kindly people, and she soon came to love them as her own. Naaman's terrible illness caused the young girl much grief. Her heart was sore because she knew that he was bound to die of it, and die horribly, unless some wondrous thing occurred.

One day she went to her mistress and said: "I would to God that my master were with the prophet that is in Samaria! For he, the man Elisha, would surely cure my lord of his leprosy."

The woman told her husband Naaman what the girl had said, and Naaman began to feel a glimmer of hope. He went at once to his king and asked if he might seek out this prophet with the gift of healing.

"Go, by all means go!" said the king of Syria, for he treasured Naaman. "I will send a letter to the king of Israel so that he will help you."

Naaman went off with the letter, ten talents of silver, six thousand pieces of gold and ten sets of beautiful clothing to offer as gifts to the king of Israel and the prophet.

He brought the letter to the king, at that time a man who knew little of the Lord and even less of the prophet Elisha. The king of Israel read the letter, and it said: "When this letter comes to you, you will see that I have sent with it my honored servant Naaman, that you may cure him of his leprosy."

When the king of Israel had read the letter he tore his clothes in great distress. "What is this?" he demanded. "Am I god, to kill and make alive, that this Syrian sends a man to me to be cured of his leprosy? Take heed! For it must surely be that he seeks a quarrel with me."

It did not occur to him for a moment to send for the prophet Elisha. But when Elisha heard that the king was troubled by the Syrian captain's visit, he sent a message to the king: "Why have you torn your clothes in such distress? Send the man to me, so that he at least shall know that there is a prophet in Israel."

The king sent Naaman off at once. The Syrian captain rode up to Elisha's dwelling place with his horses and his chariots, and waited outside the door for Elisha to come out.

Elisha did not come out. Instead he sent a messenger out to Naaman, saying, "Go and wash in the river Jordan seven times, and your flesh will become healed and you shall be cured of the leprosy."

But Naaman, the rich and mighty, was angered by these words, and said: "I had thought that he would surely come out to me himself and stand before me, calling on the name of the Lord his God and striking his hand over the diseased places to heal the leprosy! But no; he does not come out to me, and he tells me to wash in muddy Jordan! Are not Abana and Pharpar, rivers of Damascus in my own land, better than all the waters of Israel? May I not wash in them and be cleansed of this leprosy?"

And he turned and went away in a rage.

But his servants knew that simply bathing in a river was no cure for his illness; it was the prophet's very words that he must obey. They followed him, and said: "My lord, if the prophet had asked you to do some great and difficult thing to cure yourself, would you not have done it?" Naaman was silent for a moment; then he nodded. "Then why not do this easy thing?" they went on earnestly. "Is it not even better than a hard thing, only to obey when he says to you, 'Wash, and be made well'?"

Naaman listened thoughtfully, remembering what he had heard of this great man of the Lord. Then he went down to the river Jordan and removed his finery. Seven times he dipped himself into the waters of the Jordan, according to the advice given by the man of God, and seven times he looked at his body that was patched and shriveled with the dreadful leprosy. And then he rose from the muddy waters for the seventh and last time. His flesh was as clean and fresh as the flesh of a little child; his skin was clear, and all his leprosy was gone.

He went back then to the man of God with all his company of men, and he stood before Elisha with gratitude in his eyes.

"Now I know there is no God in all the earth but the God of Israel!" he said. "I beg you, take a gift from me, your grateful servant."

But Elisha shook his head. Naaman pressed him eagerly to accept a present that would show the feelings of his heart. Elisha still refused.

"As the Lord lives," the prophet said, "the Lord under whose blessing I stand, I will take nothing from you for what God has done."

"Then allow me to take something," Naaman said. "Will you not then give me two mules' loads of earth? For I will build an altar to God out of the soil of Israel, and from this time forth I will offer neither burnt offering nor sacrifice to any other gods, but only to the Lord."

Elisha was well pleased. "Take all the earth you want, and go in peace," he said.

So the Syrian captain departed from the land of Israel.

The Story of Jonah

++++++++++++++++++++++

In time the great power of the Syrians decreased, leaving the lands of Israel and Judah free to fight each other. Elisha in his time had again and again helped the Hebrews to stave off enemy attacks, only to be rewarded by ingratitude and lack of faith. But the Syrians at last declined, and never again did they recover strength to terrorize the Hebrew kingdoms. One of their last acts of war had been to sack Jerusalem and inflict a staggering defeat upon the land of Judah. Israel had then taken advantage of this situation to invade Judah, plunder the temple of its treasures, and make hostages of their fellow Hebrews of the south.

This was the state of affairs when the great country of Assyria, once only a small part of the Babylonia in which Abraham of Ur had been born so many centuries ago, began to stir like a mighty giant and cast covetous eyes upon the neighboring lands. One of the

Assyrians' first acts as a fighting nation was to invade Israel and force the king and all the rich men of the land to pay vast sums of money to the Assyrian king Pul. Not long afterward the Assyrians marched into the land of Syria, took its capital city of Damascus and carried its people away into captivity, and slew the Syrian king. Yet powerful as they were, the people of Assyria and particularly of its capital Nineveh, did not believe in the God of Israel, and they did much that was evil.

Now at about that time, in the reign of Jeroboam II of Israel, there was a prophet named Jonah who was such a dedicated Hebrew that he did not care at all what became of the souls of the Gentiles of the world.

And the word of the Lord came to Jonah the son of Amittai, saying, "Arise, and go to Nineveh, that great city of Assyria, and cry out loud with preachings, for its wickedness rises up before me." For the Lord God wanted his word to spread to the people of other lands. They were his children, too.

But Jonah did not want to go to Nineveh, to turn the people away from their sins. In the first place the Assyrians were Gentiles, and in the second place they were Israel's enemies. Jonah very much preferred to let the people of Nineveh suffer and die for their sins, worshiping their heathen idols and becoming more wicked by the year, rather than go to their rescue by teaching them to turn toward the true God.

And so, instead of going to Nineveh, he went down to the seaport of Joppa and found a ship going to Tarshish, which was in the opposite direction from Nineveh and twice as far away. He paid his fare and boarded the ship, planning to hide out in Tarshish and escape the presence of the Lord.

But it was not possible to avoid the Lord, who saw him board the ship and knew of the rebellion in his heart. The ship sailed, and Jonah went down below decks to get some rest. When the wind rose he did not hear it, for he was fast asleep. But it was the Lord who had sent the wind across the sea, and it blew into a mighty tempest that churned the waters up to throw huge waves against the ship until its timbers groaned and its decks were awash with swirling seas. The little ship tossed and creaked like a toy upon the waters, as if it would shatter into pieces at any moment and take every man aboard down to the bottom of the ocean. The sailors were terrified, for they had never in all their lives seen such a frightful storm. Each member of the crew prayed earnestly to whatever god he believed in, but no man's god could stop the storm. In desperation they threw the cargo overboard to lighten the load so that the ship might bob more freely on the raging waters. But nothing helped. And Jonah, fast asleep below, neither heard the wind nor felt the wild heaving of the ship.

So at last the master of the ship went down to him and said, "How can you sleep at such a time, O sleeper? Call upon your God, so that he may think of us, and then perhaps we will not perish."

Jonah arose, but he did not call upon his God as all the sailors had called upon theirs, for he was fleeing from his God and wished to have no speech with him. Therefore the storm went on raging bitterly about the ship until it seemed that the battered timbers would surely split into a thousand pieces.

The sailors talked among themselves with great misgivings. "Come, let us cast lots," they said, "so that we may know who is the cause of this evil that has come upon us." For they were sure—and they were right— that someone on board was responsible for their troubles.

So they cast lots, and the lot fell on Jonah.

They said to him, "You, who have caused this evil to come upon us, pray tell us why! What is your occupation? Where do you come from? What is your country? Of what people are you? And why did you bring this trouble?"

"I am a Hebrew from the land of Israel," Jonah answered. "I serve the Lord, the God of heaven, who made the sea and the dry land." And he went on to tell them in all honesty why he was aboard their ship.

Then the men were exceedingly afraid, knowing that he had fled from the presence of the Lord and was being pursued. "Why have you done this to us?" they asked reproachfully. "And what shall we do to you, that the storm may be calmed?" For the waves were wild and thunderous, and the tempest raged with even more violence than before.

"You will have to take me up and cast me into the sea," Jonah said unhappily. "Then the sea will calm itself for you, for I know that it is my fault that this great tempest is upon you."

But the sailors, though they did not worship Jonah's God, were good men and they did not want to throw him overboard. They took up the oars and rowed with all their strength in a desperate attempt to race the storm and bring the ship to land. It was impossible; the strong winds roared and great waves rose like walls of water to crumble down upon the small ship and deluge it until it seemed that it must surely break and sink to drown the lot of them.

Then their cries of fear and anguish rose to the Lord God of Jonah, and they said, "We pray you, O Lord! We pray you not to let us die for the sake of this man's life. We beseech you, Lord: do not cause us to let the innocent die, nor blame us for their blood, for you, O Lord, have done as it pleased you."

And at last, when all their rowing and their praying failed, they took up the prophet Jonah at his own command and cast him forth into the sea. At once the wild wind died and the sea ceased from her raging.

The sudden calm was almost as terrifying as the storm. The men were struck with the fear of the Lord and his great might. They offered up sacrifices to the God of Israel and made vows to serve him. Thus had Jonah persuaded a boatload of Gentiles to turn toward the Lord without even preaching to them.

Now the Lord had prepared a great fish to swallow up Jonah as he fell into the sea, and the fish did swallow him without a bite. Jonah was alive inside the fish for three days and three nights, moaning with fear and praying to the Lord his God out of the fish's belly.

"I cried by reason of my affliction unto the Lord,
And he heard me," Jonah said hopefully.
"Out of the belly of hell cried I,
And you heard my voice.
For you had cast me into the deep,
In the midst of the seas;
And the floods surrounded me;
All your billows and your waves passed over me.
Then I said, 'I am cast out of your sight,
Yet I will look again toward your holy temple.'
The depth closed me round about,
The weeds were wrapped about my head,
I went down to the bottoms of the mountains.
When my soul fainted within me I remembered the
    Lord;
And my prayer came in unto you,
Into your holy temple.
I will sacrifice unto you with the voice of thanks-
    giving;
I will pay what I have vowed.
Salvation is of the Lord."

And the Lord spoke to the great fish, so that it opened up its huge mouth and spewed forth Jonah upon the dry land.

It was some little while before Jonah was ready to face the hazards of another journey. But eventually the word of the Lord came to him a second time, saying, "Arise, go to Nineveh, that great city, and preach there as I command you."

This time Jonah went to Nineveh. At least he did not have to go by sea. Yet still he went with resentment in his heart, for he hated Nineveh and all Assyria, and he did not want the Assyrians to repent and thus escape the wrath of the Lord. But the Lord had spoken, and Jonah had already had one unpleasant experience resulting from his disobedience. He was genuinely contrite.

Nineveh was an exceedingly large city housing many very wicked people. Jonah entered into the heart of it and began to cry out his message to the people: "Turn from your evil ways! Nineveh shall be overthrown at the end of forty days! Nineveh shall be destroyed! Turn from your false gods and believe in the Lord, the one true God!" Assyrians flocked after him as he strode along the streets; they stopped and listened with awe upon their faces as he talked in the market places and on street corners, and they gathered round him in all their numbers to hear his vehement, warning words.

So inspired was his preaching, and so urgent was his warning of destruction, that they came to believe in God and to repent of their sins. From the smallest to the greatest of them, from the beggar in the street to the king in his fine palace, they turned from their heathen idols to worship of the Lord. The king himself rose from his throne and took off his costly robes. As a symbol of his sorrow for his past wickedness he covered himself in sackcloth and sat humbly among ashes. Then he and his nobles sent a proclamation to all the people of the city:

"Let neither man nor beast, nor herd nor flock, eat or taste of any food, nor drink a drop of water. Let every man and beast be covered with sackcloth and cry mightily unto God for forgiveness. Let everyone turn from his evil ways and from all the violence of the past. If we repent, we may be saved. Who can tell if God may not turn his fierce anger from us so that we will not perish as the prophet says?"

And every man prayed, and put on sackcloth, and declared a fast. The days passed into weeks, and still they served God with all their hearts.

God saw their deeds, and how they had turned from their evil ways, and he forgave them for their sins. Jonah looked on at Nineveh and the works of the repentant people, and saw that the city showed no sign of forthcoming destruction.

Now God's mercy displeased Jonah. He was very angry. That the Lord could consider sparing the enemies of Israel so that they might attack his land again seemed terrible to him. Then, too, he had told the people of Nineveh that their city would be destroyed, and he did not wish to become known as a prophet whose prophecies were false.

He complained bitterly to his Lord. "I pray you, O Lord," he said, "is this not what I said when I was still in my own country? That is why I fled to Tarshish, for I know you are a gracious God and merciful, slow to anger and of great kindness, quick to forgive when people seem to be repentant. And these Assyrians, it is not right that they be spared!" He was particularly resentful that it was his own eloquence that had turned the people of Nineveh away from evil to earn the forgiveness of God. "Therefore now, O Lord," he went on, "I beg you to take my life away from me, for it is better that I die than live."

"Is it right for you to be angry?" said the Lord, then was silent.

Then Jonah went out of the city and made a rough shelter for himself. It was hot there, and extremely uncomfortable, but he wanted to see what became of the city at the end of the forty days. So he sat down in the small shadow of his shelter, and waited.

Nothing at all happened to the city. Jonah was outraged.

Then the Lord made a gourd to grow, and caused it to become tall and large so that its leaves would shelter Jonah from the blazing sun. And Jonah was very glad of the shady shelter of its great green leaves, so much better than the crude roof he had made for himself. But early on the following morning God sent a worm to gnaw at the plant's heart, and the cool green leaves began to wither. When the sun rose there was nothing but a limp, dead plant to shield the prophet from its rays; and as the day wore on God sent a violent east wind that brought with it a terrible heat. The sun beat down upon the head of Jonah with such terrible, burning force that he fainted under its blaze, and when he recovered consciousness he wished again that he were dead. "It is better," he said mournfully, "for me to die than live."

"Is it right for you to be so angry about the gourd?" God asked his narrow-minded prophet.

"Yes, it is right for me to be angry, even unto death," said Jonah. "For why should this plant with its green leaves die? What has it done? And why should that wicked city be spared?"

Then said the Lord: "You have had pity on the gourd which was of use to you, though you neither planted it nor made it grow. It came up in a night, and it perished in a night, a mere plant that knows nothing and is nothing. Yet you wished it spared. Therefore why should I not spare Nineveh, that great city in which there are one hundred and twenty thousand people, among them many little children, and also many herds and flocks? And all of them not knowing what is right from wrong until it is told to them?"

And thus did Jonah learn a lesson from a dead plant and a living city. All men, all women, and all children are beloved by the Lord whether they be Jew or Gentile, if they will listen to his words and choose to follow God.

By the Rivers
of Babylon

****

The people of Assyria learned their lesson well, so well that they grew great and strong while Israel became weak and sinful.

Under King Hoshea the Israelites broke every commandment of the Lord and committed every sin of idol worship. And because of these sins the Lord permitted King Sargon of Assyria to sweep down upon Israel, capture its capital city of Samaria, and utterly destroy Israel as a nation. Then King Sargon, to make quite sure that this conquered people would never rise again, carried thousands upon thousands of them into exile in Assyria. All the leaders, all the nobles, all the few remaining wise men, all those who might have rallied their countrymen to revolt against their Assyrian masters were driven from Israel to Assyria, where they scattered like dry leaves in the wind.

Only a few Israelites, the poorest, most humble, and

the least in learning, were permitted to remain in their ravaged land. The victorious Sargon looked upon his captive land and decided that it was not good to leave the cities empty and the fields untended. Therefore he sent families from Babylon and other heathen people of the east to take the place of those who had been transported forcibly to Assyria. In time the few remaining Hebrews married among the heathens in their midst, and a new half-heathen, half-godly race resulted from the union. Its people became known as Samaritans, and because they were of mixed descent they came to be regarded with contempt by certain other peoples who themselves had little, if any, reason to feel superior.

As for the Israelites held captive in Assyria, they were allowed a measure of freedom that was more than they were capable of handling. Instead of uniting, they parted; instead of becoming a great new group within the alien land, they separated and dispersed into the far reaches of Assyria. Never again did they come together as a nation, and never again did they return to the land of their forefathers. From the day of their banishment until this very day they have been referred to only as the Ten Lost Tribes of Israel. For they are lost indeed: no one knows what has become of them.

Apart from the mere handful of Israelites left in and around Samaria, only the peoples of the land of Judah were left of the twelve tribes which had once been united into the one great nation called Israel.

The little, shrinking land of Judah struggled on as a nation for more than a century after the fall of Israel. Surrounded by enemies, it sometimes lost great bites of land to foreign armies, and sometimes it even succeeded in biting back and retrieving some of its lost soil. One or two of its rulers were upright, God-fearing men who tried to lead their people in the paths of righteousness. Once in a while, when they listened to the counsel of the prophets of the Lord, these kings did prevail upon their people to turn back to God, and at such times the land of Judah knew victory and prosperity. But there were not enough God-fearing kings.

Now it happened, in the reign of Hezekiah over Judah, that King Sargon of Assyria died. Sennacherib became Assyrian king in his stead and launched what promised to be an overwhelming attack against Jerusalem. But Isaiah the prophet interceded with the Lord his God so that the city held, and Sennacherib departed in defeat after a strange disease had laid low his forces.

Judah's fortunes waxed and waned. As the years passed, great changes began to take place in the country first known as Mesopotamia, then as Babylonia, and next as the Assyria of Sargon and Sennacherib. Within the land two mighty powers were constantly battling for supremacy: the Babylonians, also known as the Chaldeans, and the Assyrians. Under Sargon and several of the kings who followed him, the Assyrian empire reached great heights of might and splendor, but eventually the Babylonians regained the great power they had known centuries before. They revolted against their Assyrian masters, destroyed the city of Nineveh, and built up a new and even greater Babylonian empire. Nebuchadnezzar, the powerful, became king in Babylon. Thus the Chaldeans, or Babylonians, achieved supremacy over the Assyrians, and began to look around for other fields to conquer.

In the land of Judah the good kings had gone their way, giving place to those who were weak and sinful. Prophets and warnings came and went: Micha, Nahum, Habakkuh, Zephaniah, Jeremiah, and Ezekiel all tried to persuade their wayward people that they were heading for disaster, but to little avail. Some helped to stave off trouble, others prophesied inescapable doom, yet Judah learned no lesson from their words. Few men even listened.

Now the end came for the land of Judah.

King Nebuchadnezzar of Babylon attacked the city of Jerusalem with his vast army of Chaldean soldiers. They sacked and burned the city, carried away the treasures of the temple, and left the temple itself in ruins. And they took the king of Judah in chains with

them to Babylon, and drove his people after him into
captivity. Only a few remained amidst the crumbled
stones that had been the city of Jerusalem. All the
rest—the king's family, all the princes, all the nobles,
all the wise men, all the young men of great promise, all
the best among the people of the land—were made
captives in the city of Babylon. The Chaldeans called
their captives Jews because they had taken them from
Judah, and since then all the people of the Hebrew
race, all the descendants of Abraham, Isaac, and Jacob
who was Israel, have been known as Jews.

In their captivity the Jews mourned for their lost city
of Jerusalem. And they lamented:

"How lonely sits the city that once was full of people!
How like a widow she has become, that was great
    among the nations.
And a princess among the provinces.
Now she is a vassal.
She weeps sadly at night, and her tears are on her
    cheeks.
Among all her lovers she has none to comfort her."

And they sang sad songs for themselves also as they
endured their captivity in the beautiful city of Babylon:

"By the rivers of Babylon,
There we sat down, yea, we wept,
When we remembered Zion."

Yet Nebuchadnezzar was not a cruel king compared
with others of his times, and he treated his captive
people well. As soon as his conquest of Judah was
complete he gave orders to the master of his household
to select certain of the finest young men among the
captives so that they might be taught the language and
sciences of the Chaldean people. "Choose from the
king's family, and of the princes," he ordered. "Look
for those of good health and pleasing countenance;

young men who are skillful in wisdom, cunning in knowledge, and able to learn."

His servant made a careful choice. And among those chosen were four young men who were not only wise but faithful to their Lord. Their names were Daniel, Shadrac, Meshach, and Abednego.

The king in his generosity served them with good food and wines from his own table, so that they would be well nourished and grow strong to serve him. But Daniel and his three friends were forbidden by the laws of their religion to eat such foods, and Daniel requested of the master of the household that they be supplied with simpler fare.

Now the master of the household had taken a great liking to Daniel, and therefore he said: "I fear my lord the king, who has given orders regarding your food and drink, will be much displeased. When you stand before him with the other children of your sort, he will be greatly angered if you are pale of face and unhealthy in appearance. The king will have my head if you do not look as strong and well as all the rest."

"Try us for ten days, I beg you," Daniel said. "Let us have beans and lentils to eat and only water to drink. Then look at us, and also at those who eat the food from the king's own table, and deal with us according to what you see."

So the king's man agreed to this request, and for ten days he allowed the four young men to eat the plain foods they had asked for. And at the end of that time he saw that they were fairer of face and stronger in body than all the young men who ate the king's meat and drank wine from the royal table. Therefore he took the meat and wine away and gave them instead the foods requested by Daniel.

As for the four young men, God gave them knowledge and skill in all learning and wisdom, so that they quickly learned the sciences of the Chaldeans and mastered the Chaldean language. And to Daniel, God gave understanding of dreams and visions.

When they had completed three years of study the

king sent for the young Jews chosen for training, and he talked with them for many hours. Among them, Nebuchadnezzar found none like Daniel, Shadrach, Meshach, and Abednego. In matters of wisdom and understanding they were ten times better than the magicians and astrologers in the king's own realm.

Now it happened some time later that Nebuchadnezzar dreamed strange dreams that broke his sleep and left his spirit sorely troubled. He sent for the astrologers, the magicians, and the sorcerers among his people and demanded that they help him. "I have dreamed a dream that troubles me," he said, "but I do not remember what it was. You are magicians; you tell me what I dreamed, and what it means."

"O king," they answered, "we cannot tell you the meaning until you tell us what you dreamed."

"I have told you, the thing is gone from me!" the king said angrily. "Answer me, and you will be rewarded. If you do not, you will be cut in pieces!"

"But we cannot answer," they protested. "Let the king but tell his servants the dream, and we will show the interpretation of it."

The king's rage was mounting rapidly. "How will you be able to interpret it if you are not even able to tell me what it was? If you tell it to me I will believe your interpretation. But if you will not make it known to me, there is but one decree for you!"

The Chaldean sorcerers shook their heads. "There is not a man on earth, neither magician nor astrologer, who can answer such a thing," they said. "Nor is there any other king, lord, or ruler on this earth who would ask so rare a thing of his magicians. Only the gods can answer you!"

"Then you must die!" said the king, now wild with fury. "Every wise man in this land shall die!"

Now Daniel was a wise man, and thus he also was in danger though the king had not asked for his advice in the matter of the dream. When he heard the king's decree he begged for time, and with his friends he prayed to God for help. And the secret of the king's dream was revealed to Daniel in a night vision. He went quickly to the king before any of the wise men in the kingdom could be slain.

"And you are able to make known the dream to me?" the king demanded.

"I am able," Daniel answered. "Know first, O king, that no wise man, astrologer, magician, or soothsayer can show the secret which the king demanded. But there is a God in heaven who reveals such secrets, and who will make known to you what shall happen in the future. This is what you dreamed, O king."

The king listened closely so as to miss no word.

"The God of my fathers," Daniel said, "has made known to me that in your dream you saw a great image whose brightness was excellent and whose form was terrible to see. This image's head was of fine gold, his breast and arms of silver, his belly and his thighs of brass, his feet part iron and partly clay.

"As you watched a great stone rolled against the feet of this fearsome image and broke the feet of iron and clay. And then the whole image shattered. The iron, the clay, the brass, the silver, and the gold became as dust, and the wind carried them away so that they were found no more. The stone that broke the image remained. It grew, until it became a great mountain that filled the earth."

At last the king remembered. That, indeed, had been his dream. "Now the meaning," he demanded.

"This is the interpretation," Daniel said. "You are the head of gold, a king of power and strength and glory, ruler of the greatest kingdom now upon this earth. After you will arise a lesser kingdom, one of silver; and then a third kingdom of brass, which shall rule over all the earth. Then there will be a fourth, a kingdom of iron that shall be strong in the beginning but will become as weak as clay.

"And in the days of these kings the God of heaven will set up a kingdom which can never be destroyed. It will fill the earth, and destroy all other kingdoms, and it will stand forever. That, O king, is the dream God sent to you, and that is the interpretation."

The king was amazed, but he believed in Daniel's words. "Of a truth," he said, "your God is indeed a God of gods, and a Lord of kings, and a revealer of secrets, seeing that he has given to you the power to reveal this secret."

Then the king gave Daniel many gifts and made him a great man in the land, setting him up as ruler over the whole province of Babylon and as chief of all the wise men. And at Daniel's request, the king gave Shadrach, Meshach, and Abednego much power in the affairs of Babylon.

All went well for many years. Nebuchadnezzar became great in conquest and in might. His power grew, his riches grew, his kingdom grew, and his pride grew also.

Forgetting all about the God of gods and the Lord of kings, he made a massive image of gold and ordered all the captains, judges, treasurers, counselors, sheriffs, and rulers of his provinces to come to the dedication ceremony and bow down to the golden idol he had made. And a herald cried aloud: "O people of all nations and all languages, to all of you it is commanded that when you hear the sound of the cornet, flute, harp, dulcimer, and all kinds of music, you will fall down and worship the golden image that Nebuchadnezzar the king has set up! And whoever does not fall down and worship shall be cast into the midst of a burning, fiery furnace."

When the music sounded all the officers and all the people of all nations and all languages fell down and worshiped the golden idol of their king. Daniel was not there, for he had business affairs elsewhere in the land, but his three friends saw the vast image on the plain. Their own hearts, not the herald or the king, told them what to do.

Then certain Chaldeans went to Nebuchadnezzar and accused the Jews. "O king, live forever!" they began. "You, O king, made a decree that when the music sounded every man must bow down and worship the golden image or be thrown into the midst of a burning, fiery furnace. Now there are certain Jews whom you have set over the affairs of the province of Babylon, whose names are Shadrach, Meshach, and Abednego. These men, O king, did not obey. They do not serve your gods, nor do they worship the golden image which you have set up."

Then Nebuchadnezzar, outraged and furious, commanded the three Jews to be brought before him. When he saw their calm, wise faces, his anger cooled slightly and he spoke in almost reasonable tones.

"Is it true, Shadrach, Meshach, and Abednego, that you do not serve my gods nor worship the golden image I have set before you? Did you not understand what I commanded? Now I shall give you one more chance. This time, when you hear the sound of the music, you will fall down on your faces and worship the image I have made. If you do, then all is well. But if you do not, you shall be cast within the hour into the midst of the fiery furnace. And who is the God who will then deliver you?"

The three men answered readily. "O Nebuchadnezzar, we have but one answer to give you. We do not want a second chance, for you must know that we will not serve your gods nor worship the golden image you have made. Our God is able to deliver us from the fiery furnace if it is his will. But if it is not his will, we would still gladly die rather than serve your gods or bow down to the image."

Then Nebuchadnezzar's fury knew no bounds and his face became twisted with rage. No longer was he reasonable when he spoke to these disobedient Jews. "Then the furnace shall be heated until it is seven times hotter than it has ever been!" he shouted.

And he sent for the most mighty men in his army to bind Shadrach, Meshach, and Abednego, and cast them into the burning, fiery furnace. The three men submitted without struggle and let their captors lead them to where the hot fire blazed as it had never blazed before. But the mighty men who led them were too hasty and came too close to the furnace that was blazing with a heat seven times hotter than usual; they flung their captives deep into the heart of the crackling flames, but in their zeal to fulfill the king's urgent command they allowed themselves to be caught by the furious heat and the leaping tongues of fire. And they died where they stood while the three Jews fell down, still tightly bound, into the midst of the burning, fiery furnace.

But the three Jews did not burn.

Nebuchadnezzar watched from a safe distance as they rose in the heart of the fire and began to praise and glorify and bless God in the furnace:

"Blessed art thou, O Lord God of our fathers;
And to be praised and exalted above all for ever.

O ye heavens, bless ye the Lord;
Praise and exalt him above all for ever.

O ye sun and moon, bless ye the Lord;
Praise and exalt him above all for ever.

O ye fire and heat, bless ye the Lord;
Praise and exalt him above all for ever.

O Israel, bless ye the Lord;
Praise and exalt him above all for ever.

O all ye that worship the Lord, bless the God of gods, praise him, and give him thanks;

For his mercy endureth for ever."

Nebuchadnezzar listened, and watched with growing amazement. There was something remarkable about the furnace, and it was not only that the three men were not burning. He rose in haste and astonishment and said to his counselors: "Did we not cast three men bound into the midst of the fire?"

"True, O king," they answered.

"Then why do I see four?" said the king. "Look! Four men, unbound, walking about in the midst of the fire, and they are not even hurt! And see, the form of the fourth is like the Son of God."

Then he went close to the mouth of the fiery furnace and spoke into its depths: "Shadrach, Meshach, and Abednego, you servants of the most high God, come out! Come here to me."

The three men walked out of the heart of the fire, and there was no one left behind. All the princes and governors, captains and counselors, gathered around to stare at the men, those men of God upon whose bodies the fire had had no power. Not a hair of their heads was singed, neither was there any sign of scorching on their clothes, nor was the smell of fire on them. Yet the ropes that had bound them had been burned away.

Then Nebuchadnezzar said, before all the nobles and rulers who were with him: "Blessed be the God of Shadrach, Meshach, and Abednego, who has sent his angel and delivered his servants that trusted in him! Blessed be these three men who defied the king's word and risked their own bodies that they might not serve or worship any god except their own! Therefore I make a decree: that any people of any nation or language, which says anything amiss against the God of Shadrach, Meshach, and Abednego, shall be cut in pieces and their houses leveled to the ground. For there is no other God who has such power to save!"

Then the king promoted Shadrach, Meshach, and Abednego to higher office in the province of Babylon, and they were respected by all men for the rest of their days.

Daniel

++++++++++++++++++++++

When Nebuchadnezzer died, his son Belshazzar became king in his father's place. Now Belshazzar was a foolish and extravagant man who thought only of his worldly pleasures. Even though the mighty armies of the Medes and Persians were threatening the land of the Chaldeans, he made no preparations to defend his kingdom. In his pride and arrogance he was sure that Babylon was safe from any attack.

Belshazzar the king made a great feast to a thousand of his lords, and drank much wine before the thousand. Again and again were the wine cups filled, and when Belshazzar was flushed with drink he rose unsteadily to his feet and issued a command to his servants. "Go," he said to them, "and bring me the gold and silver vessels which my father Nebuchadnezzar took out of the temple which was in Jerusalem. Then shall I, your king, and my princes and my wives and all the other women of my household drink wine from these vessels of the Jews!"

So his servants brought the holy vessels which once had adorned the house of God, and all the people drank from them. As they drank the wine they praised the gods of gold, of silver, of brass, of iron, of wood, and the gods of stone, and the false gods despised by the true believers in the Lord.

But suddenly the noise and merriment died down. Every man and woman at the feast saw the king's eyes turn and stare at the wall of the banquet hall. They followed his gaze and gasped with astonishment and fear.

Near the great candlestick that shed its light upon the wall of the king's palace, the fingers of a man's hand had appeared. The fingers moved and wrote strange words upon the plaster of that wall, and the king saw the part of the hand that wrote. But no other part of the writer could he see, only the moving hand with the finger making letters on the wall beyond the candle. A great fear came upon Belshazzar. His face froze and turned pale with terror, and his mind troubled him so sorely that the joints of his legs were loosened and his knees knocked against each other. The finger wrote, moved on, and disappeared, leaving on the wall four mysterious words in letter that no man present could read, much less understand.

The king cried aloud for his astrologers and soothsayers. When his wise men came to him he said, "Whosoever reads this writing and tells me the meaning of it shall be rewarded with scarlet robes, and have a chain of gold about his neck, and he shall be the third ruler in the kingdom."

The wise men looked long at the writing, but they could make nothing of it. Belshazzar and his lords stood in the banquet chamber shaking with fear, not knowing what to do or where to turn for help.

Now the queen his mother came into the room where the feasting had been so merry only minutes before, and spoke soothing words to King Belshazzar.

"Oh king, live forever!" she said to her trembling son. "Do not let your thoughts trouble you, nor let your face be pale with terror. There is a man in your kingdom who has in him the spirit of the holy gods. In the days of your father this man showed himself to have wisdom and understanding like the wisdom of the gods. Nebuchadnezzar your father, the king, made him master of all the magicians, astrologers, and soothsayers. Therefore, because your father found in this Daniel such an excellent spirit, such knowledge and understanding, such wisdom to interpret dreams, and such skill in clearing up doubts, let Daniel now be called. He will show you the interpretation of this writing."

Daniel was brought in. The king said to him: "Are you that Daniel who is one of the captives from Judah? I have heard of you, that the spirit of the gods is in you, and that light and understanding and excellent wisdom is to be found in you. All of my wise men have been brought before me that they should read this writing, but not one of them is able to interpret it for me. Now it is said of you that you can make interpretations, and I say to you that if you can read it and explain its meaning, I will clothe you in scarlet and place a chain of gold about your neck, and you shall be the third ruler in my kingdom."

"Keep your gifts," said Daniel, "and give your reward to another. I will read the writing for you and explain its meaning. But remember first, O king, that the most high God gave Nebuchadnezzar your father a kingdom and majesty, and glory and honor. And because of this majesty given by the Lord, people of all nations and languages trembled and feared before him, and his might was very great. But when his heart was lifted up and his mind was hardened in pride, he was deposed from his kingly throne. And they took his glory from him until he came to know that the most high God ruled in the kingdom of men, and that the Lord appoints over his kingdom whomsoever he will. And at last King Nebuchadnezzar blessed and honored the most high.

"But you his son, O Belshazzar, have not humbled your heart, even though you knew all this. Instead, you have lifted up yourself against the Lord of heaven, and have even sent for the vessels of his house. You and your lords and your wives and your concubines have drunk wine in them as you feasted in this place. And you have praised the gods of silver and of gold, of brass and iron, of wood and stone, which neither see nor hear, and you did this even while you drank from the holy vessels of the Lord. But the Lord himself, the God who holds your life in his hands, this God you have not glorified.

"It was a part of God's hand that was sent from him, and this writing on the wall was written by that hand. And these are the words that were written: MENE, MENE, TEKEL, UPHARSIN. And this is the interpretation of them. MENE: God has judged your kingdom and numbered its days, and has finished it. TEKEL: You have been weighed on the balance scales, and you have been found wanting. UPHARSIN: Your kingdom is divided, and given to the Medes and Persians."

In spite of this dire warning, Belshazzar commanded his attendants to clothe Daniel in scarlet and place a chain of gold around his neck, and then he proclaimed to all his people that Daniel was to be the third highest ruler in the kingdom.

But it was too late for sudden belief in God's servants upon earth, too late for gratitude or lavish reward; and far too late for change.

That very night the city of Babylon was attacked. Belshazzar the king of the Chaldeans was slain by the soldiers who scaled the city walls while the rulers and the nobles feasted. The combined forces of the Medes and Persians swarmed through the city and the land of Babylon and made it all their own. And Darius, the Mede, took the kingdom and the throne.

Unlike Belshazzar, he took immediate note of Daniel.

It pleased Darius to set over the kingdom a hundred and twenty princes, and over these he set three presidents of which the wise Daniel was first. Thus Daniel, a Jew of captive Judah, was preferred above all presidents and princes because the new king thought so highly of his wisdom.

But the other rulers of the land were jealous of Daniel's high office. Time and time again they tried to find some fault in him, or some excuse for speaking evil of him to the king, but they could find no fault or error in him.

Therefore the presidents and princes gathered together and devised a plot against him.

"There is only one way we can find fault with him that will turn the king against him," they told each other, "and that is in some matter concerning the law of his God." In this they were correct, and soon they found a way. They had noticed that three times each day Daniel went into his house to pray in front of the window that looked toward the distant, ruined city of Jerusalem, and this was all they needed.

The nobles assembled before the king and humbly bowed down low.

"King Darius, live forever!" they said. "All the presidents of the kingdom, the governors, the princes, the counselors, and the captains, have consulted together so that you may draw up a royal statute. This shall be a firm decree that will require every man in this kingdom to acknowledge you, and only you, as the supreme being in this land."

What Darius heard was pleasing to him, and he told the speakers to continue.

"We ask you to establish a law," they went on craftily, "that for thirty days no one shall ask anything of any God or man but of you, O king. All prayers, petitions and requests must be addressed only to you. And if anyone should disobey your royal statute, he shall be cast into the den of lions. Now, O king, establish the decree and sign the writing of it so that it cannot be changed, for all the people of your kingdom know that no law of the Medes and Persians can be altered."

Darius saw no harm in this request, for it was flattering to him, and after all he was king of the great empire that had toppled the mighty Babylonians from power. Nor did he notice that his first president, Daniel the Jew, was not among the company that stood before him. Therefore he signed the writing and the decree they had prepared for him.

"Now when Daniel heard about this harsh new law he went into his house as usual to kneel, three times a day, before the open window that looked toward far-off Jerusalem and the ruins of God's temple. He could see neither house of God nor ransacked city, but he knew that they were there, and in spite of the decree he prayed and gave thanks to his God as he had always done.

The envious presidents and princes saw him kneeling before the open window and heard him praying to his God and asking for guidance from the Lord. At once they hurried off to Darius to remind the king of his decree.

"O king!" they said, scarcely able to contain themselves, for triumph was now in sight. "Have you not signed a decree that for thirty days any man that asks a petition of any God or man but you, O king, shall be cast into the den of lions?"

The king nodded. "That is true," he said. "It was signed according to the laws of the Medes and Persians, which cannot be changed."

"Ah! Then know that Daniel, one of the people of the captivity of Judah, does not regard you, O king, nor does he respect the decree that you have signed. In his disobedience he prays three times each day to his God with his petitions and requests, instead of asking you."

Then King Darius saw the trap into which he had been led, and he was mightily displeased with himself. There had been no thought in his mind of the wise old Daniel, whom he truly loved, when he had signed the foolish law. He set his heart on trying to save him, and he thought and labored until sundown to find some way of keeping Daniel from the dreadful fate awaiting him. But it was useless. The stern law of the Medes and

Persians left no escape for even the finest and most deserving of men.

At sunset the jealous nobles went back to the palace and stood again before their king. "Know, O king," they said, "that the law of the Medes and Persians is that no decree nor statute which the king has made may ever be changed, not in any way nor for any man."

It was true. With great reluctance King Darius sent for Daniel and commanded that he be thrown into the den of lions. When it was done he spoke down into the deep pit, where the innocent Daniel stood fearlessly among the growling lions, and said with both hope and sorrow in his voice: "Surely your God, whom you serve so faithfully, will deliver you from death."

Then a great stone was rolled over the mouth of the pit so that no man could look in nor any man climb out, and the king sealed it with his own signet so that the stone would not be moved until he himself gave the command.

King Darius went back to his palace and passed the night in torment and in sorrow. In his great anguish of spirit he could neither eat nor listen to music to soothe his troubled soul, and though he lay upon his bed of luxury he could not sleep throughout the long and terrible night. His every thought was with Daniel and how he must be faring in that dark pit with the snarling, hungry lions. After a night of torture and remorse he arose very early in the morning and went in haste to the den of lions, dreading what he might find when the sealed stone was rolled back.

In a voice full of grief he cried out to Daniel in the silent pit: "O Daniel, servant of the living God! Has your God, whom you have always served with faithful heart, been able to deliver you from the lions?"

Then to his great relief the voice of Daniel answered from the lions' den: "O king, live forever! My God has sent his angel and has shut the lions' mouths so that they have not hurt me, for I was innocent in the sight of the Lord. And I am innocent before you also, O king, for to you have I done no harm or wrong."

Then the king was exceedingly glad for him, and his heart rejoiced that Daniel had been spared. He called for his servants and commanded that Daniel be taken at once from the den of lions, and it was done as soon as spoken. King Darius and his men looked with awe upon the living Daniel. There was no wound nor sign of any hurt upon him, because he had believed so firmly in his God.

The king was full of gratitude, but he was also angry. By his command the men who had accused Daniel were brought before him. And at a second command these false men and their families were thrown among the lions to suffer the fate that Daniel had so miraculously escaped. This time the lions did not spare their victims.

Then King Darius wrote and signed another statute which he sent out to all peoples and all nations of the earth. It was very different from the first, and it read:

"Peace be multiplied unto you! I make a decree: that in every dominion of my kingdom, men shall tremble and fear before the God of Daniel, for he is the living God, and steadfast forever. His kingdom shall not be destroyed, and his rule shall be even unto the end. He delivers and rescues, and he works signs and wonders in heaven and in earth, he who has delivered Daniel from the power of the lions."

And from that time on Daniel prospered in the reign of Darius. And when Cyrus the Persian became king of Babylon he dealt with justice and kindness not only toward Daniel but to all the captive peoples of Judah.

For it had been said of Cyrus many years before when the prophet Isaiah had spoken God's words in the land of Judah, that the Lord had appointed him to do great things, saying:

"I am the Lord that saith of Cyrus, 'He is my shepherd,

And shall perform all my pleasure;
Even saying to Jerusalem, thou shall be built;
And to the temple, thy foundation shall be laid.' "

Daniel knew of this prophecy. He also knew the words of the prophet Jeremiah, who had written the Lord's saying down in a book so that all Judah would know and remember that God had not forsaken them. And these were the words written down by Jeremiah:

" 'For lo, the days come," saith the Lord, 'that I will bring again the captivity of my people, and I will cause them to return to the land that I gave to their fathers, and they shall possess it. I will have mercy on their dwelling places; and the city shall be builded upon her own heap, and the palace shall remain after the manner thereof. And out of them shall proceed thanksgiving and the voice of them that make merry: and I will multiply them, and they shall not be few; I will also glorify them, and they shall not be small. Their children also shall be as aforetime, and their congregation shall be established before me, and I will punish all that oppress them. And you shall be my people, and I will be your God.' "

And because he believed in the Lord God of Israel and understood the sayings of the prophets, Daniel knew that the days of the captivity were numbered. Though he himself was old and the day of his death was drawing near, he was happy and he prospered in the reign of Cyrus. He might never see the new Jerusalem. But he knew that it would come.

The Homecoming of the Jews

✠✠✠✠✠✠✠✠✠✠✠✠✠✠✠✠✠✠✠✠✠✠

Now in the first year of Cyrus, king of Babylon and Persia, the Lord stirred up the spirit of the king so that the word of the Lord might be fulfilled according to the sayings of Jeremiah.

Cyrus made a proclamation throughout all his kingdom and put it into writing so that all his people would know of his decree. These are the words that he proclaimed:

"Thus speaks Cyrus, king of Persia: 'The Lord God of Heaven, the most high Lord, has given me all the kingdoms of the earth, and he has commanded me to build him a temple at Jerusalem in Judah. If there be any here among you that are of his people, may the Lord your God be with you. May you go up to Jerusalem that is in Judah, and build the house of the Lord of Israel: for he is the

Lord that dwells in Jerusalem. And whosoever remains of the people of Judah, let him be helped by the men of the place where he lives. Let him be given silver, gold, goods, and beasts, besides any offering which his neighbor may wish to give for the house of God in Jerusalem.' "

Great was the rejoicing among the captive people when they heard this proclamation by Cyrus and knew that their prophets' words were coming true. Not all the Jews wished to return, for now they had been in Babylon for seventy years and most of them had never seen the city of their forefathers. Many had become settled and prosperous in the land of their captivity. But many more exulted at the thought of going home.

The first to rise up and cry out his joy was the chief of the leaders of Judah and Benjamin. Then the priests rose up, and the Levites who remained of the scattered tribe of Levi, and then all the people whose spirits God had lifted up with the desire to go back to build the house of the Lord in the city of Jerusalem. At once they started preparations for the journey into Judah.

Their fellow Jews who were remaining, and their friends and neighbors in Babylon, poured gifts into their hands: gold, silver, goods of all kinds; sheep and cattle, donkeys, horses; vessels for the temple, precious things, and offerings for the house of God in Jerusalem. Cyrus himself brought forth the holy vessels which had been in the Lord's house, those which Nebuchadnezzar had stripped from the temple and taken out of Jerusalem to put into the house of his own gods, and gave these priceless treasures to one of the princes of Judah. When they were counted it was found that there were five thousand and four hundred vessels of silver and gold to adorn the temple when it was ready for adornment.

A great and joyous procession of men, women, children, and domestic beasts started out from Babylon and wound its way across the many miles of hills and plains to the land of Judah. Well over forty thousand people

were returning to a home most of them had never seen.
Among them were their handmaids and their servants,
as well as two hundred singing men and singing women.
The horses and the mules, the camels and the asses
numbered more than eight thousand among the many
families. And the treasures of gold and silver carried by
some of the chief men among the elders of Benjamin
and Judah were almost beyond counting.

Daniel was now a very old man and remained with
Darius in Babylon instead of returning with his people
to the land of his forefathers. He watched them go
until the sounds of their singing faded into the distance
and the clouds of dust settled behind the feet of their
animals. Then he turned away and gave thanks to his
Lord for delivering his people.

Zerubbabel of the family of David and Jeshua the
priest led the vast cavalcade on its triumphal way. It
was a long journey but a happy one, for not only were
the Jews returning home but they were taking with
them out of Babylon all the stolen treasures of their
temple and mule-loads of precious gifts from generous
friends. Surely it would not be difficult for them to start
new lives in the city of their ancestors.

They came at last to the ruin of Jerusalem and
looked at it with mixed feelings of deep gratitude and
love and sorrow. Some hearts sank and others leaped,
but to even the most uncritical eyes it was a pitiful
sight. Imagination had not warned them it would be so
devastated. The few half-Jews, half-heathens living in
the city, and the foreigners who lived nearby, had done
nothing to rebuild Jerusalem. Nebuchadnezzar's war
had done it's dreadful damage, and time and negligence
had done the rest. The walls were crumbled piles of
stone, the temple was a heap of rubble, and weeds grew
among the ruins of what had once been a palace surrounded with fine houses. Those who had known the
city in its days of glory and those who had been born in
Babylon were horrified and heartsore.

But there was no time to mourn. Homes must be
built, the city mended, the walls repaired, and above all

the temple must once again be made into a house worthy of the Lord and be filled with its ancient treasures.

The Jews began at once to make homes for themselves within the city and in the small towns outside the walls. Zerubbabel and the priests built an altar to the Lord and made burnt offerings upon it every morning and evening. When all the people were settled in reasonable comfort they got down to the main task at hand. To the people of Tyre and Sidon they sent meat and drink and oil in return for cedar trees from Lebanon for the rebuilding of the temple, and they chose carpenters and masons to begin the work.

And when the builders were ready to lay the foundations of the temple of the Lord, the priests came with their robes and trumpets and the Levites came with cymbals so that they might praise the Lord. They sang together, as David and his priests had done so long ago, praising God and giving thanks for all their blessings. "For the Lord is good!" they sang, "and his mercy endureth forever toward Israel."

All the people shouted with a great shout when they praised the Lord, because their hearts were glad that at last the foundation of the house of the Lord was being laid. But many of the priests and Levites and leaders among the people were very old men who had seen and revered the first temple in Jerusalem, and now, with a new foundation before their aged eyes, their memories made them weep out loud while the rest of the people shouted for joy. Those who heard the great noise could not distinguish the cries of joy from the sound of the bitter weeping. And many people heard the noise, for it sounded far beyond the fallen city walls.

Work on the temple began in earnest then, with a vast flurry of activity and much cutting of cedar logs and blocks of stone. But the Samaritans and other people who lived in the land of the returned captives were not glad that the Jews were back, nor that the temple was to be rebuilt. Therefore they did all they could to harass the builders, troubling them in many ways and hiring counselors to defeat their purpose. It was not long before conditions became so difficult that the Jews were obliged to stop building, for the man who became king after Cyrus had listened to the pleas of the Samaritans and decided against the Jews.

But in time another Darius of Persia came to the throne. When he discovered how the Jews were being frustrated in their attempts to build the temple in spite of King Cyrus' decree that the Lord's house must be built, he himself issued a new and stern decree:

"Let the work of this house of God alone! Let the governor of the Jews and the elders of the Jews build this house of God in his place. Moreover I make a decree that the goods and monies sent in tribute to the king be given instead to these men for the building. Also: young bullocks and rams and lambs, wheat and salt, wine and oil, and whatever may be required by the priests, shall be given to them every day without fail for the burnt offerings of the God of heaven. Whosoever shall defy this decree and hinder the building of the Lord's house shall have his own house torn to the ground and be hanged upon its timbers. I, Darius, have made a decree; let it be done with speed."

And it was done with speed. The Jews, no longer troubled by their enemies, went back to work with a will. And the house was finished in the sixth year of the reign of Darius the king. The children of Israel, the priests and the Levites, and all the people of the captivity kept the dedication of this house of God with joy and songs of thanksgiving to the Lord God, the God of Israel.

Yet there was still much work to be done in the city of Jerusalem. After the temple was finished there was little gold and silver left for other work, and indeed it was necessary for the people to spend the greater part of their time in tending to their lands to provide food for their families. The Samaritans and other jealous people again harassed the Jews of the city so that they became discouraged and weary, and left the ruined walls and buildings where they lay.

Now it happened that one Artaxerxes became king of Persia and its many possessions, one of which was the land of Judah. He ruled his kingdoms from his capital city of Shushan in the land of Persia, and he had in his Persian palace a young cupbearer. The name of the youth was Nehemiah, and he was a noble young man of Judah.

For years he heard no word of distant Judah. But one day Nehemiah's kinsman Hanani and certain other Jews arrived in Shushan from their homeland, and Nehemiah eagerly asked them about the Jews who had left captivity and of conditions in the city of Jerusalem. "Does all go well?" he asked.

They shook their heads sadly. "The people there are in great difficulty and shame," they said, "for they are poor and troubled by their enemies. Some have even married among the heathen round about them. The temple is built, but the walls of the city still lie in ruins and the gates are burned with fire as they have been these many years."

When Nehemiah heard these words he wept and mourned for several days. Then he fasted, and prayed before the God of heaven. "Forgive us, Lord, for our many sins, and hear my prayer. O Lord, I beseech you, grant me mercy in the sight of the king so that I may help my people."

And it came to pass, on this day in the twentieth year of Artaxerxes the king of Persia, that Nehemiah performed his usual task of taking wine before the king. For the first time in all his years of service his face was sad and his manner expressed deep sorrow.

"Why do you look sad?" said the king, turning upon his cupbearer a penetrating gaze. "I do not think that you are sick, therefore this must be nothing else but sorrow of heart."

Then Nehemiah was afraid that his cheerless look had angered the king.

"Let the king live forever!" he said. "I grieve because the city of my forefathers lies waste and the gates are burned with fire. How shall I not be full of sorrow when the place of my father's tomb is yet in ruins?"

The king looked at him shrewdly. "And what is your request?" he said.

Nehemiah breathed a silent prayer to God that he should find words that would not displease the king. And then he answered: "If it please the king, and if I have found favor in your eyes, I beg that you will send me to Jerusalem in Judah where my ancestors lie buried so that I may help rebuild it."

Then the king, who was sitting with the queen beside him, asked the royal cupbearer: "How long will you be gone?"

This was difficult to answer, for Nehemiah could not judge how long it would take to rebuild the city walls he had never seen. But he set a time, and to his great joy the king granted his request.

"If it please the king," Nehemiah added, "give me letters for the governors beyond the river, so that they may give me safe conduct through their lands. And let me also that a letter to Asaph, keeper of the king's forest, that he may give me timber to make beams for the gates of the palace and for the walls of the city."

The king agreed to everything he asked, for the good hand of God was on his servant Nehemiah.

Accompanied by a small company of army captains and horsemen supplied by the king, Nehemiah made the long journey from the land of Persia and arrived safely in Jerusalem. He did not, at first, make known his presence to the people of the city, for he knew that there were enemies round about who had no wish to see the walls rebuilt and the city fortified.

He remained in hiding for three days, resting from his journey and quietly making plans. Then he arose and went out silently in the night to view the city by moonlight. And still he told no one what God had put in his heart to do. In company with some few chosen men he rode out upon his sure-footed donkey to inspect the ruins. He left the city by way of the Valley Gate, whose fortified tower had long since fallen into dust, and rode quietly past the Dragon Well to see the entire wall from outside.

For as far as he could see it was broken down and lay in useless heaps. The gates, nearly all of them, had been almost totally destroyed by fire. Piles of shattered stone lay everywhere about. He rode on, toward the Gate of the Fountain and the King's Pool, hoping to re-enter the city at that point, but the rubble was piled so high that his donkey could find no path. Any number of enemies on foot, however, could easily climb across the stones if they had a mind to.

Nehemiah rode on toward the brook Kidron and viewed the section of the wall that faced the river. Then he turned back and re-entered the city through the Gate of the Valley. It had not been a heartening survey. Yet he was not dismayed.

In the morning he went to the priests and rulers and told them what he had seen and why he had come. "You see the distress we are in!" he said earnestly. "You see how Jerusalem lies in ruins, and how the gates of the city are burned by fire. Come, let us build up the wall of Jerusalem so that we may no longer feel shame, so that we may hold our heads up high!" He told them, too, of God's answer to his prayers, and how the king of Persia had encouraged him with words and deeds. And his listeners were inspired.

"Let us rise up and build!" they cried.

And, led by Nehemiah, they started work at once upon the walls. First they cleared away the fallen rubble and the debris of the years of neglect. Then every man who was capable of working, and even every woman, set to work upon the walls. Nehemiah parceled out the work according to the clans and families. Some men worked on the walls nearest their own homes; others worked in groups to repair long sections of the walls and replace the many broken, burnt-out gates.

Eliashib the high priest worked with other priests to repair the Sheep Gate, through which the sheep for sacrifice were brought into the city. The sons of Hassenaah built the Fish Gate, with its great beams and solid doors and heavy locks and bars. Next to them worked Meremoth, repairing the wall; and next to Meremoth, Meshullah; and next to them worked Zadok; and next to the men of Gibeon repaired Uzziel of the goldsmiths; next to him worked Hananiah the son of one of the apothecaries, and so on around the great circumference of the wall. Hanun and the inhabitants of Zanoah repaired the Valley Gate and a thousand cubits of the wall. Shallun, ruler of part of Mizpah, repaired the Gate of the Fountain and the walls of the Pool of Siloah by the king's garden. Priests, merchants, nobles, gatekeepers, and all the people of Jerusalem worked together to rebuild their city wall and replace the devastated gates with sturdy beams and bars.

At first the Samaritans and other adversaries of the Jews mocked them for their efforts. "What do these feeble Jews?" they asked each other. "Will they fortify themselves against us? Will they make the wall in a day? Will they restore the stones out of the heaps of rubbish? What a poor wall it is! If a fox should leap upon it, their stone wall would break and fall."

But when they saw the great progress that was being made in filling up the breaches and raising up the walls, they became exceedingly angry. For the stone wall did not fall; it grew stronger every day. So now the enemies of the Jews conspired to come out and fight against Jerusalem before the wall was finished, for they knew that if they did not do it now they would never again have free access to the city.

But Nehemiah heard about these plans and made his own. From the moment the conspiracy came to his ears he set a guard to watch day and night for any sign of attack. During the workday, he set half of his builders to labor at the wall, and the other half to stand guard and hold spears and shields and bows in readiness. Even the builders and those who carried loads of stone and timber to the walls worked, each one of them, with one hand always ready to grasp the sword that was girded by his side. Nehemiah himself kept constant watch, urging his men on to even greater effort and yet never allowing his alert gaze to falter for a moment. A trumpeter walked always by his side, ready to sound an alarm if it were needed.

The threatened attack was never launched. It was obvious to the enemies outside the walls that there was nothing they could do to stop the work. Neither Nehemiah nor his kinsmen, nor any of the builders and servants, nor any of the guards, permitted themselves to rest beyond their barest needs. They did not so much as remove their clothes, except to wash, while the wall was being built.

And after fifty-two days of vigilance and unrelenting work, the wall was finished.

Great was the rejoicing when the work was done. Nehemiah gathered together all the people and the priests to dedicate the wall with gladness. They came with thanksgiving in their hearts, and with singing and with cymbals, and with psalteries and harps, and they sang joyful songs of praise to the Lord their God.

Their city, with the plains and countryside and towns around it, was all that was left of the land of Judah, and of the very much greater nation that had once been Israel. And even the small portion still left to them was ruled by a foreign king who counted them among his subjects.

But yet there was cause for happiness. The tribes of Benjamin and Judah had come back to the holy city of Jerusalem. They had rebuilt many of the damaged homes; they had repaired the city wall; they had built a great new temple to their Lord. As they sang they remembered God's promise, spoken through the mouth of the prophet Jeremiah: "For lo, the days come that I will cause my people to return to the land that I gave to their fathers. I will have mercy on their dwelling places; and the city shall be builded upon her own heap. And out of them shall proceed thanksgiving and the voice of them that make merry. Their congregation shall be established before me, and I will punish all that oppress them. And I shall be their God."

Thus had God's promise come true for the captive peoples of Judah. And they had yet another promise to remember: that some day a savior from the line of David, son of Jesse of the tribe of Judah, would come among them and cast his light upon the world.

So, that day by the city wall, they offered sacrifices and rejoiced: the priests and all the other men who had worked so diligently, the wives, the children, the scribe Ezra, the cupbearer-builder Nehemiah, the singers, and those who made music with the cymbals and the harps —all praised the Lord with love and gratitude. And the joy of Jerusalem was heard even afar off, across the plains and pastures of the land of Judah.

God's Promise
to Israel

✝✝✝✝✝✝✝✝✝✝✝✝✝✝✝✝✝✝✝✝✝✝✝✝

Years passed into centuries. The land of the Jews became known as Palestine. Kings of many countries fought each other, and Palestine changed hands like any spoil of war. The Jews remained in their own land, sometimes suffering oppression and sometimes benefiting under the rule of their foreign rulers, but always clinging fast to Jerusalem as their holy city. The prophecies and promises of old were not forgotten, least of all the stirring words of the prophet Isaiah:

"The people that walked in darkness
Have seen a great light:
They that dwell in the land of the shadow of
 death,
Upon them hath the light shined.
Thou has multiplied the nation, and not increased
 the joy;

They joy before thee according to the joy in har-
    vest,
And as men rejoice when they divide the spoil.
For thou hast broken the yoke of his burden,
And the staff of his shoulder,
The rod of his oppressor,
As in the day of Midian.
For every battle of the warrior is with confused
    noise,
And garments rolled in blood;
But this shall be with burning and fuel of fire.
For unto us a child is born, unto us a son is given;
And the government shall be upon his shoulders;
And his name shall be called Wonderful,
Counsellor, the mighty God, the everlasting Fa-
    ther,
The Prince of Peace.
Of the increase of his government and peace
There shall be no end,
Upon the throne of David, and upon his kingdom,
To order it, and to establish it
With judgment and with justice
From henceforth even for ever.
The zeal of the Lord of Hosts will perform this."

And Isaiah also said:

"And there shall come forth a rod out of the stem
    of Jesse,
And a branch shall grow out of his roots:
And the spirit of the Lord shall rest upon him,
The spirit of wisdom and understanding,
The spirit of counsel and might,
The spirit of knowledge and of the fear of the
    Lord;
And shall make him of quick understanding in the
    fear of the Lord:
And he shall not judge after the sight of his
    eyes,
Neither reprove after the hearing of his ears:

But with righteousness shall he judge the poor,
And reprove with equity for the meek of the
earth.
And he shall not judge after the sight of his
mouth,
And with the breath of his lips shall he slay the
wicked.
And righteousness shall be the girdle of his loins,
And faithfulness the girdle of his reins.
The wolf also shall dwell with the lamb,
And the leopard shall lie down with the kid;
And the calf and the young lion and the fatling
together;
And a little child shall lead them.
And the cow and the bear shall feed;
Their young ones shall lie down together:
And the lion shall eat straw like the ox.
They shall not hurt nor destroy
In all my holy mountain:
For the earth shall be full of the knowledge of the
Lord,
As the waters cover the sea.
And in that day there shall be a root of Jesse,
Which shall stand for an ensign of the people;
To it shall the Gentiles seek:
And his rest shall be glorious."

The Jews of Palestine waited: waited for a child to be
born from the stem of Jesse and David, a child who
would grow in wisdom and understanding until he
became known as the Prince of Peace.

SIGNET and MENTOR Books of Special Interest

☐ **THE STORY BIBLE: VOLUME I by Pearl S. Buck.** The winner of the Nobel and Pulitzer Prizes retells the Greatest Story Ever Told in the living language of our times. In VOLUME I the immortal stories of the Old Testament are brought to life with a power and immediacy for the modern reader. (#W8247—$1.50)

☐ **THE STORY BIBLE: VOLUME II by Pearl S. Buck.** This superlative rendering of the New Testament brings the crowning achievement of Pearl Buck's career, *The Story Bible*, to a triumphant conclusion. Here, adding relevance to its wisdom and freshness to its beauty, is the story of the birth, life, death and resurrection of Jesus. "Compelling, moving!"—*Library Journal* (#W8248—$1.50)

☐ **THE SERMON ON THE MOUNT According to Vedanta by Swami Prabhavananda.** A fascinating and superbly enlightening Hindu reading of the central gospel of Christianity by the renowned author of books on Indian religious philosophy. (#MW1518—$1.50)

☐ **WHAT THE GREAT RELIGIONS BELIEVE by Joseph Gaer.** An enlightening account of the basic beliefs of the world's historic religions—Hinduism, Jainism. Christianity, Islam, Zoroastrianism, Confucianism, Judaism, Zen Buddhism and others—with selections from their sacred literature. Bibliography. (#E8588—$1.75)

☐ **THE VARIETIES OF RELIGIOUS EXPERIENCE by William James.** James' classic work on the psychology of religion and the religious impulse, with an introduction by Jacques Barzun. (#ME1603—$2.25)

Buy them at your local bookstore or use this convenient coupon for ordering.

THE NEW AMERICAN LIBRARY, INC.,
P.O. Box 999, Bergenfield, New Jersey 07621

Please send me the books I have checked above. I am enclosing $_____
(please add $1.00 to this order to cover postage and handling). Send check or money order—no cash or C.O.D.'s. Prices and numbers are subject to change without notice.

Name_____

Address_____

City _____ State _____ Zip Code _____
Allow 4-6 weeks for delivery.
This offer is subject to withdrawal without notice.